# Adrian Bell:
# Voice of the Countryside

# ANN GANDER

First published on 4th October 2001 by Holm Oak Publishing
St Michaels, Narrow Way, Wenhaston, Suffolk IP19 9EJ
Telephone: 01502 478702

British Cataloguing in Publication Data.
A catalogue record for this book is available from the British Library.

ISBN 0 9533406 1 9

Typeset by Karen Kohn
Printed by Barnwell's of Aylsham, Norfolk

*By the Same Author*

Top Hats and Servants' Tales
A Century of Life on Somerleyton Estate

**For Matthew**

# Acknowledgements

My sincere thanks to Anthea, Sylvia and Martin Bell for their kind support and permission to quote extensively from their father's writings. An extra special thank you to Anthea, who has been so generous with her time and hospitality.

Thanks also to Dr Alex Bell, without whose expertise in genealogical research this book would have been much poorer in detail.

I am grateful to Mrs. Cynthia Peacock for permission to quote from her late husband's memoirs, and to Mrs. Hilary Bond for her late mother's essay on the Gibsons' life in Potchefstroom. My thanks to all those relatives and friends of the Bell family who have kindly given their time and memories.

I am grateful to Peter Franzen, Editor of the *Eastern Daily Press*, for permission to use the quotations from Adrian Bell's articles and the famous picture of Adrian that appears on the inside back cover. My thanks to Colin Self for permission to use his evocative picture, The Ploughman.

My research in Stradishall was much aided by Mr. Dennis Kiddy, for which I am most grateful. My thanks to the Reverend Mr. John Howard for conducting research into Glengorse School, Eastbourne, and to Mrs Kathleen Hanna for local history information about Steeple Aston.

I am grateful to the following people, organisations and institutions for their help and advice: Mr H. Spry-Leverton, Librarian, Uppingham School; Ms. Margaret Ecclestone, Librarian, Alpine Club Library; Ms. Kathleen Cann, Department of Manuscripts, Cambridge University Library; the Syndics of Cambridge University Library; the staff of Suffolk Record Office, Bury-St-Edmunds; Glenn Clarke, Property Administrator, Greene King plc; Nicholas Mays, Deputy Archivist, News International plc; Geoffrey Warren and Anne Williamson.

Thanks to Sutton Publishing for permission to quote from Anne Williamson's book *Henry Williamson: Tarka and the Last Romantic*.

My thanks to Dr Keith Snell, Dept of Local History, University of Leicester for his interest and encouragement. Lastly, my hearty thanks to James Hayward, proof-reader and general counsellor par excellence.

# Contents

# 1. Cold Start

The baby was dead, they said.

They had smacked it, chafed it, patted it, but there was no sign of life at all. The little thing lay lifeless as a mucky wax doll. Blue-tinged, blood-smeared, a baby boy, too tiny to have survived the trauma of the last forty hours.

There was no time for ceremony. The woman wrapped the pathetic scrap in newspaper and laid him at the foot of the bed, against the cold iron bars. The warmth of the womb soon began ebbing from the puny body that lay in a shroud of printed pages.

The frock-coated doctor and his grim nurse still had a battle on their hands to try and save the fading mother. She was exhausted. Her own child-like body lay drained, and her beautiful long golden hair was dark and matted with sweat. She was hardly breathing.

They had wrenched her baby from her, with metal tongs. There had been no other way, or the two would have been buried as one. But it was as if they had torn out her soul, and she had nothing left to fight for.

Somehow, as the minutes ticked by on the new clock Robert had bought her, she clung on. Everyone was silent now, listening to the shallow breaths. Only the ticking could be heard above it, as if someone sat knitting in the shadows.

And then a miracle happened.

A sound, perhaps a faint rustle of paper or a tiny gasp, alerted the nurse. She looked again at the discarded bundle and cried out - the baby was breathing.

It was Friday the fourth of October 1901 and Adrian Hanbury Bell had come into the world.

If the first vision he saw was words on a page he must have formed a subconscious bond with them, because words were to become his lifelong companion. He would one day joke that he had ink in his veins and it was true that words would seem to course onto the page, words that came straight from the heart. His writing would bring crispness and colour to the otherwise damp litter of novels about country life and farming. His characters would be so real that readers could see the dirt under their nails and smell the hay on their sleeve, and through it all he would weave humour and his joy at being a part of it.

Some would dub him a Poet in Prose, others the Sage of Suffolk. As a messenger of Mother Nature, his keen senses would collate every sight, every smell and sound and, endowing the most insignificant happenings with metaphor and rhythm, he would share the wonder of them with those who otherwise could not see, or could see and yet had no means to express. He would become an interpreter, a translator, a diplomat; he would be the Voice of the Countryside.

But for now, Adrian Bell was simply a feeble little bairn being nursed in a Victorian Lancashire semi.

In the days following the astonishing birth, there was an air of reverence in the Bells' house at 5 Birch Avenue, Stretford. Fanny, gaining strength slowly, would look silently upon her precious child, anxious to overcome the horrors of his birth, and willing herself to love him. Fanny had a strong will, as time would tell.

Motherhood was something that Fanny was determined to master. In the six years since her marriage she had re-invented herself, changing from carefree, gay party-maker to attentive wife, delightful hostess and charming entertainer. She had followed Robert around the country as he made his way in the newspaper world and she had given up her first love, art, for his sake. Now there was another role for her to play and she would give it her all. She would forgo those other interests and she would employ her artistic skills in dressing the little child.

The name she had chosen for her boy came from a book by one of her favourite authors, George Meredith. In his novel *The Ordeal of Richard Feverel: A History of a Father and Son* the character Adrian appears, a rather sneaky young man in a tragic tale. The basis of the story, about an overbearing father and an interfering family who ruin the life of a boy, could never apply to Robert and his son, but perhaps Fanny was making a point about her puritanical Scottish in-laws.

Possibly she simply enjoyed the book for its black humour, as when the household staff are forbidden to show any affection for fear of polluting the boy's mind. Perhaps she just liked the name Adrian. In any case, Robert had objected to it, he preferred George, after his younger brother. As he would say later 'the woman had her way'.

There was one more dispute to overcome yet, and that was the registration of the boy's birth. Fanny would later tell her son that Robert could not bring himself to go into the registrar's office, he was so excruciatingly shy, and so on the last day possible Fanny had to do it herself. 'Ill as I was,' she told Adrian, 'I could hardly stand, but I had to get up and dress and somehow drag myself to the office and register your birth.' This was something of an exaggeration, in that Adrian was registered on 8th November and there was another two months' grace yet in law, but it was indeed Fanny who made the declaration. It was a grievance she held forever more.

Adrian was Fanny's sole concern now and he had to be dressed in the crispest, nattiest and even frilliest of dresses, as was the vogue for baby boys then. From the start he had to stand out from the rest as the finest boy in town for in Fanny's eyes at least, Adrian was much more than just an ordinary baby. Not only was his birth something of a miracle, he was the first grandson of her father, Charles John de Witt Hanbury, and so he was practically nobility, in her eyes.

The Hanbury family story was laced with tales of notable ancestors and above all, a sense of outrage at the doing down of Fanny's own grandfather Thomas James Hanbury. The son of a stockbroker, Thomas had been made bankrupt through an unwise choice of friends, and so the family had been deprived of their rightful place in society. Still they maintained their fierce pride and they held on to the hope that one day their fortunes would be restored. Fanny must have thought that having shown such fortitude in the face of birth, Adrian Hanbury Bell might be just the one to do it.

While the tiny child slept, Fanny spent many long hours alone with her thoughts. Her mother had died some years before and her only surviving sister was abroad. Her father had re-married and his new wife did not get on with his daughters. Oh, how Fanny missed the sensible guidance and jolly humour of 'the dear old Dad', with his ready store of opinions and endless high hopes. No-one else could offer her the same quality of advice and stimulation, and nobody could replace him in her esteem. Fanny felt badly in need of his paternal approbation.

In fact, what Fanny needed most was company. She was a woman of sparkle and fun. She was a card, a jester and fond of japes; but what use was wit in a lonely house?

Robert, her husband, was rarely home. He came and went like a shadow, dodging the maid, Edith, and snatching cautious moments with mother or child. As if clocking in and clocking out, he would drop a kiss on his wife's cheek and pass by.

At times he was so introspective he hardly seemed aware of others around him. Slightly deaf, he could easily slip into another world where music and poetry absorbed his mind. Outside, Robert had a knack for being anonymous. Closing the front door with the softest click the earnest, bespectacled man would make his way along the unmade road and into the Manchester metropolis. If anybody ever noticed him they would not have recognised the editor of the brand-new *Daily Dispatch* newspaper, or realised that he was bound for the world's biggest newspaper plant at Withy Grove. He would not return until well after dark.

In the office his creativity would flow onto the page and his boss, the great Edward Hulton, saw that Robert had a talent for writing short, sharp paragraphs and thought-provoking notes that delivered a punch. The smart style appealed to their growing mass of middle-class readers who were rising out of the slums and demanding clear, concise information on world affairs and politics.

Robert's own socialist and pacifist tendencies had to be kept to himself during that jingoistic time as the Boer War was coming to a conclusion. Although the most self-effacing of men in public, Robert concealed a maelstrom of internal emotion and he had ambitions to make his mark. He wanted to be at the hub of news-making, he wanted to reach out to the masses and cause them to stop and think about the world and where it was going. He felt that if everyone pulled together the common man could have his day. In his ideal world, the monarchs would be the first with their backs to the wall.

While Robert was mentally rising up against injustice and inequality, Fanny's spirits were sinking ever lower. The baby wasn't sleeping well at all and even with help around the house, Fanny was feeling exhausted. Robert had said they could not afford a full-time nurse for the boy, and she must take care of him herself. The responsibility and stress was too much for her. Depression stole up and enveloped her like a creeping fog, and before she knew it she was on the edge of a precipice. In February 1902 Fanny went back to Leeds to stay with one of her painter friends, Bertha Doyle.

Replying to a letter from Robert, she wrote, 'I am glad to see you write to me, although I know it is only to know how the son is. Well he is behaving much better than he ever did at home, simply because someone is always nursing him. Mrs. Doyle says she never saw a baby so good before, but she puts it down to my disposition during the making, she says it is my easy go lucky style.'

Thanking him for the money he sent her, much of which she had 'blued' on paints, Fanny went on to describe the fun she was having: painting, visiting the art gallery, and going ice-skating. According to Adrian, the picture she worked on was one of Lady Godiva, with a curtain of yellow hair that Fanny could have copied from her own mirror image. In fact she copied the picture from Leighton's original in the Leeds art gallery, but Fanny may well have envied the historical character her nerve and daring, for she too liked to cause a stir. Later, Adrian would say that she had painted two copies of Waterhouse's Lady of Shalott, and again she no doubt identified with the subject.

Mother and son returned home, and the two had found a new closeness born of calmer times. Fanny was so restored to health that the following year she agreed to spend some time in Edinburgh with her in-laws, and promised to be on her best behaviour. The family travelled north in June 1903 and Robert, having installed them, went back to his work in Manchester. Fanny wrote to him, '...Baby is really very good. He is greatly taken up with a stag's head that is over the dining room door but he won't stroke it...I went to church this morning and again this evening. Ta ta.'

The very fact that Fanny had willingly set foot in church was a sign that she was trying very hard to please her devout hosts. Two weeks later she was still with them, and wrote to her husband, 'I have just got our boy to sleep and he looks fine, so peaceful and rosy with his dummy and his chubby hands all in a tangled heap....I look forward to you coming again, as I shall be all alone. Lizzie will have Mamie and you and I could share the kid. When you come, come for a fortnight and then take a week later...Don't forget to write to me if it is only to ask how Baby is. Much love dear. Fanny.'

Lizzie was Robert's sister who took on the care of various nieces and nephews in her time, including the children of their brother

Hay, who had gone to Portugal to find his fortune. He would regularly send back crates of sardines, and occasionally a child, to be raised and educated in Edinburgh.

When Fanny went home she hardly needed to unpack her bags, as the family was about to move again. Robert Bell was going up in the newspaper world, and a new opportunity had arisen that should suit his culture-starved wife too.

One can easily see why Robert jumped at the chance to go to London and join the staff of Arthur Pearson's *St. James's Gazette*. Pearson, who had won his first job on *Tit Bits* in a competition, was the epitome of a self-made man. Still in his thirties, he was rapidly building an empire which already included the *Daily Express*, and he offered Robert a part in his next push. He was about to buy the *Evening Standard* and secretly intended to amalgamate it with the *St. James's Gazette* to form a great new, penny journal. Robert could not resist such an opportunity to be at the heart of the new organisation, and at an excellent salary of nearly £500 a year. Naturally, Fanny was delighted when he gave her the news.

The Bell family headed south when Adrian was just a toddler, so his first real memories of growing up centred on their large apartment in Norfolk Mansions, Prince of Wales Road, Battersea, and the parks around. He would remember Chelsea Bridge from where he looked down on the strong-armed shouting barge-men. He was impressed by the marching bands and the little, pricked-thumb dot of a dressed-up monkey on a barrel organ in the street. It was a time when aeronauts were taking to the air in gas balloons and whenever weather permitted they would launch from the parks and rise up above the astounded crowds. Adrian recalled seeing a silver airship one day, and his mind had flown with it on a voyage to fantastic discoveries.

Motor cars were increasingly appearing but mostly he would see horses of all kinds, from prancing thoroughbreds in the park, to sad old drudges plodding on the wooden-paved road. As the nodding beasts strained against their load, Adrian listened to the wheels of the drays 'rumbling like thunder - with an interval of silence when there was straw down because somebody lay gravely ill within', as he later wrote. There were the rich and privileged folk: ladies in finery, gents in satin-lined cloaks - he recalled seeing his neighbour, the author G.K. Chesterton, in just such garb - and there were the tragic, down-and out families, hanging around in the hope of a few spare coppers.

Adrian took everything in, but he was slow in learning to speak, which caused great consternation to his mother. He must be cured, she insisted, or her plans for his illustrious future would be severely curtailed if he turned out to be dumb. She need not have worried: he eventually worked out how to put his thoughts into sounds, and in time would more than make up for his late start.

And now he had a nurse, Miss Evans, who would say later that 'Adrian was rather a difficult little boy'. Certainly, he was strong-willed, and occasionally given to tantrums. He hated the taste of the iron tonic he was given to help his I.Q. and he often resisted drinking up his milk. But was it really so naughty to refuse to eat a dish of sheep's brain? Apparently so, in those days.

Part of Adrian's problem was that reality so often failed to match up to his eager imagination. If he had a kite, he would expect it to sail up into the blue sky and bob about, waggling its bow-tied tail at him from on high. Sadly, he tried it on a day when there was no wind.

The abject failure of his scheme led him to throw himself on the ground and thrash about like a drowning boy. His mother, horrified, rushed him home and threw the kite on the fire. Another time, instead of being overjoyed at the gift of a new rocking horse, he eyed its wild, snorting expression and shrieked in fear. It was not the most gentlemanly behaviour.

Of course Fanny loved being back in London, with its eclectic mix of fashion, culture and wealth. While her infant boy was being cared for by his nurse, Fanny went to sales, hunting for bargains in tasteful old furniture that had yet to be elevated to the class of 'antique'. She had an eye for craftsmanship and style, albeit a little chipped or faded. There was the Empire couch, the great sideboard which would dominate their dining room, and the dainty gilt girandolas for wall-mounting candles. The effect was perhaps a little eccentric, but it suited her fine.

Fanny would buy clothes from a dressmaker who was good at recycling the outfits of minor stage artistes. The dramatic colours and designs appealed to Fanny's artistic eye. It was some years since she had been a serious painter; she had been trying so hard to devote herself to being a housewife, but art burned in her and made her restless. The great passion she felt would well up inside until it spilled into urgent gushes of affection over her boy child. Such was the power of her emotion that it frightened him; he caught glimpses of an abyss inside her that he knew could engulf him.

Conversely, if he offended her she shunned him, sometimes for days, leaving him sad and confused by her silence. He was her life, and his education her life's work. She saw the cruelty only as kindness.

Determined that Adrian would grow up to be a gentleman, Fanny watched his every move and he particularly remembered the painful lessons in etiquette, when his mother would surreptitiously pinch his arm to remind him to say please or thank you, or to ward him away from some social faux-pas. She chose dandy clothes for him and had him buttoned into starchy shirts and strangling collars. Once, as a sweet little tot with curling fair hair, he had been voted the bonniest baby in the park and from then on he had a reputation to uphold, which he did at great cost to his comfort.

By this time, Adrian's memory was beginning to set pictures in his mind. He would later recall the balcony of the flat, where he spent much time peering through the iron railings at the scenes of life below. There were the carriages and the trades vans, and on foot the beggars, passing along the road and calling out for pity. Adrian did not understand. His nurse hustled him away, dismissing the people as 'the unemployed' and threatening that they would take him away if he didn't drink his milk. He found a lot to fear both in the unknown and in the adult threats, but then he detected something exciting in his environment, and it was the spark that would lead him on to inspiration.

Adrian had always viewed nature from a distance, either seeing the beauty of the parks from his stifling wrappings and springing pram, or later from the path as he was marched out for his daily walk. The ranks of bedding plants left him unmoved, and the tall trees of the park seemed to stand to attention too rigidly. But up on the balcony, a clump of dowdy mignonette had been planted in a window box, and one day its sweet scent found its way into Adrian's senses.

Standing gazing at the street below, the little boy caught the faintest whiff, and turned his head this way and that to catch it again. He traced its direction and sniffed curiously at that elusive scent which no man could have manufactured. The wafting siren smell liberated a bird in the little boy's soul, one that had been imprisoned by the constraints of daily routine and training. In an instant he knew there was more to life than his home and family, than the streets of London and the parks. Somewhere out there was a different kind of green. Somewhere there was love, but he didn't yet know its name. He would remember that sensation forever, and one day he wrote a poem about it.

Whence the vision in the flower
No experience tells,
When than I so little lower
Hung its peal of bells

Passing all the flare and flourish;
Poppies with hearts of jet,
I was halted dream-nightmarish
By grey-green mignonette.

When was put that spell upon me
By that small scented spire,
Too young for sentimentality
Or memory or desire?

Threatened by beauty as by thunder,
In that hour I knew
Both the danger and the wonder
Of years-hence loving you.

Perhaps he inherited that gift for poetry from his sensitive father, but Adrian hardly ever saw him nowadays. Robert's work on the *St. James's Gazette* kept him out most nights until dawn. He had joined the newspaper during a turbulent time in politics, and with the latest technology of telephones and telegraphs, reporters were sending in up-to-the minute news, which had to be fed to the avid readers. Robert was certainly at the hub of the action and it occupied his mind every minute of the waking day. When he did come home his racing brain would resist sleep, so that for relaxation he would sit and play the piano, soothing his nerves with strains of Bach.

It might seem that Robert's standing should have made Fanny proud of him, but his absence and distraction were getting her down once more. Her expression was adopting a permanent look of impatience while Robert's was increasingly withdrawn and closed.

Their former good-natured sparring at the dinner table had turned to sniping and Robert was constantly reminding his wife of the need for frugality. He simply could not appreciate her passion for fun and excitement. His puritanical parents had scorned those who idolised fashion, and denounced frivolity as the work of the Devil. He had been brought up to respect hard work and education, not leisure and games.

In the early days of their marriage they had found common ground in the arts and music, and their opposing views on social matters had presented no barrier to their good humour. While he would promote the right of the proletariat to be given a fair chance, she would counter with a caustic remark such as 'If they had it in them to be anything better they would not be servants.'

Guests at their table would laugh, and Robert had to smile graciously. But they had both changed, and neither felt so inclined to compromise any more. Fanny began seriously to go off the rails.

Even from his earliest years, Adrian thought he noticed the sweet smell on his mother's breath that signalled her strangely animated moods. The gales of laughter held a frightening tone for him, even though he was well used to her outbursts of song and music hall humour. To see her get up and dance on the table was nothing short of terrifying. His father hardly seemed to notice.

Fanny was drinking, and she was constantly going to the doctor's and coming back with tablets to boost her spirits. Her highs and lows were becoming more hyperbolic and when she walked out to meet friends, she put on a joie de vivre that was as empty as the discarded bottles left behind. Yes, she could be a good sport and fun to be with. But she was going out and coming back alone.

Adrian did not pick up the tension between his parents then, but one event occurred which he later pinpointed as the start of his own troubles. His beautiful mother had gone out in a shimmer of evening wear and perfume, and he had waited in the darkness of his room for her return. The hours passed and she did not come home.

All the tales his nurse had told him came crowding in on him, of how naughty boys were abandoned by their mothers. Could it be that his loving comforter had gone for good? As his anxiety mounted, he imagined his fate as a darkness enveloping him. It closed around him and a pain stole into his head, gripping tighter and tighter. He screamed. The black agony and long, slow recovery would become a regular feature in his life from now on: Adrian had experienced his first migraine.

The story as Adrian recalled it was one explanation for the disabling headaches that dogged most of his life. In fact, despite many and various unsuccessful attempts at finding a reason or a cure for them, the most likely cause seems to be a head injury through the use of the forceps at birth. Even so, he did have a very traumatic parting from Fanny when he was only two, and this was one he never mentioned.

Fanny, it seems, had been spending so much time in the company of her doctor that she had fallen in love with him. The relationship was in danger of becoming an affair. Fanny was too loyal to her family to bring shame on them for her own personal gratification, so she turned to her bottled consolation for solace. If life could not be as she dreamed, she would remove herself from its reality and shut the pain inside. But the pressure was building dangerously.

Robert foresaw that there was trouble ahead and he arranged for his little son to go to Scotland, to stay with his father at Alva, Clackmannanshire. Adrian was a little frightened of the old man whose deafness caused him to bawl too loudly for most people's comfort. Daily postcards reported Adrian's progress, stating that he was gradually settling in, that he didn't scream too much, only cried at times. Clearly he was missing his doting mother. It would be many weeks before he saw her again.

Fanny had a nervous breakdown in July 1904 and was sent away to her uncle's rectory at Swanmore on the Isle of Wight to recuperate. Uncle Fred was always to be dubbed the Two-bottle Parson, but his clear-headed wife sent regular notes to Robert and eventually Fanny herself managed a letter from her exile.

She wrote, 'I am getting very like myself again but shall always carry the inward feeling that I have passed through a great tragedy. Although the name of it is simply hysteria. Don't ever sneer at those poor women again, believe me when I truly say it is <u>Hell</u>. To be more cheerful, I am looking forward to coming home and shall take up my duties with a real relish, I hope.

'...I can't tell you how awfully sorry I am to have caused this experience. I still wonder if it could have been avoided... We shall see what we shall see...I believe I have another fortnight to stay here, then I shall come home and talk things over. Meantime I have not much to write about. I am relieved to know the kiddie is well (I wonder really how he looks, am dying to see him)!

'Ta ta - for I don't know for how long but I really will write in a day or so again. Kiss the boy for me and please burn my letter.'

For much of the time Adrian stayed with his grandfather, Alex Bell. He was too young to know what was going on, and later he made no reference to any memories of that time. Alex wrote to Robert, 'I feel for you in your wife being so sorely afflicted. It is a satisfaction to us here if we can contribute one iota to lessen her anxiety...Room in abundance is here, and dwelling on the hillside facing the open as far as man can see is the A.1. position for health. A dual bodyguard should be enough to keep his eminence in order, and afford him pleasure too.'

Adrian was being cared for by an elderly aunt, Alice Brown, and also enjoyed being spoilt by others of the Bell clan. But it was not the same as home.

One can only guess what effect this all had on Adrian. Night after night he went to bed without his goodnight kiss from the lovely lady who called him 'My darling boy.' She had always sung to him, lately it had been a new song with undertones which had been ominous for the intense child: 'Goodbye, Dolly I must leave you, Though it breaks my heart to go...' Without this strange lullaby he slept uneasily until, after many days of weeping, the memory of the sweet chanteuse began to fade.

Alone in London, Robert was at a loss to know what to do. He must carry on with his work and hope against hope that his wife would recover her senses and come home. If he lost her now, his father Alex would have every right to say 'I told you so.' Of course, the fervently religious man would do nothing of the sort, but Robert must have felt that his mother, even in her grave, was grieving for his pain and reproaching him for his reckless choice of a wife.

Because his parents had certainly made it clear to him that Fanny was not their idea of a good woman, when he took her home to Scotland that first time.

## 2. Roots of the Tree

'Austere' would be the best way to describe the Bell family home in Edinburgh. Austere, even by Victorian standards. In the twilight years of the nineteenth century, the household was draped in a quiet gloom, untroubled by laughter or joy. On the Sabbath, even the too-cheery sun was expelled, with the blinds snapped down in its face. Inside, the Good Lord was being praised with puritanical passion.

While the upper classes were vying to outdo each other's opulence and throwing lavish parties, and even the middle classes were enjoying themselves on a lesser scale, one dour house in Hartington Place played host only to God. Singing was reserved for hymns. Dancing was banned. Tobacco, cards, the theatre, even bagatelle and carpet bowls were considered to be entertainments of the Devil. As far as they were concerned, Satan could have all the fun - the Bells were a more serious lot.

Admittedly life had not been easy for the head of the household, Alexander Bell junior. His first wife had died within a year of their marriage. His second wife, Jessie Brown, also died within a year of her wedding, just three days after giving birth to a sickly son. The motherless child, called Alexander Brown Bell, was wet-nursed by a formidable matron who wore black-and-white tartan and had a taste for stout. On her fortified milk he thrived, and was handed into the care of his grandmother and doting aunts.

Lovingly, they filled him with rhubarb, castor oil, senna tea and what he would call a 'horrible powder' called Gregory's Mixture, along with various forms of nourishment including, of course, plenty of porridge.

In 1864 Alexander found a third wife, a shoemaker's daughter named Catherine Hay. At the time of their wedding the twice-widowed Alexander was only 33, and his bride nine years younger. Thankfully, she survived the century out. Almost exactly nine months after this lucky marriage, a baby boy was born to the Bells, and they named him Robert.

More children came along, mostly at one and two year intervals: Elizabeth, George, Mary, Charles, James and Hay. Charles did not survive, but the others did, which in itself was a blessing at that time, as one after another the doting aunts and other relatives succumbed to the diseases of the age, with tuberculosis - known as consumption - being the most common. Granny Bell never opened a window again, for fear of letting in the Grim Reaper and his arsenal of diseases, along with the chill wind.

As for thunderstorms, she seemed to view these as 'a manifestation of Divine power or wrath' according to her grandson. Or rather, she chose not to view them at all, insisting that the blinds be drawn down and the members of the household gather in the dining room where they would sit 'in solemn silence till the storm ceased, as if they were preparing for the Last Judgement.'

But her son Alexander Bell was not for worrying about impending doom - his solace lie in the devout belief that his wives, his sisters, two brothers, two nephews and his own little son had gone to a better place. God would take good care of their souls. Here on earth, he had his own problems to think about.

In middle age, Alexander was feeling that duty to The Lord should come before most other things, including the need to make a living. His grip on the family ironmongery firm was slipping, as he was reeled in by the inexorable pull of the Church.

One of Alexander's sons described him as having 'an almost morbid religious seriousness' and added, 'apart from his business...seemed to find little or no interest in life outside religious matters.'

One can imagine Alexander, sitting at his great desk, with the account books at his left hand and his Bible at his right, torn between the need to earn his daily bread and the passionate desire to be led away from temptation and delivered from evil. It was a tough dilemma, with filial loyalty at its very root.

His father, Alexander Bell senior, had built up the Edinburgh business from scratch, first in Princes Street and then moving round the corner to Frederick Street, where locals knew it as 'The Wee Shoppie.' By the time Alexander senior died in 1870 he was worth a small fortune - around £10,000 - including several properties.

The old man had had his religious beliefs too, of course; he left various legacies to church funds, including £5 to the 'Scheme for Converting the Jews.' But he had never lost sight of his faith in his business acumen, and his son had been set to continue in the same shrewd way. It was not to be. Alexander junior had discovered Calvinism, and it was gradually taking over his whole life.

To cut down his responsibilities to the business, the younger Alexander took on a partner in 1878, which backfired slightly in that the firm grew stronger still. Messrs. Bell, Donaldson and Company, now in George Street, gained a reputation as the best ironmongers in Scotland. Mostly they supplied metal goods to builders, cabinet makers and farmers, but they had a firm foothold in Edinburgh's domestic trade too; 'articles of sanitary ironware a speciality.'

So he turned to his children to lend a hand. But his eldest son, the erstwhile sickly child Alexander Brown Bell, was warned that his unhealthy heart - later found to have been wrongly diagnosed - must constrain him from taking an active part in the hardware business. The young man turned his attention instead to hard facts, and went off to a life in journalism.

Then young Robert, the next son, followed that path too. Always dreaming of poetry and fine words, and with the strains of beautiful music filling his head, Robert was forming strong ideas and priorities. He soon ducked out of religion and ironmongery.

At Edinburgh University, Robert had taken an Arts course and also studied music, developing a style all of his own when immersing himself in his beloved piano concertos. For a career he too had chosen journalism, starting on the *Fifeshire Journal* before moving around England with his sights set on Fleet Street.

It was left to the younger brother George to try his hand at running the family business, much to Alexander's relief.

Alexander was no despot, but he made it clear he thought one of his sons ought to be doing their duty by carrying on the family trade. Surely he had brought them up to respect their elders, as the Good Lord commanded?

His wife Catherine supported his views, but she had a softer side to her nature too, so that the children had a good balance of discipline and care. Catherine was quite beautiful, with auburn hair and a healthy pink complexion. She made large quantities of good, plain porridge, and dreamt of making even better porridge, the 'Shearer's porridge' as she called it, that sustained the rough-tough farm hands at harvest time. The quality of Shearer's porridge was a product of the vast amount required, which was boiled up in the washing copper with a domestic constantly stirring it with a broom handle until ready to serve. Unfortunately even her large, hungry brood would make little impression on this amount, so it had to remain a treat for harvest holidays spent on a farm.

Catherine's sons remembered her most for her sharp intelligence. Refusing to send them to school before they were six, Catherine encouraged them to read widely at home. She certainly set them an example in this, with her diverse choice including Calvin's *Institutes*, Byron's *Don Juan* and lengthy newspaper reports of Parliamentary debates.

Catherine's health declined later in life, and by 1890 she was almost an invalid. From then on, her pleasure lay in sneaking a crafty game of whist while Alexander was out, for she knew he would not approve. She had been pleased to see her stepson Alexander Brown Bell married the year before. Her eldest daughter Elizabeth then wed in 1892, and three years later there was more excitement for the frail old lady; her own boy Robert had become engaged, and he was bringing his fiancee Emily Hanbury to meet them all.

Typically, Robert had told them virtually nothing, and his betrothal had come as something of a surprise. Both Alexander and Catherine must have wondered about the only woman to have captured their son's heart - was she a good, God-fearing girl? Humble, modest, meek and mild? Surely she must be respectful, quiet and sensible.

They were in for an almighty shock.

The Hanburys: what a complex, colourful and unwealthy family they were. How far back to go? To the putative connection with Sir Charles Hanbury-Williams, eighteenth century ambassador who was a favourite of Catherine the Great, but came home to England and killed himself? This son of the ancient Worcestershire Hanbury family was renowned for his wit, and that if nothing else was inherited by the other Hanburys on his family tree.

Possibly there was also some money around when Thomas James Hanbury, son of a stockbroker, was working as a clerk to an attorney in London. But then Thomas lost the lot by standing security for a friend - it is said he was a peer - whose charm and enthusiasm outweighed his business acumen.

Thomas was lucky in one respect: he was declared bankrupt in 1862. Had it been a year earlier, before a change in law, he may well have found himself incarcerated in a debtor's prison like Dorrit of Dickensian fame. But Thomas' family did suffer as a result of his fall from grace. His daughter Gertrude, engaged to a gentleman, found herself having to release the panic-stricken chap from his bond. She would remain a spinster.

Of his other five children, Ada, a talented artist, would become a recluse albeit a contented one, William 'Fred' Hanbury would settle on the Isle of Wight as a parson who worshipped the amber spirit as much as the offertory wine, and James 'Gus' would emigrate to Australia. Blanche, farmed out to an aunt, was to marry a notable schoolmaster, and the eldest son, Charles John de Witt Hanbury, would do his best to hold his head up high. He is the one we are concerned with.

There are various family stories about the de Witt side of Charles' name, which came from his mother's side. Some say that old man Witt was 'flogged through the streets of Amsterdam' - his crime is unspecified. Others say that Uncle Richard Witt was 'captured by the Chinese' and there may well be a connection with the Opium Wars of the 1840s. Certainly he died at sea. His sister, Emma Lydia Witt, was the one to marry Thomas Hanbury.

Their children became known as 'The Hanbury Six.' Today that would have criminal connotations, but Thomas managed to stay out of prison, as mentioned, and maintained his dignity in spite of penury. Yet the Hanburys held fast to the belief that there was still some money hidden away in a convincingly heavy, locked wooden chest at the end of Thomas's bed. Unfortunately, when he died, it was broken open and found to have been nailed to the floor, empty.

So his son Charles had to work for a living, disgraceful though that seemed, and his occupations are variously recorded as architect, surveyor, and estate agent. He made enough money for the family to uphold its middle class status and he never lost his sense of breeding, or his eye for decorum.

'No gentleman', he declared, 'would ever come down to breakfast in his carpet slippers.' This and other pearls of propriety were scattered before his daughters, for whom he had great hopes that one day, something would come up. The trouble was, the girls would later insist, he was just too good a man to be successful in business. But even if he could not provide the high life in practice he made sure that the family saw it from the outside, and hungered for it inside.

Charles and his wife Georgiana had three daughters, and the 1881 census shows them living with their servant in Peckham, London, while the birthplaces listed for their children indicate that they had moved around in the last ten years or so. The two younger girls, Emily, known as Fanny and Katherine, always called Katie, were close confidantes and co-conspirators. Their eyes were kept wide open to the beauty and finery all around them in the streets of London, and no doubt in their own home they play-acted and dressed up, teetering in their mother's shoes, a boa slung round their neck and borrowed necklaces dangling to their tummies.

Fanny, a bubbly child with a golden waterfall of hair, loved colour and beauty, and most of all she adored attention. She especially admired the ladies of the stage, who got to wear the most outlandish and decorative outfits, and obviously enjoyed life to the very full. Not for those women the dignified, sit-down-and-be-served stiffness of the Army and Navy store, where the Hanburys did most of their shopping. The showy women had private dressmakers, and wherever they went they were feted by the public and adored by wealthy, dashing gents who heaped gifts on them. That was the life for Fanny and Katie, the girls decided.

Their bid for freedom was daring but disorganised. Instead of going to school one day the pair set off on the road to stardom, but they did not get far before their legs tired and they stopped for a rest. A passer-by realised they were truants, and 'rescued' them, much to their chagrin. Another time, Katie did manage to get away and secure work as a dancer, but again she was soon discovered and brought back.

Perhaps the girls' escapade was linked to the recent death of their mother, Georgiana. At the age of only 38 she had succumbed to a chest infection; at the time of her passing Fanny had been ten and Katie only six. Fanny's only memory of parental bliss was the way her mother, a former music hall artiste, used to lie with her feet up on her husband Charles' lap and he would stroke her legs lovingly. She would fall asleep and he would not dare move for fear of waking her.

Fanny did pursue her dream to some extent, she moved north to become a student at the Leeds School of Art. Her father had re-married and moved to Leeds, but the stepmother took a dislike to the daughters. Fanny moved in to lodgings, and financed herself and her studies by painting antique furniture. It was at one of the weekly students' dances that she was to meet Robert Bell, then a journalist at the *Leeds Daily News*.

Apparently these dances were quite simple affairs, with music provided by a pianist and sometimes a violinist too. The students had little money but a great deal of enthusiasm, and with the whole world at their feet, they danced away the night to whatever music was on offer. Except on the night Robert Bell went along with a friend. Short of a musician, they had cajoled the young introvert into playing, but as he became carried away, he became oblivious to the needs of his audience and he pounded the waltz and the polka beyond anyone's physical ability to follow. Fanny volunteered to distract him.

Had she ever stopped to consider the possible consequences, she might have thought twice about her actions. What she was about to do was tantamount to opening the tomb of an Egyptian king. She would cast light into the dusty darkness of the young man's soul and find treasure there, but also, in some ways, a curse.

Such was Fanny's success in capturing the attention of the startled young Scot, he turned up at every possible event after that. Standing by the wall, fingering his moustache and staring at his feet, he represented a challenge to the girl whose friends were all so amused by him. His large drooping eyes seemed to hold a twinkle that suggested humour and yet his rumpled, ill-fitting apparel showed he had no-one to take care of him. She, Fanny, liked to bring out the best in people. To her surprise, the information she winkled out of him revealed a man of real depth and intelligence, which was, she had to admit, lacking in many others of her acquaintance.

One has to assume they went on a number of dates, but it seems that Fanny was keeping quiet about it. She would not introduce him to her father, and this bothered Robert. He wanted this courtship thing done properly.

There came a day - it was the 11th March 1895 - when Robert, tense yet determined, handed Fanny a letter. It was an ultimatum. In tiny, loopless writing, he begged, 'Dear Miss Hanbury, I see only one way out of my dilemma. I enclose a note to your father asking him whether I may have his consent to continue your acquaintance....' In particular, he wanted to take her to a concert, but did not feel he could do so without permission. It ended, 'yours, Robert Bell. P.S. Have I got your father's name right?'

Fanny had a choice: if she posted the note, it would be a signal that she wanted the relationship to become serious. If she tore it up, she would go back to her footloose former life and an uncertain future. It was a tricky one.

She had been in love once, but had known the man was 'a bounder'. She had terminated the affair and admitted to friends 'we would have ended in the gutter'. That could never happen with Robert; dear, inoffensive little man that he was. In giving her this letter, he had put her whole future into her hands.

Fanny hesitated. Should she post it, or shouldn't she? Finally, with a shrug, she popped it in the letterbox.

Fanny's father duly received the letter and, after hearing more about the young man made the pronouncement, often repeated in the family, that 'Journalists are a shady lot and seldom sons of gentlemen.' He approved the match, with condescension.

The couple soon became engaged and all that remained before the wedding was for Fanny to be taken to Scotland and introduced to her future in-laws. For the journey she dressed smartly in a swirling skirt and saucy French cape. That was her first mistake.

Fanny's initial appearance must have alarmed the staid Bells and from then on matters went from bad to worse. Undaunted by the sharp scrutiny of Catherine Bell, or the mutterings of Alexander, Fanny was determined to show herself to be a valuable addition to the family. At every opportunity she displayed all her powers of jollity and charm, and chattered gaily, throwing in some witty music-hall verses to break up the solemn, philosophical conversations. Politely, the family waited for her to finish before continuing their discussion.

One afternoon, finding the younger brothers at their quiet pursuits in the drawing room, she burst in with her usual gusto, and prattled on merrily. Finally she bet they couldn't turn a cartwheel like she could. In a whirl of petticoats she whizzed across the room, to the utter horror and amazement of the lads.

Soon her behaviour brought her a special mention in the family prayers. Fanny, a devout atheist like her father, was unconcerned about their fears for her soul; 'We go out like a candle,' she would say. Life was for living in the here and now, as far as she was concerned. When the visit was over, Alexander declared 'That young woman knows nothing of Godliness.' Fanny would have taken it as a compliment.

Fanny, who summed up the Bells as being 'All porridge and prayers' was nevertheless married to Robert Bell in March 1896. She was then 23, and Robert seven years her senior.

For the next five years the unlikely couple seemed happy enough. They had their sad times - Fanny's elder sister Ellen died in 1897 and Robert's mother passed away in 1900. But mostly they lived in rented rooms while Robert freelanced as a journalist and Fanny painted, and planned dinner parties. They felt free and at the same time secure. At first Robert had been shocked to find himself spending more money in a month than he might previously have done in a year, but it was worth it to see the pleasure it gave his pretty, vivacious wife.

For her part, Fanny had always made it clear that she had no intention of becoming a drudge. Wherever they went, they must take rooms so that she would not have to worry about keeping house. She saw it as part of the deal for agreeing to marry him.

Robert might have agreed at the time but when he took up his challenging job at the *Manchester Daily Dispatch*, he decided it was time they put down roots. They had a baby on the way, so their carefree times must end, he said.

The house in Birch Avenue, Old Trafford, seemed the right sort of move to make. There were only eight houses in the road, semi-detached three-storey properties occupied by professional people, with at least one servant apiece. This was the place where Adrian Hanbury Bell would make his dramatic entrance to the world.

Their next home, the apartment in Battersea, was commodious enough, and at a rent of £65 a year cost more than many people earned. But Fanny would insist the family were poor and her word could never be doubted, least of all by Adrian.

The little boy must have been devastated when his gentle mother became a changeable enigma. First she was dull and desolate, then gay and loud, and one day Adrian would look back and admit that at least she was happy when she was drunk.

His love for her was like a living entity that grieved when they were apart. When he was sent up to Scotland and her life lay shipwrecked on the Isle of Wight, she still remained a part of him, and neither time nor space could shift it.

For them both, the weeks of separation served only to strengthen their bond and when the two came together again, it would be as momentous as the first fusion that begets new life.

# 3. Glengorse Days

As Fanny recovered from her breakdown, she and Robert were reconciled too. Another baby was born to them in February 1906. It was a son, Francis De Witt Bell.

Little Adrian didn't have much to do with his baby brother. He was going to kindergarten school now and, encouraged by his mother, he was developing a love of painting. His blossoming talent expressed itself in a charming rendition of a snowy daisy which he would remember and keep all his life, long after his artistic creativity had been trampled underfoot.

Meanwhile Fanny was continuing his education of Life, pointing out to him all the beauty of the London parks - see how the geraniums look like scarlet-clad guardsmen, she might say - and see how the guardsmen look just like geraniums.

His father would take him for walks, too, but these were more like expeditions, with maps, time-tables, supplies, and - most important of all - money for the sweet shop. It did not take Adrian long to realise that the choosing of the sweets was a serious matter, so that man and boy must deliberate carefully over the relative merits of each kind.

Then, flicking open his pocket watch as one might toss a yo-yo, Robert, dressed in his city suit, would take them on a bus trip to the starting point of their ramble. From there, losing track of time, and peering myopically at the map, he would lead his son away through hedges and over the green hills of Surrey and along the banks of the River Mole. As they rambled on, Robert would be talking all the while about his current hero - he went though a number of them - starting with Gladstone, and eventually ending with Winston Churchill. He would march along with his hands clasped behind his back, or with his ever-restless fingers fiddling with the map, or his glasses, or the change in his pocket.

Those were the best days, Adrian would recall, when he tried to match his father's hypnotic, on-and-on stride and fervently agreed with his every idea. His pa was an important man, he knew.

Robert was associate editor of the *Observer* now, so in the little boy's eyes he knew all there was to know about the world.

In an article written much later in life Adrian would describe his father in detail, unveiling the shy man inside the newsmaker. In public Robert could be invisible, he said, a non-person. He loved travelling, because then he had no duty or definite place of being, he could simply withdraw into himself and compose poetry.

'He lived a double life', Adrian wrote. 'Some men of his age vanished into the arms of mistresses...His mistress was the Muse: he "vanished" to enjoy her in third-class railway carriages or in municipal trams. How happy he was, gazing through steel spectacles at an advertisement for soap while his hidden self was fitting line to line of sonnet, triolet and ballade.'

Fanny saw only a 'disreputable pedestrian' in her husband on holiday. Adrian saw a happy man, a man borne along on a wave of mysterious ecstasy. He added, 'No man's spectacles were so eloquent as my father's. I can swear we felt his mood by the way the light fell on the lenses within the circlets of their steel frames...' Adrian explains that his father would often walk with his head tilted to the sky, causing his glasses to flash in the sunlight. At other times, in the home when he had had a tiff with Fanny, he would walk monk-like to the piano, and the shadows of the room would reflect in the downcast lenses.

While Adrian's father could be remote, there were few other opportunities to make friends, and so Adrian too learned to exist in another world, like a little cosmos of his own he said, into which other children made sudden appearances like meteorites. Mostly they bemused Adrian, but one boy succeeded in turning him into a gangster, or so he imagined.

Adrian's escapades with Berwick 'Turks' Holt were really little more than normal boyish scrapes, such as fighting with the neighbouring gang, or firing missiles at passing cab drivers. But as their pranks became more and more daring, or in his parents' eyes, downright dangerous, so Fanny and Robert became concerned about the influence of his playmate.

Not only was their erstwhile natty chap increasingly resembling a tramp, often coming home covered in mud and with clothes in disarray, Adrian says that on one occasion they found a policeman at the door, come to report some misdemeanour. Drastic steps were taken: Adrian was packed off to stay with his Aunt Katie in the beautiful countryside of Steeple Aston in Oxfordshire.

The decision would turn out to be another life-changing moment for Adrian. As soon as he arrived in the village, he felt the same stirring of excitement that the mignonette had aroused on the balcony of their flat, only magnified many times. In Oxfordshire there was not just a clump of spindly greenery, here the whole eye was awash with it.

Instead of manicured parks and paltry window boxes, here was the stronghold of nature. It was a tangible force that oozed out of every grain of soil, springing forth under every footstep. The pretty, mushroom-soup-and-crouton coloured stone cottages had enticing gardens of tumbling pastel hues, not garish primary colours, and each boasted neat rows of vegetables all tended by sure and knowing hands. In no time, Adrian had laid down his bow and arrows and fallen to his knees to scrabble in the soil and marvel at its potential.

It was just as the most informed biographer of Richard Jefferies, Samuel J. Looker, said: '...town experience seems essential in the evolution of men who write glowingly of the countryside.' Only those who have lived in towns seem to appreciate truly the beauty of the countryside, because the contrast strikes them as it cannot strike the country-dweller, to whom those experiences are everyday, and therefore overlooked. City living, said Looker, engendered a 'restless urge' and ambition. Of course, restlessness and ambition were also in Adrian's genes.

Aunt Katie was a fascinating lady. Her proud surname - Peacock - was apposite but inside she was a Hanbury through and through. The younger sister of Fanny, she had displayed a curious lack of prudence when, at the age of 17, she was asked by the gallant Doctor William Ernest Peacock for her hand in marriage. Trying her best to be tactful and sophisticated, she had declared that she could not marry anyone who lived in England. She wanted to live somewhere with a warmer climate.

As their son Carlos would later say, 'She underrated his determination.' The good doctor went and secured a job in Chile and Katie had run out of excuses.

The early days of their marriage had not been easy. Carlos recorded in his memoirs, 'She found herself as a young married woman marooned on the hurricane-swept peninsula that straggles out into the grim desolation of Tierra del Fuego and Cape Horn.'

The couple had lived in a corrugated iron hut and Doctor Peacock went on his all-day rounds on horseback, carrying a loaded shotgun, says Carlos. His patients were the sort who would shoot him if his cures failed.

It was a wild country but there were opportunities too. Doctor Peacock became involved in the sheep-rearing ventures that British settlers were starting in Patagonia. In that lawless land, Peacock would sit up all night and keep watch over the sheep, aware that out on the shadowy pampas, fortune-hunters high on cheap spirits would soon kill him for a quick buck. But, with a partner called Alec Cameron, Peacock's business had developed and soon even the Bells were buying shares in the deal.

So the Peacocks had come home somewhat richer and in 1903 they had a son, Thomas, born at Steeple Aston, in the three-storey house locally known as 'the Doctor's House.' The house stands atop a steep hill which caused many a problem for the doctor in his state-of-the-art but virtually brakeless De Dion motor car. Peacock had an irascible temperament and he would jump from the car, leaving his manservant to wedge chocks against the wheels.

His front door opened straight off the street and he would go crashing in, causing the paintings and ornaments to shiver all around the beautifully-furnished house. For Katie had an eye for quality and taste; she decorated the drawing room in white and gilt and the rest of the house was filled with antiques.

It was here that Adrian first came in 1907 to be diverted from his wayward path. In fact he had been there before, once with his mother when she was pregnant with her second child in September 1905, and again at Christmas that year just with his nurse, Miss Alice Evans, nicknamed 'Chunky.'

Then, writing to her 'Dear Little Baby', Fanny had asked, 'Are you a good boy and do you do what Alice tells you? Or does she have to make you stand in the corner till you are good? I hope not.' In another letter she enclosed a not very representative drawing of their pet cat, and wrote, 'I have just given Pokenose some egg that your wasteful Daddy left at breakfast time and a saucer of milk.' Robert was still finding it hard to please his wife.

Adrian seems not to have remembered that visit, but in 1907 every detail imprinted itself on him. Although he adored his Aunt Kate, it was the local carter's daughter who made the most impact on him then. Her family were poor and she was treated badly -

Adrian would always remember his horror at her being beaten for coming home late for tea. But he would also tell the tale of how she had shown him her secret collection of pottery fragments, and he had been entranced. Referring to her as 'Tetty' he would later reminisce about their days spent exploring the countryside, especially down by the stream. 'Tetty' he said, 'became of course my companion - my little mother, my girlfriend, my everything. She knew all the wild flowers, she taught me to catch minnows...' What more could a little boy want?

In the face of this feminine charm, all thoughts of Turks and fighting and derring-do paled like a flickering lantern in sunlight. From this moment on, the warmth of a woman's heart would ever take precedence in Adrian's esteem over the competitive motivations of a man's mind. Inevitably, when he suggested to his aunt that he might invite the girl to visit him in London, she quashed the notion. 'She's not our sort' was the reason given.

Over the next four years Adrian made several visits to Oxfordshire and each time he fell in love with the countryside anew. Then the Peacock family had to leave Steeple Aston so with Tom and their new baby Charles, always called Carlos, they moved to London. Eventually Kate would part from her restless, explosive husband.

For Adrian too, a separation was imminent: the love of his life was about to send him away from her again, and it was to be the most painful parting yet.

Robert and Fanny Bell had a third child in 1908, a daughter whom they named Eleanor Stephanie. She is mentioned little in Adrian's memoirs but he states that it became hard to bring up two babies in their Battersea flat, where the lady living above them would bang on the floor if they made too much noise.

Signs of strain were showing in Fanny once more and Robert took the initiative in finding them a home that he thought would bring them some peace and relaxation. He moved the family to a semi-detached villa in Streatham, with a rough patch of grass that served as a garden, and the golden gorse common of Tooting Bec across the way. The rent was much cheaper - only £24 a year, and the family took on a steady stream of servants, usually three were needed to cope with all the jobs of scrubbing, cooking and childcare. Fanny's critical and forthright manner in dealing with them meant they rarely lasted long.

This was a new and fascinating world for Adrian and at first his parents agreed, it was the right decision for them all. While Fanny had less need to worry about housework, she was determined to excel at household management. This being a less wealthy suburb she found she had nothing in common with her neighbours, and, feeling condemned to social isolation once more, she focussed all her attention on her children, and in particular on her first-born.

Of course Robert, as always, was oblivious to the domestic dramas. Every working day he caught the L.C.C. tram from Streatham High Street to the office, and he derived a curious pleasure in doing so, for he liked to sit among all the other dark-suited men and be camouflaged for a while. He returned home with a faraway smile on his lips and a weekly paper under his arm - the *Spectator*, the *Cornhill* or *Blackwoods* being typical of his choice of reading matter.

The parents saw that Adrian was happier with the freedom to roam in the rough grass of the common and play in the bushes with his friends. However, they were not entirely of one accord when they discovered that Adrian was raiding their larder. To save the maid from being accused, he admitted he was stealing the food for a tramp who had taken up residence in the gorse bushes on the common. Fanny was convinced the man must be on the run, whereas Robert's reaction was to quietly slip half a crown to Adrian for the poor man. It was typical of their diverging views on humanity.

The next great event in Adrian Bell's memory came in 1910. The boy had turned eight, and it was as if the click of the big hand on the twelve had started the cogs whirring in the time machine of his life. At eight, he must move on towards his destiny of becoming a gentleman.

In spite of Robert's protestations and arguments against privilege, Fanny set about finding a private school for the boy. First he was lodged down in Bournemouth, where a branch of the Hanburys were living, and he attended the High School there. It was an all-girls school but exceptions could be made, and the wide-eyed little boy spent two terms most probably in a state akin to shell-shock, assimilating little in the way of education.

He records nothing of his time there, but his Great Aunt Blanche was a kind lady who had shown admirable determination in securing the husband of her choice.

The man Blanche Hanbury had picked was the Reverend Theophilus Barton Rowe, then a schoolmaster at the illustrious Uppingham public school in Rutland. He had been widowed, and Blanche set about becoming wife number two. She succeeded eventually, in 1888 when she was 36 and he 55. But there were times when it seemed that the spectre of the first Mrs Rowe would not relinquish her hold so easily, such was the Reverend Mr Rowe's habit of talking about her.

Even so, three daughters were born to them, and by the time the Reverend Mr Rowe died in 1905 the family were to be found living comfortably in a large house called St Annes in Bournemouth. Adrian had visited on a number of occasions and did remember tennis parties with his aunts, two of whom would be left spinsters by the First World War. He also warmed to his Great Aunt Blanche, who took a keen interest in his continuing education.

Meanwhile, Fanny was in search of a suitable prep school for him. Her first instinct was to go to the place where she obtained just about every other necessity: the Army and Navy Store. There, a helpful assistant informed her that a school in Eastbourne was spoken of highly. Its name was Glengorse. Fanny took herself there on a fact-finding mission and one look at the school with its population of polished little page-boys all resembling Little Lord Fauntleroy was enough for Fanny.

In September 1910 Adrian was escorted to the railway station, where they were greeted by a 'bristly old gentleman', as Adrian described the Scottish headmaster of Glengorse, William Morrison. Their destination was Chesterfield Road, Eastbourne, near South Cliff; but this was to be no seaside holiday. Adrian's ensuing misery is documented in his autobiography, with images of spartan accommodation and iron rule.

The taste and smell of bread and dripping, and bedtime cocoa after prayers were abiding memories. Strangled by his uniform, stifled by the despotic regime, Adrian one day erupted in hysterics, bringing down upon himself the sharp, stabbing wrath of the heron-like Morrison. Speared by the collar, he was hooked out of class and rattled until his teeth chattered then plopped into his bed, where an agonising three-day migraine kept him pinioned.

There were brighter flashes in this swamp of youthful dismay. At the back of Glengorse was the girls' school, Hilcote, and every glimpse of these lithe, shining creatures left him curiously excited.

The sight of a whole shoal of them, white-fleshed in white dresses, filing demurely into church on Sundays, created in him a desire which surely bore no link to the crude boasting of the older boys who knew the 'facts of life'.

Adrian made some friends among the more sensitive lads, and recalled that one boy had kissed him and run away, leaving him startled among the coat-pegs. One of the less sensitive boys had riled Adrian to the extent that he punched the boy on the nose. The impulse was out of character but boxing lessons were part of the curriculum, so Adrian could at least say he had learned something. Apart from that, he felt that he was wasting his life away in a fuddle of incomprehensible facts and figures.

Salvation came when two young men named Jones and Appleton bought the school. The maths lessons continued but now, taught by the rotund Mr Jones, they seemed less daunting. As for Mr Appleton - his resemblance to the idolised character Sherlock Holmes meant he was an instant hero to the boys.

Adrian willingly attended extra Latin and Greek studies in Appleton's study and late one day, as he translated the ancient love poems and classic tales, he looked out at the dusky sky through an open window and the first star of evening winked at him. The dead languages as he had called them, were reborn.

An assistant master who also made an impression on Adrian was Ernest Raymond, who went on to become a well-known novelist and was awarded the O.B.E. In his early twenties he taught at Glengorse for three years, and Adrian remembered his skill at telling thrilling stories that transported the boys into new realms of adventure. Raymond was a devotee of Dickens - he would one day become president of the Dickens Fellowship - and he was a lover of poetry too, later writing a book entitled *Two Men of Rome, The Story of Keats and Shelley*. He understood what was in Adrian's heart, but he left in 1911 to take holy orders and so had little chance to influence him further.

Adrian's artistic soul had some more suffering to do before it could start to live and breathe in its own right. Now he must move on to public school life, to Uppingham, where masters waged a war against individuality with as great a gusto as the British military showed in sending its young men to fight the Boche.

On balance, Adrian was better off at Uppingham than at home, where hostilities had escalated and the wounds were growing ever deeper. It had begun with the good-humoured sparring between Robert and Fanny, and then a phase of bickering had set in. Now it was all out war.

Robert, having escaped the excesses of his religious upbringing, had turned into something of a preacher himself, holding forth on weighty political and philosophical matters. As a Fabian he had pledged never to hold savings of more than £150 (rising as time went on to £500) and, his neo-socialist views conflicting with his pacifist temperament, he would call for the execution of all the crowned heads of Europe.

Adrian wrote in his diary of one such occasion, when Robert's brother Jim was present, as well as a journalist friend, Charles Beattie, then of the *Daily Mail*. 'I remember their attempts to stem the torrent with faint expostulations. "But the facts, Robert. What are the facts?" My father, rocketing on, would not hear - or if he deigned to - snapped, "I know the facts. I am in a position to know" and continued headlong with sonorous quotes from Dr Johnson - or Whitman - or any verbal missile that came to hand. Then, having slammed all down, he would open the piano - take Bach at the gallop - then - quieting mysteriously, go for a seraph stroll in the evening light.'

Adrian added that his mother 'would occasionally shoot him down in mid-flight with a shaft of wit. On other occasions he would let it glance off him. Thus, to a visitor who did not know the household well, and was uncomfortably divided between paying attention to my father's exposition or to my mother's parallel but Collins Music Hall type of Monologue - "Mr ... - my wife has three jokes. Now that she has told them all, we can continue the discussion."

'My mother had a fund of sayings which she would produce independently of any relevance to what my father called The Discussion. My father, exasperated by these interpolations, would liken her to a parrot reacting mechanically to certain stimuli. Thus - if the word 'father' came up, my mother was apt to exclaim "It's a wise child who knows its own father." '

Adrian had begun to realise that all was not well with his mother. Even from the age of nine he had started to sense it, when she would leave him outside Streatham Station while she popped into the buffet for a 'quick one.'

At home she played the part of the assiduous housewife but

even in that she overdid it, obsessively polishing her veneer of efficiency.

Adrian's cousin Carlos wrote in his memoirs of a stormy Christmas celebration in the Bell household. He, his brother Tom, and their parents had come over from London to spend time with the Bells.

Carlos wrote, 'At the beginning of the meal we children were, as we expected to be, the focal point of the proceedings. We were shepherded to our chairs, presents were dealt out to us, crackers rattled in our ears to enhance the mystery of their contents. All this was as we expected, the traditional Christmas ritual that was so delightfully flattering to our little egos. But as the meal went on, our elders became so irritable and argumentative that we children were gradually thrust into the background and in the end completely forgotten.....

'At some stage that afternoon the conversation got round to Hinduism and to the customs of the Hindus generally. Someone (my Aunt Fanny, I think, who had a propensity to shock) threw in the statement that the floors of Hindu homes were made of compressed cow-dung. The effect was disastrous.'

Carlos goes on to describe the expostulations of his own father, a doctor with strong views on hygiene and coloured people. Opposed to him was Robert, liberal-minded and philanthropic, but equally adamant.

Their quarrel raged and spread like fire across a forest of topics, while the children cowered among the ruins of the gay decorations and half-eaten meal. Apart from anything else, Carlos could not believe that grown-ups could say 'cow-dung' so publicly.

He added, 'I was appalled, and also frightened at the sight of these two grown-ups glaring at one another over the carcass of the dismembered turkey.'

The event was imprinted on Carlos' mind and so was the dining room, which he describes in exquisite detail, with its maroon walls and crimson silk hangings. On the Regency sideboard an artistic arrangement of fruit in bowls particularly caught his eye. It was no wonder that Carlos should go on to become a curator at the Tate Gallery.

Adrian also wrote about that Christmas family debacle, although he tinkered with it and put it into *The Balcony*, one of his semi-autobiographical novels. He recalled that Charles Hanbury, father of Fanny and Kate, was there too, adding fuel to the flames of temper. The Hanburys en masse always posed a serious threat to Robert's equilibrium.

It was true that Robert did know a lot about world affairs - after all, he was now assistant editor of the *Observer*, working with the famous editor J.L. Garvin. As one commentator would say, in many ways Robert effectively was editor, for he ran the office for most of the week.

Certainly, when the newspaper's owner Lord Northcliffe appointed Garvin in 1908, he wrote to the new editor, 'I hope you will speedily make the acquaintance, if you have not already done so, of Mr Bell in the Observer office. You will find him a most industrious, amiable and capable colleague, very quick at adapting to a suggestion. He will relieve you of an immense amount of detail...Mr Bell will do all the drudgery for you.'

Garvin preferred to work at home, sending in his great works of political wisdom along with lengthy letters of instruction to Bell so that by the time he put in his weekly appearance on Saturday, the paper was virtually ready to roll. Bell acted as midwife while Garvin was in labour, said one later commentator.

The new team was a great success - the paper rapidly went from making losses such as a deficit of over £8,000 in 1906-7 to making a healthy profit, and increasing sales from twenty thousand to almost thirty thousand in six months. Garvin, it was said, saw Bell as a 'lieutenant who could help him in every kind of detail connected with the paper.' High praise indeed, but, even at the relatively high salary of 16 guineas a week, Robert never became rich by it, and Fanny found that hard to accept. While others rode around in hansom cabs or even motor cars, the Bell family still went by bus. 'We are poor' she told Adrian, many a time, and he believed her.

Robert enjoyed his job, though. While politics was the strict preserve of Garvin, 'Lieutenant' Bell, apart from carrying out orders, was in charge of book reviews which brought him into contact with many literary celebrities of the day. Also, he was able to write a column of thoughtful notes called *At Random* - a typically modest, dismissive title - and often he included poems of his own composition. These were very well received by the readers. However, Adrian would reflect that his father had probably sacrificed 'what I believe would have been a considerable power of literary expression' in the pursuit of news.

In 1910 the mutual admiration between Garvin and Lord Northcliffe had disintegrated and the editor, unable to raise the £40,000 needed to buy the *Observer*, persuaded Lord Astor to dip into his pocket instead. Northcliffe, on taking his leave, wrote personally to Robert Bell saying, 'Your work was one of the essential causes of the success we all achieved in raising the old wreck, refitting her and starting her on what, if the existing combination of men and enthusiasm be not disturbed, must continue to be a valuable and prosperous voyage.'

Sales continued to rise and in 1911 the circulation of the 36-page paper was quoted as being well over sixty thousand. Perhaps just as importantly Garvin would later say that with Bell's help they had made the *Observer* 'the happiest office in Fleet Street'.

The stormy internal politics of Britain were soon overshadowed by threats from overseas and in 1914 Garvin's view on war was eloquent and direct - he wrote in his leader article that the United Kingdom must enter the fray to safeguard its own future or be labelled 'deserter' by its allies.

Robert was in a quandary. He had always insisted, fiercely in the case of arguments with his father-in-law, that no nation would be so insane as to wage war on Britain. When the old man had declared 'It will come; war will come', Robert had leaped to his feet, shouting, 'Mr Hanbury, this is the greatest balderdash you've talked yet!'

But war did come, of course. Adrian remembered even in the first year of it, seeing the lines of soldiers at the railway station, 'on leave, counted in hours, the mud of France still on them. And another line in an opposite-going train, returning from leave - and each line of faces looking equally like doomed cattle, while London's gaiety went on above ground regardless.'

In Adrian's home, the threat was less from the Kaiser than from Robert himself. For a while he kept a loaded gun by his bed, ready to shoot the family and himself if the invasion came. One night, the crash of a falling picture had caused him almost to annihilate them all in their beds, and after that the gun was kept locked away.

It was in the midst of wartime, in 1915 that Adrian said goodbye to his familiar and now in some ways, beloved school at Glengorse. If the masters had carried out their promise to 'make a little man of him', then his next school would turn him into an automaton.

He was to go to Uppingham, the renowned school in Rutland

where Fanny's uncle, the Reverend Theophilus Rowe had once
been a housemaster. Rowe's widow, Adrian's Great Aunt Blanche,
gave him a copy of *Tom Browne's Schooldays* beforehand, and
Adrian's hair stood on end at the tales of cruelty and oppression.
He little guessed that she had given it to him to prepare him - for
he would find that Uppingham was just the same.

# 4. Mastering Uppingham

If Adrian, like his young cousin, was shocked at the term 'cow-dung,' he was utterly horrified by the language he heard at Uppingham. He later recalled with the humour of hindsight that he had never even dreamed that such words existed in the English vocabulary. They sullied his dreams of Greek tales and Latin romance; they stained his thinking altogether. But that was a minor problem.

At Uppingham Adrian was beaten, bullied, robbed, swindled and taunted. Nothing new in that, according to most reminiscences of early public school life. But Uppingham was going through a particularly difficult time owing to the advent of war and the departure of its fit young masters. The elderly men left in control of over 400 highly-charged pubescent boys had no control at all.

In the days when Adrian's Great Uncle Theo had been a master at the school, he had worked under the Reverend Edward Thring, one of the most celebrated names in the history of British education. Thring had arrived in 1853 and he became known as the 'second founder' of the school because of his genius and motivation in turning around its failing reputation. The numbers of pupils would rise from 43 to over 300 during his term of office and the school itself would expand, with new building works paid for by subscribers.

Thring had a talent for charming money out of people. One of those was the Reverend W.F. Witts, great uncle to Fanny Bell. It was customary for masters to buy into the school, retaining ownership of their 'boarding house' which Thring filled with paying pupils. Having promised to put in £1,000, Witts duly became a housemaster and had the dubious honour of thrashing one of his junior relatives. When Fanny told the story to her young boy, Adrian detected a note of relish in her delivery. It was all part of the great old tradition.

In teaching, Thring's ideas were revolutionary, and not always popular with the governors. He believed in helping poor achievers as well as bright ones and he taught a whole new curriculum including French, German, drawing, carpentry and music. Even if he was still a harsh disciplinarian, he seemed to like children and he seemed to have their best interests at heart. This was virtually unheard of at the time.

The Reverend Theophilus Rowe had been there as owner and master of Old Constables house from 1861 and he eventually went on to become headmaster of a school in Kent. Rowe left Uppingham in 1875 and in 1888 the school was taken over by a new headmaster who swept away Thring's philanthropic culture.

Dr E.C. Selwyn's time at Uppingham was, according to one historian, 'a disaster and a betrayal of Thring's principles.' The author Dr Tozer wrote in his book *Physical Education at Thring's Uppingham,* 'The Selwyn years saw all that was worst in public schools; athleticism, militarism and immorality came to Uppingham. Dulling uniformity replaced individual attention, esprit de corps ousted the ideal of manliness.'

Sensitive boys suffered immensely during this time, and many were taken away by their parents.

A new headmaster, H.W. McKenzie was appointed in 1908 and his aim was to restore the school's fortunes. He was a traditionalist - his wife used to walk ten paces behind him as he strode out in frock coat and top hat - but he is said to have had a sense of justice and humour that was refreshing to the sullen and oppressed boys. Uppingham became popular with parents once more.

The advent of war in 1914 saw six masters immediately join up to do their duty and although the rallying cry was 'school as usual,' anyone could see that could hardly be possible. In his history of the school, entitled *By God's Grace* Bryan Matthews wrote 'The replacements found for these officers were clearly not as capable nor as firm as they. Furthermore most of the activities which add sparkle or variety to a term disappeared - the visiting lecturers, the trips to exhibitions, away matches...there was little left but dull routine.'

And so it was when Adrian Bell arrived in 1915. McKenzie's health had broken down and the masters were floundering in their attempts to keep order. Like McKenzie they were suffering enormous stress which worsened every time they heard that one of their 'old boys' had been killed. Supplies of just about everything were becoming difficult to obtain, including food.

The new head of this lamentable situation was a handsome young man of 28, named R.H.Owen. As he stood before the school, the first question in everybody's mind was: 'Why isn't he doing his duty at the Front?'

There was never really an answer to that, although his wife said he had failed a fitness test. No evidence of it was found in military archives, then or since. The man was adjudged a coward by staff and pupils alike. His brash manner did nothing to endear him to parents either, and Owen's secretary intercepted many abusive letters before they reached his desk.

Adrian's housemaster was Hubert Champion, an elderly relic of the pitiless Selwyn era, who himself had no means of keeping order in the riotous classes. The pink-cheeked new boy in his smart new uniform was in for a very rough ride indeed.

Adrian wrote in his autobiography, 'I think my house was one of the worst at that time, due entirely to half a dozen fairly vicious boys of sixteen who persecuted the fags. Pocket money was extorted from new boys by the forced purchase of worthless objects, such as broken lampshades and dud fountain pens.'

A letter from the housemaster to Adrian's father, apologising for these events and promising to put matters right, still exists in the family archives.

In fact, 'Champ' as the boys called him was anything but a champion for the weaker boys. His prefects, called Praeposters, forced him to sign a charter in which they agreed to behave only if he kept to his side of the house and left them to their own devices.

Eventually he would be persuaded by Owen that his talents lay elsewhere, and he moved on in 1919 to become an Inspector of Schools. The school magazine carried a farewell that described him as 'individual in his methods and opinions,' and it noted the 'unusual fullness of interest and friendship which he showed to those who came into closer personal relations with him.' Adrian noted nothing of this, but he did receive several letters from 'Champ' in later life, when the elderly man enjoyed reading his former pupil's books.

Uppingham itself is a delightful place. The town, spread like butter over a green hill, consists of many attractive old houses and shops built of local ironstone, which is the colour of sucked honeycomb. The school is spread out too, with the main building right on top of the hill and the later additions dotted around it.

Strolling along the main street, one would hardly guess that one of the first things Adrian had to learn was on which side of the street he was allowed to walk. Only older boys from Constables house could take the direct route to the main school, others were not permitted to contaminate that pavement, so must cross and re-cross the road. Adrian recalled in his diary, 'trying to keep a speckly straw hat on in a snow-blizzard on Uppingham's bitter hill, for which purpose we bent them till they crackled and clamped them down on our heads like bonnets, as we made our way once a week to the Art School, symptomatically through the graveyard.'

Even art gave Adrian no pleasure at Uppingham, where they were given dull subjects to draw by a crackled old master. As Adrian mooted, 'What could he do with twenty rude, rugger-playing boys each presented with a wilting buttercup to paint?'

Adrian took his frustration out on the paper, firing paint at it with a thud. 'It was like a little world exploding,' he said. Certainly the days of delicate daisies had passed.

At meal times those rude, rugger-playing youths had a special game to play with Champ's spinster sister, who was a matron at the school. With outrageous double-entendres they held a seemingly innocent conversation with the plain, middle-aged woman, while those in the know sniggered at their daring.

There was little else to enjoy at the table. Adrian wrote of the dire lack of supplies in his diary for 28th February 1918. 'The food situation is becoming rather acute and Champ has gone mad about food. What annoys me is that he collared 30 scones and half a pound of <u>real fresh butter </u>which Rush had sent him, and gave him 1/- for the butter and 6d for the scones. He then proceeded to eat them himself. If he rations us so strictly why should he not be rationed himself? Rush has just got licked for throwing a piece of bread to Pope at tea. The matron was terribly fed up.'

Adrian was still suffering recurrent migraines, and after this entry he was ill for several days. His next entry came on 6th; March '..We are now rationed for bread.....Champ has also started not allowing us second helpings of pudding on certain days. We live chiefly on potatoes.'

Adrian's days spent in the school sick-room were not all wasted. As he lay on the hard bed, drifting in and out of awareness, he had time to dream inside the safe haven that was his real self. He wanted to be a poet when the war was over, and to write breathtaking verse like his heroes, Browning, Wordsworth, Tennyson and Keats. In his dream world he lay down under whispering trees and draped his hand in silken pools. In the cool moonlight behind his closed eyelids, love stepped gracefully in silver shoes, holding out her hand to the shy youth. It would be a pure love, not bawdy or brash, but deep and everlasting. When he came out of his suspended animation he felt reborn, and ready to face the real world in all its ugliness.

Back out in the school, it was business as usual. On 12th March 1918 Adrian noted, 'Escombe is getting hopelessly mobbed. He had to climb on to the roof of Fircroft fives court after his hat today amid showers of stones. He has taken to filling his pockets with stones which he flings at all aggressors. If he could throw straight he might be dangerous.'

Of course, the boys were being taught to improve their aim; the war was still going and there was a good chance they would be among the next cohort of schoolboys-turned-soldiers. Inside the classrooms, the dark, stained desks carried the inky inscriptions of many boys whose names were now being etched on the roll of honour. Outside, army drill was taking place.

Later Adrian made this note about the lads' preparation for a cavalry charge. 'Recalled today one of the more lunatic moments in my education at Uppingham. Officer Training Corps 1917 - an order to "Prepare to receive Cavalry!" Down we went on one knee in the mud, rifle with bayonet pointing somewhere towards the North Star. Like at Waterloo. No cavalry came of course.'

For Adrian, it was a case of mental survival as much as anything. In the early days, there had been no respite from persecution even in the earth closets that served as toilets, for there were no locks on the doors. Adrian later described these closets, 'the seats of which were on springs which were supposed to liberate a sprinkling of earth after each session. But in fact boys being mischievous boys - all the earth was exhausted on the first day of the week - and on the seventh day the gardener was seen puffing a strong pipe, emptying the 'bog' into a wheelbarrow from doors at the back. Our changing-room window looked on this operation at close range.'

Boys being boys, they found all matters scatological most interesting. Not until they were married men would they ever be so intimate with another human being.

Luckily, old headmaster Thring had had the wisdom to see that boys needed privacy sometimes and he had included study rooms in his new building projects. These were like little brick cells but they offered boys at least one small sanctuary where they could work in peace.

Now though, Adrian was older and so he was no longer bullied. He could slip away from the crowd and lie out in the sun on the sloping school grounds, and watch the clouds drifting overhead. His gentle nature still nestled inside his hardened shell, and he could commune with it in moments of perfect peace. Music and art had fallen by the wayside in these times of strife, but Adrian still had poetry inside him.

In his final terms, Adrian and his close friends began to make a difference at Uppingham. For most boys, senior status meant the opportunity to mete out the same kind of horrible treatment they had received as new boys. Adrian's group refused to do so; they rejected the fagging system and Adrian himself never beat a junior boy at all. He could see no pleasure in it.

There was one activity brought about by the war which would add another cobble to his road of destiny: that of the harvest camp. The Ministry of National Service had appealed for all able-bodied citizens to help bring in the year's crops and in 1917 Uppingham responded. Adrian did not record his reaction to the work, but he would have been amused by the debacle caused by a London government dictating to other areas of the country.

The Uppingham School Magazine noted that, because the authorities had declared that harvest should start on August 1$^{st}$, they had overlooked the fact that northern climates meant a longer growing season. So when dozens of boys were dispatched to camps in the Lake District, they spent the first three weeks cutting thistles and waiting for the corn to ripen. The following year, they started on August 20$^{th}$.

Sadly, this time they were confronted with non-stop rain and returned home thoroughly disheartened. It was noted in the magazine 'If we learnt nothing else at the Harvest Camp, we learnt to sympathise with the troubles of farmers.' Of the gruff Cumbrians themselves, the journalist reported, 'The farmers were not lavish in their praise...Most of them were nice people and easy to get on with, but they seemed to be surprised that we were not keen to take up agriculture as a profession.'

Adrian did not go far afield to help with the harvest on account of his propensity to be afflicted by migraine. He did help locally though and wrote in his diary of September 1918 'It was very healthy exercise but not so tiring as I thought. For the most part I was engaged in stacking and carting the corn.'

There is no hint in Adrian's reflections that a seed had been sown in his ambition. Farming and nature would one day become his whole life's impetus.

The spindly little boy had grown into a lithe, healthy youth, except for his prostrating headaches. One of the most precious gifts that a fit young man could be offered in 1918 was a future, and on 11th November the boys of Uppingham were granted their wish. Armistice came and the school was ecstatic. Adrian and his friends made torches out of newspapers and candle grease and paraded through the town whooping and yelling, gathering a crowd of onlookers and followers. Back at school there was a huge bonfire, fireworks, and explosions caused by boys throwing blank cartridges into the inferno. Tragically, one boy was hit in the eye and all further fires were forbidden.

Nothing could dampen the boys' excitement. For the following two nights, sudden bangs and flashes demonstrated their rebellion. Adrian wrote 'Champ was simply furious. He beat half the house, degraded all the pollies (prefects) and made Measures captain of the house with myself as a sort of half polly to help him. He had us in his study every evening and gave us long lectures on our behaviour, said that we were dishonourable and that he was a broken old man and even had the cheek to say that we were drunk! Altogether there was an awful row.'

The lengthy Armistice celebrations ended when almost every boy and master caught flu and was confined to bed. The pranksters still managed some mischief: they lobbed their milk puddings and porridge out of the windows which, Adrian commented, 'made a fearful mess down below'.

As the memorable year came to a close, Adrian concluded that he must give up any idea of becoming an author, because his poems were simply too childish and his sketches he found 'nauseating'. He added that this disillusion might be just a passing phase.

More vivid than any other memory of post-war Uppingham was the one that featured bare female flesh. 19th July was designated 'Peace Day' and in 1919 the boys were taken to Sutton-on Sea in

Lincolnshire for a celebratory day out. They picnicked and explored, taking care to avoid the sewer outlet, and the day concluded with sports on the beach. There, the teenage daughter of one of the masters won a race, and to speed her way she had hoisted up her skirt above her knees. This, said Adrian, 'caused a sensation', which was the highlight of the day, and all the way home on the train, the feverish thoughts of the pubescent youths turned the vision over and around in their minds.

Adrian left Uppingham in 1920. To modern thinking, he had had a torrid time there but he admitted to himself that he had enjoyed some aspects of it. Looking back at the end of term he knew that most of all he would miss the friends with whom he had become necessarily close. He said 'It all seems like a badly constructed tragedy, to have firm friends for five years and then suddenly to lose them all, probably forever...Shall we ever meet again or hear of one another again, I doubt it; each will go his own way, make other friends, marry, settle down and die. What can it all mean?'

All of this heavy emotion was poured into a poem entitled 'Vale' which Adrian sent to the school magazine. Part of it went:

To-day a sterner battle is begun
Whence I return not; and though now I'm bold
In glory of a goal that's never won,
Some day the fight will tire, and I'll grow old.
Then even as a widening, mud-dimmed stream,
Troubled with traffic, wandering to the sea
May glitter in a gust and seem to dream
Of the swifter, sun-wed brook it used to be,
So I'll remember thee, thy quiet ways,
Thy well-loved names, thy vanished yesterdays.

Now Adrian had to think about his future, and what kind of career he might pursue. He jotted down his thoughts. 'I have two ambitions, to write poetry and to have a small farm. About farming I know nothing and very little about poetry.' He added that he was unlikely ever to make money as a poet, and that his parents were urging him to take up journalism.

There had been talk of university, although only briefly. Robert finally asserted himself and declared that his son should not follow that privileged course, even though he himself had studied at

Edinburgh. Robert, having lost the fight against public school, was determined to win on this one. Against him, Fanny rallied her Aunt Blanche, widow of housemaster Rowe, who begged to no avail. If Adrian had survived Uppingham, she argued, he could go all the way through the system. And think of the opportunities that would open up.

Blanche had three daughters to support, but she even offered to pay the tuition fees, or at least lend the money if it were needed. Robert would have none of it. Much as he respected Blanche - they had even made a pact that whoever should die first would try to make contact with the other - he still would not listen to her. He could not have known that soon she would have her opportunity to try out their agreement, for even as she sat discussing the matter at hand, she had only three years to live. For his part, Adrian had never felt so close to her before, or so cared about.

The arguments at home swung back and forth over Adrian's head: could he make any money as a poet? Were there any other openings as a writer of articles, or as a journalist? What about his headaches, which had increased in frequency of late? The fact had to be faced - Adrian was virtually unemployable.

Adrian had already noticed that the tenuous sympathy that his father had for him was being stretched to breaking point. In his autobiography, Adrian wrote, 'My father ... looked at me when he came home as if I were a letter very difficult to answer, to which a reply was overdue.'

In exasperation, Robert declared that he would take the lad under his wing and find him a desk in the offices of the *Observer*. But then it became apparent that wartime Uppingham had not provided a budding journalist with the necessary skills of shorthand and typing. In fact Uppingham had been preparing its young boys for nothing beyond the trenches. Adrian would have to go back to lessons.

Before he could attempt a college course in journalism, he must pass his matriculation, his entry exam, and to get him ready for this, Fanny made the necessary arrangements. She enlisted a tutor named Mr Borland to teach her son the basics, at his 'crammer' school in Victoria.

Meanwhile, Robert had found a desk in the *Observer* office, in his very own office, and he stationed Adrian there in the afternoons to watch and learn. His son did watch, and he soon learned that he never, ever wanted to be a journalist. In his diary of March 1920 he reflected, 'I was there for about a month, in which time I came to detest journalism with all my heart. There was I, shut in an office in a London back street looking through proofs all day; it was ghastly. Then my father, seeing that I was not learning much, thought I had better let it drop.'

Adrian was continuing to suffer from migraines, and Fanny, afraid that he might die prematurely if his health declined any more, determined to get him away from all the stress. In any case, she had had another idea for her son's advancement. Instead of taking Adrian on a 'grand tour' of Europe or other foreign parts as rich parents did, Fanny would take him for a weekend in Brighton.

Of course, Robert would have no part in his wife's plan to turn their boy into a gentleman, so Fanny saved up her housekeeping money and called on her well-heeled and worldly brother-in-law, Dr Peacock, to take them in his smart de Dion motor car. The car was a temperamental beast, with a snorting engine that boiled and raged, and lights that flickered and flashed, but they made the journey and to Adrian, it was the most exciting experience of his life.

During their weekend stay at the Grand Hotel, Fanny gripped him by the soft upper arm and urged him to 'Look at the people', as she had so often before. He did look at the people and no doubt they in turn cast a sideways glance, and probably another, at the lad in the strange garb, being propelled about by his mother - or was she his lover? The whispered conversations, the urgency in their closeness - it was apparent there was a special bond between them. And yet he called her 'Mother' and sometimes 'Mater.' To outsiders, it could be confusing.

There they sat, Fanny in her actress' hand-me-down dress and Adrian in his white linen spats and green, humbug-striped waistcoat of a passé fashion, watching the rich and famous. Fanny was now his tutor, first in the art of dress and then on the arts of women. She warned him against those who set out to entrap foolish young men and part them from their money. He must be constantly on his guard, she counselled. Love she dismissed as nothing more than animal attraction. He must marry the right kind of woman according to wealth and social standing, never mind beauty or brains. She couldn't abide 'clever' women at all.

Later they went out on the town, with Adrian dressed in his

father's eveningwear. Fanny hooked her hand through his arm and, hissing in his ear, bade him absorb everything he saw. He looked at the people until his eyes ached, and he was grateful when finally it was time for bed.

Robert himself had agreed to visit them on the Sunday, arriving with the 'hoi polloi' on a day-trippers' train. He refused point-blank to set foot in the Grand Hotel and instead the group dined in a nearby restaurant of lesser pedigree.

It has already been shown that Robert could never meet up with his brother-in-law Ernest Peacock without it ending in verbal war. This was to be no exception. For a while Robert sat silently biting his moustache, eyes alert and restless, as if expecting an ambush. Adrian would describe that look as if his father was 'almost ready to shoot the first unmistakable rich swell he saw.'

It would not take long before the sight of his wife cooing agreement with Dr Peacock's seemingly pompous remarks riled him and when the waiter was treated with their customary disdain, Robert mounted his high horse and rode to the rescue. Needless to say, the event came to a premature end.

Uncle Ernest took Adrian and his mother on to see Kate, his estranged wife, in the Wye Valley, where they spent another two weeks in more tranquil bliss. Before leaving them, he slipped a card to Adrian, on it was printed the name of a lady he knew who, he said, would be kind to Adrian and charge him a preferential rate if he mentioned his uncle's name. Adrian kept it for some years but never took up the offer.

In the Wye Valley Adrian saw all the beauty of nature as described by the poets he idolised and he voiced the impulse that he should like to farm there. Aunt Kate offered him the chance to make a start on her own land but it was a short and abortive attempt. He and a labourer made half a bracken stack and spent the rest of the time dozing.

On their return to London, Adrian and his mother found a letter from Mr Borland suggesting that, with Adrian's unexplained absence from lessons, he should perhaps assume that their agreement was at an end. They had quite forgotten about him.

So it was back to Plan A: Adrian would have one last shot at becoming a poet, and with an air of resignation Robert agreed to show some of his son's poetry to a Fleet Street associate. For weeks Adrian threw open the shutters of his soul and let the sunlight stream in. All kinds of tender thoughts and phrases were cultivated, until poetry sprouted on page after page. Every possible epithet for fervent emotion and profound sensation was employed, so that the most mundane events became a veritable ballet of froth and magic under his pen.

Not one piece was accepted for publication.

Young master Adrian had spent too long lounging on his parents' sofa, puffing a pipe as he read Shelley and Tennyson, and the pastoral epics of Virgil. Now his time was up, and he must find gainful employment - somehow. Even the surprise acceptance of a sonnet to be printed in the *Westminster Gazette* in September 1920 was not enough to stay his fate. He was excited, of course, but he noted in his diary, 'As I read the proof through I wondered how they could be such fools as to want to print it.' His own confidence in his ability to 'make it' as a poet had trickled away, and the last few drops of his ambition lay inert in the dust of his parents' scepticism.

All he had left was the beauty of his thoughts, which he would now keep to himself and save for private moments. 'I love going to bed', he noted. 'I like being shut away from the world by darkness and silence, so that I can enjoy my own imaginings undisturbed. As soon as I get into bed I turn over on my side and jam my face into the pillow. Then I dive right down to the very depths of my soul wherein is stored all the loveliness I have gathered from life. ...Herein I may wander all the night through, herein is a sure refuge from the world, from pain and cruelty and the hand of tyrants... From all harsh and ugly things I turn inward and find gentleness... I have a cure for every evil.'

But what cure could he find for the evil of unemployment? And where might it be found? The improbable answer to the latter lay in the small ads. page of the *Daily Telegraph* newspaper. What is more curious, it was a newspaper the family rarely took, and so there is no telling why one day, as he headed for home, Adrian made a short detour to the paper shop and picked up a copy. There he spotted an offer by a farmer in Suffolk to take on a young man as apprentice for one year, in exchange for hard work and a fee.

With images of Virgil's worthy country folk still fresh in his imagination, he stopped and considered the possibility of becoming a part of that great poem of life.

Suffolk - the county of rolling green fields and gentle rustics swinging their scythes and clanking their milk churns. Suffolk, with its proud Punch horses and its red-headed Polls in beauteous herds of chestnut splendour. Suffolk, the artists' county - for had not Constable and Gainsborough made it their home?

Suffolk, ah, yes, Suffolk - that was the place for a lad with poetry in his soul. As for the farm work - well, why not?

# 5. In a Land of Corduroy

*October 26th 1920.* A tap at the door and a voice rousing him. Adrian stretched, and his fists made contact with an unfamiliar bed-end. He twisted, looking around him, and his spine creaked and complained. It had been a long journey yesterday to Great Lodge, Hundon: his home for the next year.

Time to get up, the voice had said.

What was that ringing? He had left behind the bells of London. No - it was a clanging, a jingling, now a gruff voice, boots clomping. He peeled himself off the bed and padded to the small window, raking back the curtains and peering into the grey early dawn. He wiped a porthole in the condensation and peered again. Men were making their way from the harness-room, with leather and brass hanging from their shoulders, and calling out as softly as gruff voices can. An answering snort and whicker. A clunk of bolt and bang of stable door. It all had the air of familiarity, of routine. But it was new to Adrian.

Yesterday, on his laden, ex-WW1 dispatch rider's Douglas motorcycle he had rumbled into the yard of Great Lodge, Hundon, to move in with his new employer, Victor Savage. He had had to apologise - he had underestimated the journey time from London. That was not his first error of judgement, certainly it would not be his last.

But for now he was happy, excited, nervous. As he had puttered out of the smoky city and wound his way towards the flat acres of East Anglia, he had sensed a falling away of constriction and control that was as liberating as the fresh air was invigorating. His mother, worried about his sickly mien of late, had loosed her grip on him only with the greatest reluctance and immediately he had felt a rush of freedom, almost as tangible as the wind in his face.

Finally coming into West Suffolk, with its plaster-and-thatch hamlets and pot-holed roads, he had rejoiced in the wide open spaces and the informality of the clustered cottages and remote farmsteads. He might have smiled to himself, except that his teeth were chattering at every vibration and his hands, already nettled by excruciating pins and needles, juddered in time as he bounced along the rutted lanes. When he reached Great Lodge he had climbed gingerly from the saddle and unbent his tall, thin frame from the crouched position in which it seemed to have fixed itself. He'd taken a good look around him and allowed himself a deep sigh. He had left London and all its artifice behind; he was among genuine, no-frills, country people now. On his journey towards manhood, he had made it to base camp.

When on that first evening he had sat down to a hearty meal, Adrian looked around at the stout forms of Victor Savage and his brothers who were visiting. Sitting there like a willow among oaks, he nevertheless felt confident that his spindly legs and delicate wrists would soon toughen and fill with the aid of rich fodder and healthy exercise. He would become confident, learn to banter like these men, and, swapping his dandy silver-topped cane for a gnarled stick, he would stride the fields with a firm tread. There was so much to look forward to, it's a wonder he slept at all that night, but sleep and sustenance would become vital for his survival in the coming months.

The food was certainly plentiful. He would look back on it as though seeing the daily table spread before him once more. 'Three eggs for breakfast on top of thick home-cured bacon floating in its own fat; this after a large plate of porridge made with milk, with cream added. For dinner was set on the table an enormous joint of prime English beef, followed by an enormous cold apple pie, with cheese to follow. The same, more or less, at about nine o'clock for supper, after a five o'clock tea notable for a fruit cake that rather resembled a Christmas pudding. But I forgot to mention also the pudding that proceeded, not followed, the meat at dinner; an old Suffolk custom now I think quite gone out - pudding and gravy.'

Hard work would give him the appetite needed to brave this mountain of food but Adrian was naturally wiry and in time Victor, comparing him to a fattening pig, would describe him as a 'bad doer' - for no matter how much he ate, he could never look plump.

Even if he could not 'do' much about his weight, Adrian, with the eager miscalculation that accompanies youth, was convinced he would soon be doing his share of the work. He knew that Victor had had serious doubts about his ability to contribute, but he would show them what he was made of. After all, the work didn't look very difficult - guiding horses, forking hay, driving a wagon... He would soon pick it all up, he gauged.

That would take a little longer than he anticipated. As Adrian was about to find out, farming would be harder to the soft-handed city boy than anything he could ever imagine. He would come to discover that it took a great deal of skill to make a job look so easy.

And now, on his first day, he really must get on with it. Quitting his reverie, he quickly splashed his face with cold water poured from a jug. Shivering, he pulled on the clean, fresh 'country' clothes he had bought in London, and hurried downstairs.

No breakfast yet. It was straight on with the boots and straight out the back door. He stopped. Was he dreaming? A carnival of men and beasts approached and passed by him in the yard. '...I saw them all come in a procession,' he would write one day, 'through the farmstead from the stables - two by two with chains chiming as they swung, and a ploughman seated on the off-side horse of each pair.'

He would add, 'They came home plastered with mire to their flanks. Yet next morning they walked out as clean as before.'

He spent the day with the men and horses, learning their methods and their tricks, striving to harrow the cloying clay land into neat rows until it looked like a length of corduroy on the cutting table. Soon he was berating the author Thomas Hardy for his glib dismissal of the farm horse 'that stumbles and nods, Half asleep as they stalk'. Adrian could see the great effort that went into pulling the clanking implement, the rhythm and the power in the straining muscles that bulged and shuddered under the red hide. He came to the conclusion that Hardy had never come close to the business end of a horse in his life.

However, he did not swing round to the romantic view either. Trudging behind a pair of huge, windy buttocks, or wiping away a gobbet of masticated chaff after a snort in the face, he could admit that 'gentle giant' was also a cliched misnomer for the massive monster that had a knack for standing on one's foot. He came to respect the old horseman with his secret potions and his murmured commands that seemed to work like a spell in the furry ear of the most recalcitrant beast.

Adrian worked all day alongside men whose choice of hard-wearing clothing was mostly corduroy, or a thick moleskin cloth. He, who had been kitted out by the Army and Navy Store in

London, had unusual but once-stylish breeches and completely inadequate boots. Nevertheless he determined to fit in with the men. His first obstacle was one of the most basic - that of communication. To him, they spoke a completely foreign language.

The West Suffolk accent, sometimes slow and considered, occasionally excited or bellicose, had its very own vocabulary which could be impenetrable to an outsider. The rising cadence could make a command sound like a question, or a comment sound like exasperation. Their pronunciation of the commonest words could render them incomprehensible to Adrian.

Before transport opened the gate, the 'rustics' as he described them lived in a world all of their own. A trip to nearby Haverhill was a day out, and London was a place they had often heard talk about but few felt the desire to go there. Some of their men had gone away to the Great War but many had stayed to tend the fields and it is true to say their lives depended on their land. Times were tough, and they were becoming tougher still.

Among the natives, Adrian stood out like a white crow. Everyone soon heard that he was from London and it was immediately obvious by his 'posh' accent that he was 'not from round here'. Of course, most of them assumed straight away that he must know nothing about farming. The others soon had to agree: he was pretty hopeless. Even the local postman and baker were likely to keep a few hens or a pig or cow and so he was truly at the very bottom of the class when it came to agriculture.

There seemed to be a raft of new things to learn each day, such as the right mix of feed for the various animals. They could die if he made a mistake. He must know the right way to sow each kind of crop, how to fertilise them, how to protect them.

For Adrian's part he soon appreciated that, far from being the duddle-headed peasant so often portrayed by so-called smart city folk, his country cousins were wiser in their own way than many a great scholar. So - maybe they didn't know which cutlery to use at a banquet. They knew the real meaning of life, he felt. And he knew oh so very little.

When describing those days in his book *Corduroy* he wrote, 'I found myself transgressing in some respect at every turn. At first my ignorance was so complete that this did not worry me, but later, when I began to know a little and thought I knew a lot, these mistakes irritated me greatly and caused fits of despair. It seemed as though I should never rise beyond the position of novice, so complex were the rules of this game with nature.'

The men in the fields were merciless in their ribbing of the young apprentice, often calling him 'Dunt', a local term for ignoramus. The only way to save face was to laugh along with them, at himself. Sometimes he didn't even know what they had said but he pretended to be amused. He certainly couldn't complain, for his boss would have seen it as weakness, and his comrades all seemed to be related to one another.

Many of the farm workers, although poorly paid, had large families to support. To have eight or ten children in a household was by no means newsworthy, and from a very early age the boys would be expected to help on the land. At harvest time, comely young girls bringing tea out to their fathers and brothers would catch the eye of the growing lads, and eventually a new match might be made.

It was the norm for local families to inter-marry but in the case of Adrian's hosts, Victor Savage the farmer was one of two brothers who had married Collen sisters from Braintree in Essex. George Savage was the wheeler-dealer of the family, he had businesses all over Essex including the Braintree Radio Company, the first to offer cable wireless in the town. He was a shareholder in the renowned Crittall window company, and he had a shop in Bishop's Stortford. George kept his finger on the pulse of enterprise - it is said that when he heard wool prices were going up in Australia, he stocked up on tartan rugs in his shop. His intuition was often right and he was a very wealthy man.

George's wife Amy Collen was distinctive with her dark hair and brown eyes, and her sister Martha was similar. It is easy to imagine how Victor Savage was drawn to the girl when they met. She was delicate in constitution and it would be a disappointment that they never had children, but at least Martha was not expected to churn milk or boil up grimy work clothes in a copper like the labouring-class women. Victor was a yeoman farmer, on a social par with the doctor and the rector but not quite as esteemed as a titled man. In those days class mattered a great deal.

The Savages have no particular claim to fame in their genealogy, they were simply hard-working, jovial and shrewd business-people. In the nineteenth century old Noah Savage of Hundon was a farmer but also a part-time shopkeeper, grocer and parish clerk.

He married twice and had nine children. His second son, Walter Savage, also dabbled in a number of trades; he was a land agent, shopkeeper, maltster and fertiliser dealer as well as a church warden. Walter had six children, so when the Savage family gathered together at special occasions, it was a populous affair.

Victor Savage was Walter's eldest son, and by the time Adrian went to work for him, Victor was aged almost forty which seemed positively middle-aged to Adrian at nineteen.

Victor had built up a good reputation for himself in Hundon and beyond. A sharp-minded and penny-careful man, he had expanded his rented farm from small beginnings and the land around Great Lodge, now amounting to almost 480 acres, was kept in immaculate order by a legion of hands.

Although it was his father Walter who was technically the tenant, there was no doubt that it was Victor who was in charge. Adrian recalled how Victor would only have to shout 'Boy!' as he strode into the yard, for one to appear as if by magic. Even though he spoke with less of an accent than his men, he could summon up a rich flow of fiery dialect if their standards seemed to be slipping. His wrath could be like thunder, but in a good humour he was all sunshine, like the bright yellow waistcoat he liked to wear around his barrel-like torso.

Victor, a stocky man, or as one local commented, 'pregnant-looking,' would be turned out smartly every day. Mostly he chose to wear a check jacket, a crisp clean shirt and moleskin breeches that ended with cloth gaiters, which took the brunt of the mud in winter and dust in summer. He wore stout boots and his constant companion was a knobbly stick, shiny at the top from years of association with the palm of Victor's hand. That stick had a myriad of uses, from helping him balance his way over furrow and ditch, to poking in rabbit holes or testing the wheels of a cart.

As a boss he was firm but fair, say all who knew him or knew of him. In 1920 he was employing around 20 men and he kept a dozen handsome horses to heave a series of reluctant farm implements through the clay. It took a brave heart to invest in that land. The soil was by no means easy to handle, it could be heavy and sullen, and it had a habit of getting up from its rightful place and tagging along on the boots of anyone who set foot on it. The 'clunchy' Suffolk horses, devoid of fancy feathers on their legs, were ideally suited to picking their way through it.

With so much earthly activity, Adrian acknowledged that his former yearning for the spirituality of poetry was waning. However, when he did find time to stand and stare when resting the horses briefly on a headland, then the pastoral scene held a special beauty for him. Even the earth itself held a certain charm.

His mother had schooled him to spot potential paintings all around, so as he gazed at the bare fields and trees in that first winter, he saw not just browns but a palette of sienna, sepia, chocolate, chestnut, russet, mahogany, and even toast-brown. And just as he had admired the movements of ballet dancers only a year or two before, so now, as he worked with the sinewy, leather-skinned men, he noticed a rhythm to their movements that helped the work go with a swing as they hummed tunes, or whistled, or sang.

All the time, while heaving sheaves into a thresher or flinging muck from a tumbril they bantered and japed. It was inevitable that Adrian remained the butt of their jokes for some considerable time. In the end, he hardly dared open his mouth for fear of making a fool of himself yet again.

But Adrian was treated with respect around the house. His father had handed over £150 for his tuition and board, apparently 50% more than advertised because Vic Savage saw at a glance that he would not be much use on the land. They might be able to improve on his lack of experience and his slender frame, but those headaches he had, that sent him to bed for days at a time - well, he could barely do the year's work of half a man. For his fee of £150, Adrian would enjoy the status similar to today's bed-and-breakfast guest, and he slept in a big twin-bedded room at Great Lodge.

There were six main bedrooms in the house, and two attics. The toilet and washing facilities consisted of an outside closet and a water pump over the scullery sink. Baths would mean hot water being carried up the stairs by the nippy maid, of whom Adrian soon developed a wary respect. Lacking his mother's stern disdain for the serving class, he found himself having to jump aside whenever he saw her advancing with a cloth or broom. When she had a mind to clean, it was unwise to stand in her way.

The 'best' room, the Drawing Room, with its marble fireplace and garden outlook, was furnished with mahogany and blue plush, tasselled upholstery, and it was kept free of mud, hay or any other detritus from the outside world. It was Martha Savage's retreat from the rough reality of farm living. Great Lodge was by no means the grandest house in the area but it was a palace compared to some of the poorest living conditions in Hundon, where the only running water was down the inside of the walls, and the view of the night sky was through the roof.

These were not the conditions of Vic Savage's tenants. He was a fair man, and took care of those who worked well for him. But the Welfare State had not embraced Hundon as yet and a man without a job usually meant a family going without.

Adrian ate with Vic Savage and his family, and in the course of the year would share every aspect of their life. They were good to him - Martha is remembered as being a kindly woman, though often unwell, and Victor treated him as a slightly problematical son. But he was there to learn, and learn he would, the only way in farming - the hard way.

There were times in those winter months when Adrian's spirits reached an all-time low. The cold, the wet, the early mornings and rough work seemed to hold very few attractions. Later he would write in his diary on the subject of carting muck, '...it was always an exhausting job for me. Bodily work was always a sort of martyrdom to my flesh, the will whipping the muscles to the last ounce of their effort - yet there was a sort of glory in it. Though every day I hated starting once more - and the hours crawled.'

How tempting it must have been to run back to London and the life of warmth, comfort and pavements. Adrian would say that he had 'fled' from the spectre of office life, but as he shivered in the lee of a wall of chestnut-haired horseflesh, forcing his icy fingers to sort out the harness, the cosy glow of an office may well have presented a more appealing apparition to him. Or, as he held the wooden handles of a plough in a frozen grip while at the same time trying to guide the plodding horses with a rope rein and a shout, he could easily have hankered for the comparative ease of pen and paper. There were compensations, though, in roasting hearth-fires and heart-warming meals, and these, along with an amazing stubbornness of will and pride at his own endurance, kept him going.

Not that it would have been easy to go back to London. In a way, he was trapped in limbo now, because whenever he did return home to visit his family and friends, he found their stilted lifestyle and narrow outlook quite discomfiting. He was there at Christmas, having just spent a sweating, choking yet satisfying week threshing corn and a day at market with Victor Savage, leaning on the wooden pens to study the signs of a good pig or a promising bullock. By contrast he found himself back in his parents' house among row on row of similar houses, presenting a squat barrier to the eye. His vision had become used to roaming over great expanses of open fields and kaleidoscope skies, and now all there was to see was bricks and tiles and a narrow band above.

It was more than a physical claustrophobia. The tense, bickering ripostes between Fanny and Robert, the necessity to mind his p's and q's, and having to smile at those who called him 'Farmer Giles', thinking themselves original; all these things conspired to send him hurrying back to Suffolk.

He later wrote in an article entitled *God's Own Country*, 'I can only recall the moment when, after enduring a winter on 500 bare acres of that clay, I returned from a visit to town, and the last gate of the gated farm road clicked behind me, and I stood in a field called "Fat Cattle", and I said to myself, "My home is here now."'

It was not only his home geographically, Adrian realised, it was his spiritual home. Standing on a steaming dung heap in frosty January, he might have doubted it, but Suffolk would be the place where, but for the briefest interlude, he must live his life out. Instead of trying to master Nature, he would eventually be happy just to cohabit with her.

Spring came at length, and Adrian's world was transformed. Field, hedge, tree and ditch burst into life with green - no, not just green but emerald, jade, celadon and beryl, while blossoms of pretty pastel shades showered him with confetti as he stood in the sunshine and gentle breeze. Now his spirit was at ease; this was what he had come for, to feel the great power of thrusting growth all around him, under his feet, in his very hands as he cupped a flower or slid his fingers, squeaking, up a new leaf. The poet, the farmer, the man - all the voices inside him spoke with the same voice and assured him that he must never, ever go back to the city.

The summer of 1921 was a particularly hot and dry one, but every Sunday there was respite from the blaze that beat on the backs of the workers. No work was done on the Sabbath, only the basic feeding of animals, and Victor Savage was convinced that conducting business on that day could only bring bad luck. He would take the opportunity to stroll around his fields and check on his crops, his hedges, his ditches, but he would never do a deal.

It was a superstition born out of religion; Vic Savage was 'low church', with strong views on vicars who tried to bring in fancy ideas such as incense or modern prayers. The local reverend, unsettled by all the tales of witchcraft that still held many villagers in fear and dread, did burn incense, but Victor still kept going there because he lived in the parish and the family had their own pew reserved for them.

The Savage family, minus their atheist apprentice, would attend church on a Sunday and be warned vehemently against damnation and hell fire, after which they usually would have lunch with all the family and in summer this was often followed by a tennis party.

Victor was addicted to tennis and he was a very competent player so it was essential to have a tennis court in his garden. Many other farmers had facilities too and for Adrian it was a very social summer, with visits round the neighbourhood for genteel mixed doubles as well as competitive all-male games. It was a good opportunity to display one's skill and stamina to the ladies but Adrian was still shy and gauche at that stage. He remembered with embarrassment how he had fired a scorcher of a serve to a young lady, which by the extant Victorian rules of tennis etiquette was certainly not the 'done thing.' Interaction with these girls was a dream and a nightmare all in one.

During that year he went to all kinds of social gatherings either of the extensive Savage clan, or of the locals at hunts and sporting events, dances and parties. A most attractive young man, Adrian caught furtive glances from many a local girl, and one farmer's daughter in particular almost brought him out of his shell, except that he was just too painfully shy to speak up. He could not think what to say, or how to go about 'courting' at all. In fact, he hadn't the slightest idea about women's bodies, or how their minds worked. It had been one thing to hear the crude jokes and innuendoes of the older boys at Uppingham, but faced with the real thing, the breathing, smiling, thinking woman in the flesh, they might just as well have been aliens from another planet.

He did dance with a woman on one occasion, an older woman who kissed him and, he felt, was keen to take it further. He evaded her; even though the feel of her back and the brush of her thigh gave him a sensation he could hardly ignore, he hadn't the nerve to see it through. Besides which, he had certain principles and believed he should save himself for marriage.

It was not an easy maxim for a hot-blooded youth to uphold. A flash of leg on the tennis court or a hint of cleavage at a yeoman's ball could easily set his pulse racing but the rest was a mystery. Adrian would later comment that at twenty he held the misconception that pubic hair was something that only men had. He still had a lot to learn in many respects.

The jollity of all these occasions belied the worry that was going on in the minds of Victor, his family and all their farming friends. The oldest inhabitants had been expecting the slump that they knew came after wars, and had warned anyone who would listen, which was few. Sure enough, farming was about to go into decline, faster than a blasted pheasant.

The Corn Production Act, set up by the Government in 1917 to guarantee prices, was repealed in 1921. To most people's minds this was nothing short of betrayal, a reneging on promises to those who had sought to feed the nation in its time of dire need. They could rant in the inns and market place all they liked; their opinions counted for nothing. The farmer was on his own now and prices were beginning to tumble.

One local landowner had somehow sensed that it had been time to move on and in 1920, on Wednesday 28th July the Hundon and Stradishall Estates had been put up for auction. Nearly five thousand acres of land including 25 farms were offered in the 77 lots, and Vic Savage's farm at Great Lodge had been among them. He had gone to the sale at Bury St Edmunds but his farm, along with many others, had been knocked down to a consortium who were out to make money for themselves. With only another two years left on his tenancy, Victor saw that the end was in sight for him at Hundon.

In his autobiography, *My Own Master*, Adrian wrote of his employer's situation, calling him 'Mr Colville' as he had in his first book. 'The shrewder landowners were throwing their estates on to the market; the gentlemen among them offering the farms to their tenants first, the less scrupulous selling out to syndicates, who then tried to sell to the tenants at a profit. Mr. Colville was one of these latter tenants. He refused to pay what the syndicate wanted by two pounds an acre, and bought instead a smaller farm about two miles away for £20 an acre.'

That farm, Seabrooks, had 241 acres and part of it was let to Walter Savage already. His son Victor, who by 1921 had been at

Great Lodge for thirteen years and had built it into what was generally accepted to be the best farm in the vicinity, was about to undertake his last harvest there. It would be a time of mixed emotions all round.

In those days, corn crops were aptly described as 'seas'. The tops would shimmer and shift in the breeze just like waves, and a man, wading in, would soon find himself waist-deep. Those old-fashioned crops were far taller than today; typical breeds of wheat like Squarehead's Master were over a metre high, red headed, upright and fulsome when ripe. But some crops would fall in a swoon at the slightest provocation, a heavy downpour could flatten them, and speed was of the essence in getting them cut and stored away. The flaking ears of corn would repay this industry by depositing minute slivers of chaff into bodily crevices that would torment and irritate the whole day through.

It was all hands to the work, to capitalise on the continuing dry weather and Adrian noted, 'Stooks began to stand in the fields in place of level seas of corn. The whirr of self-binders droned in the bright, breathless air like giant grasshoppers, and tractors hummed. There, and there, and there, one saw them in the valley vista trailing around diminishing patches of corn that still retained the contours of the field. There was no sky save at morning and evening, only a pale, misty vacuity above.'

Adrian had become useful on the farm, much to his delight and pride, and he worked with zeal alongside his comrades. Finally he had been accepted, not quite as one of their own, but at least he was no longer a figure of fun. Incredibly, the men did still find time to wag each other even as they heaved the never-ending sheaves onto stack after stack, and somehow it seemed to lighten the work. Decades-old wagons rolled back and forth, and ancient farmhands reminisced at length about the men and the harvests of the past, when they had seen bumper crops one year and rain-hammered wastelands another. Bounteous crops were not always good news, as in that year, when the glut meant prices would fall even further.

The work went on and on. The horses, rabid-looking with foam on their bridles and fleck on their chests, strained and pulled at the great loads as the men, shirts open and muscles bulging, moved in harmony. Barns filled as fields emptied, leaving the golden stubble looking like the shaved head of an army recruit. High up in the webby rafters of the great storehouses, men balanced nimbly on the rising tide of sheaves, stacking them in a shimmering, slippery mound. They worked on until the sharp sunbeams ceased to pierce through the dust, and the pregnant harvest moon stood ghostly in the sky above. Only then would the men make their way home, through the shadows and the sounds and smells of a bewitching night. It was a scene that would remain with Adrian Bell for life.

If the dreaming boy had held a small yen for a country life, now the young man had a burning ambition to be a farmer in his own right. A small farm adjoining Seabrooks on the disunited Stradishall Estate was available, Vic Savage told him, and they went to see it.

Stephenson's Farm on the south side of the road to Farley Green looked picture-pretty to the eager and adventurous young fellow. Its lath-and-plaster farmhouse, white but clothed with ivy, was topped with thick, French mustard coloured thatch. Its three bedrooms, one leading into another, were beamed and cosy, and downstairs there was all that a young man could need: a living room with range, a sitting room with a stove, and a scullery with a sink and a pump. Adrian fell in love with the place.

Vic Savage, uninterested in the home comforts or the aesthetic quality of the house, had cast his critical eye over the 35 acres of land and pronounced it a suitable holding for his apprentice to get started on. Now all Adrian had to do was convince his parents to put up the cash. It was time to pay a visit to the old home.

A mini-war of attrition ensued with the Bells finding that when their son came to stay for the weekend, he seemed to talk of nothing but the merits of farming. He had been keen before, but now they were bombarded with images and anecdotes of every conceivable kind. They heard that farming was the most natural occupation for mankind, it served the most basic of needs, and the skill and mystery had to be seen to be believed. There was the health aspect too - they could not deny they had never seen him looking better, if one ignored the state of his hands and nails. The people, the animals, the crops, the farm machinery - surely the whole year's experience was laid before them in that space of time.

In passing, Adrian mentioned that there was a little place for sale that Vic Savage had said would be ideal for him if he wanted a farm. When there was no response to this he let the subject drop, only to pick it up again and again. Vic Savage said this, Vic Savage said that; it was as if there was no end to the wisdom of the man.

And Vic Savage would soon be moving to Seabrooks Farm which incidentally backed onto the little place that was for sale - had he mentioned the little place that was for sale? Yes, they believed he had.

The next stage of the campaign was an invitation for them to come and stay with Vic and Martha Savage at Great Lodge, Hundon. His mother came, only to find herself being taken over to Stradishall and along the road to Farley Green. Adrian pointed out Stephenson's Farm to her, and they stopped to look. By some gift of Fate they found the farmer in his garden and he was happy to show them around. Fanny was won over by the charm of the place.

Now Adrian had an ally in the Bell camp and before Robert really quite knew what was happening, he had agreed to part with £850 to buy his son a farm, and put another £200 in a bank account for him to use. Michaelmas 1921 was the day when the Bells would take over Stephenson's Farm.

# 6. His Own Master

So Adrian was his own master now: it was a peculiar feeling.

On the first morning he awoke in his snug little bedroom and lay staring, slightly confused initially, at the ribs of the roof above his head. Listening to the wind whispering in the thatch, his emotions twirled like brittle leaves picked up in a tiny whirlwind. He was excited, yes, but with tremors of apprehension at the realisation that he was truly on his own for the very first time in his entire life.

No mother there to urge him on; no maid, no school matron, no teacher, no farmer's wife or farmer's servant. Nobody.

His first move was easy - rising and getting dressed. Now there were a hundred decisions to be made, like whether to start ploughing, or harrowing, or carting manure. The season would not wait for him, he must act straight away if he was to keep up. Victor had advised him to get his field ready for winter oats, so that was where he decided to start.

Adrian made a fair enough job of his first day's ploughing but he could see that his lone efforts would not be sufficient. He must engage help. Similarly, he enjoyed making his own breakfast with a frying pan balanced on the living room range and toast done to a turn by means of a fork poked through it and held up like a shield to the fire. But when it came to washing the dishes, he decided to delegate that task to a local woman. Perhaps it was partly due to the fact that his mother's voice had returned to haunt his inner ear in this domestic situation, but he didn't feel up to the job of housekeeping. The wife of a farm hand, idiosyncratic but efficient, stepped in. Now Adrian Bell the farmer was an employer, too.

Certainly he needed someone to take care of him in some respects. Having no idea of store cupboard management, he had presented easy pickings for the tradesman from nearby Haverhill who had deftly steered him into ordering an array of provisions to stock his bare shelves in preparation for any possible eventuality.

Adrian might have been an amateur when it came to coping in the home, but with regard to the farm he could always fall back on the wisdom of Victor Savage. Pride deterred him from doing this too often but with his work on show for the whole world to see, it was inevitable that his former employer would make comment on his prowess whenever they met. For a couple of months, Adrian had a friend staying with him to help on the farm but he was no more experienced than Adrian had been on his first day at Hundon. A favourite tale of that time would be how the pair had toiled hard all day, trying to cut a hedge with billhooks, but making a complete mess of it. When Victor came along he noticed that Adrian was using a left-handed tool, while his friend had an ordinary one. So why were they both having so much trouble? His friend Frank was left-handed.

It was Victor who helped to choose his first heifer at market and Adrian's doubtful impression that the cow looked fiery was soon proved to be true. In spite of the problems this gave him, at least he had the satisfaction of knowing that his judgement was improving.

He had made a good choice in taking on George Hempstead to do the ploughing, but the two horses he had bought at a sale were temperamental. Jockey and Short were their names, and when Adrian had chosen to buy one, he was informed that the two had always worked well as a pair, and so he had taken the other as well. Of course, what had not been mentioned was that Jockey was easily spooked, and seemed to be constantly on the look-out for the slightest reason to bolt, dragging his poor companion along with him. Short had no reason to be grateful to Adrian for keeping the 'old friends' together.

There were other things he had not foreseen, and Adrian would look back with irony upon them. When he dismantled the valuable manure heap that he had bought as part of Stephenson's Farm, he found that the previous incumbent had duped him by piling muck over a heap of earth and stones. He had far less of the soil-enriching stuff than he literally had bargained for.

Nevertheless, the eventual joy of seeing his first crop feeling its way skyward with fragile green shoots filled him with a pleasure that was almost sensual. He could feel a man's sense of accomplishment in creating food for people to eat, but there was more to it than that, it was like giving birth. He loved the land and his little farm as though it were a fractious child. It caused him great grief at times, but it was worth it: he had a stake in the future.

On some evenings he would return home and sit by his fire, too exhausted even to take off his leathers. He would flop back in the chair and regard them in a detached way, the leggings stiffening in the heat, steam rising gently from the soles of his boots and gobbets of mud adhering themselves to the rag rug. There was a sense of satisfaction even in those small happenings.

In the early days, nothing gave Adrian more of a thrill than to see his name on an envelope with 'Farmer' appended to it. However, it would become a constant source of disappointment for Adrian to meet a local who would say 'I hear you came here for your health' or when he would overhear others saying that he was 'poisoned' with money because his father was considered rich by local standards. Yes, Robert had put up the £850 to buy the farm, and had put another £200 into the bank for outgoings. But the 'privileged' son still had to work hard.

When Adrian came to write about those days in his second book *Silver Ley* he admitted that the reader might conclude that it was all a sham. They could, he said, 'think they detect the breath that stirs the scene and betrays it to be but scenery, and see my farming as a pretty background for me as I act my "good time," with a parental cheque ever available to cushion me from the bare bones of life'. Still, he insisted, he was trying to paint an honest portrait of life in those times.

He would indeed write about the gloomier side of life, like the children of the alcoholic father who drank all his earnings and left them to scrabble in fields in bare feet, gnawing on the mangolds that were grown as animal feed. In truth, that was not the norm: the locals were poor, but these were not the Dark Ages.

One older resident of Stradishall comments that in his recollection, children always had shoes, but they might not have socks. Yes, they ate a great deal of stodgy puddings to fill their bellies, but with a little meat and plenty of vegetables they thrived. Out in all weathers in a patchwork of hand-me-downs and ill-fitting garments, the children were never bored or querulous, never demanding or disrespectful. They worked hard from an early age and had little ambition for a better life. They had not seen many signs of what prosperity might bring, and they accepted that those who were better off, simply were.

As one local lady, Violet, who was brought up in a family of ten children, said, 'We used to help pick up stones in buckets, and help in the harvest, putting shocks up. The corn was all cut with a binder, and we had horses and carts - we did a lot of walking in those days. But otherwise we didn't go anywhere, except to church, and once a year to the flower show. Nearly every village had one. It was mostly veg, but there were steam engines, and rides.' The children went along to watch, rarely having any money to take part, but, as she and her brother Dennis agreed, 'We didn't know any different.'

Adrian described the typical Suffolk farmer's wife as being thin and pale, often worn out before they reached middle age. Another local lady, Grace, agrees that her mother was exactly that. But Violet and Dennis remember their own mother as being strong, she always stood or sat bolt upright, and she was always busy, baking bread in the brick oven, washing clothes in the copper, or mending clothes for the next child to wear. There was no time to socialise with other women or pop in for coffee mornings at each other's houses. They might meet on market days, or after church, but with every job at home having to be done by hand, there was always a meal to cook or a hundred other things to attend to. The children had to do their share and at night they slept three to a bed.

Father, they said, was strict and quite often a look from him was enough to stop them in their wayward track. By necessity, life was a team effort, and it made families stick together in a way Adrian's never had.

Above all, in later years Adrian would reminisce about the spirit of the farm worker, who made every back-breaking job go easier with a song and a joke. Violet and Dennis' father always whistled, they say. When he took extra jobs hauling timber to make ends meet he could be heard coming from miles away, with four horses pulling the great clanking wagon on its iron-rimmed wheels, banging and rumbling along the rutted road.

Steven 'Bill' Kiddy was a farmer, as his father had been before him and several generations before that. His farm, just along the road from Adrian's, had not been handed down to him like many: he had rented it and then bought it from the Stradishall Estate. Farming was in his blood, it was as natural to him as breathing, although a million times harder. With twelve mouths to feed, he had to make every minute of his working day count. He had to be horseman, ploughman, stockman and accountant. He might be heaving logs one day and be midwife to a cow the next. He was no different in that respect to every other small farmer in the area, for whom his young neighbour would have a lifelong respect.

As 1921 turned to 1922, Adrian was a long way from acquiring all those attributes. Still, he was working on it. He was up with the lark and toiling on his land when in the eyes of others he could have been lying a-bed after a night on the town, dancing with fringe-skirted, flat-chested girls and drinking champagne. Instead he chose to clump out into the fields and labour until his body could take no more. They must have thought he was utterly mad.

It is unclear for exactly how long Adrian was alone, which is not to say that he was lonely. Mostly he was far too busy or too tired to notice his solitude. Now, though, certainly within a year of taking over Stephenson's Farm, he was about to suffer an invasion.

His explanations would vary - his mother missed him; his father wanted a bolt-hole away from the pressures of city life; his siblings envied his 'good life;' the family had run out of spare cash. For whatever reason, the Bells decided that Stradishall should become home for them all. That is, all the Bells except Adrian thought it was a good idea.

The news had been broken to him when he had gone home for a visit and it was like a bombshell shattering his rural retreat. His father opened fire with a salvo of philosophical and practical reasons why they should all look to the land for their future, and his mother followed up with a mortar-shell of family loyalty. She reminded Adrian that all their spare money had gone into the farm and if they could not relieve the cash crisis, they would have to sell their South American shares. This was a heavy threat, for those shares represented more than a financial investment.

Fanny's sister Kate, having divorced Dr Peacock, had by now married his business partner Alec Cameron. She had emigrated again and was living a life of luxury in Buenos Aires, in a mansion house with twenty servants. The root of Cameron's money was the sheep farming business, and by holding on to their shares, Fanny felt she still kept a bond with her sister and her good fortune. It could not be broken. They must sell up their London home and move in with Adrian in Suffolk.

The younger Bells, Francis now aged 16 and Stephanie aged 14, were in complete agreement. They could hardly contain their excitement at the thought of the adventure. When they had visited their big brother they'd found country life great fun. Francis, a lively lad with boundless energy and humour, fancied himself as a farmer one day. He was handy with a pitchfork, a rake, a hoe, a gun, anything. Already he had the makings of being a man's man, he was much more at home with the jolly leg-pulling locals than his brother had been, and he was on his way to becoming quite a lady's man too.

His sister Stephanie, pretty as the 'Princess' her mother dubbed her, enjoyed the freedom from boarding school life, which she loathed, and she laughed gaily with the local farm lads who stared at her flaxen-maned beauty. She saw herself in cotton frock and no stockings, tossing hay around and casting corn to hens that would peck about her feet. Oh, yes, she would love to live in the country.

Adrian didn't stand a chance: it was four against one.

Alarm set in as he realised they were serious, and his mother came to recce his cottage with a view to billeting them all there. As he predicted, she found it too small. Any small sigh of relief that escaped him was soon stifled when Fanny declared that they must rent somewhere nearby, for she would not have her plans thwarted so easily. In no time at all, the Bell family would be on the move.

Just down the lane from Adrian at Farley Green was a three-bedroomed farmhouse they could rent from Walter Savage. Fanny would see about the decor; Francis, in his final year at Uppingham, soon would be helping Adrian on the farm, and Stephanie would soon be finished too, although not in the way that rich girls were. It simply meant she would finish school.

Robert would have to commute to the *Observer* office on a weekly basis, and so he took a room at his brother George's boarding house in London. He would be answerable to no-one there, he would be able to come and go as he pleased, and the rent would be a small price to pay for such liberty. None of these arrangements made any economic sense at all, but reason had gone out of the window by then.

It took a while for all the deals to be made, then the day dawned when Adrian's self-sufficient, solo existence came to an end. He would write about his family's calamitous move in his book *Silver Ley*, which describes the inauspicious arrival of the furniture vans in freezing fog, late in the evening. His mother, showing the early symptoms of exposure, was adamant that she must oversee the carrying of her precious items across the unkempt garden and into the cold, candle-lit farmhouse. In time her delicate antiques, porcelain crockery and crystal glasses would be unpacked and positioned just so, and the great, square draughty rooms took on the semblance of a family home.

Adrian found himself having to take off his boots when he came in now so as not to spoil the carpets and he had to present himself washed and brushed for meals. There would be no more cosy evenings in his chair by the fire at Stephenson's Farm. He could not leave his mother and sister defenceless in the old farmhouse at Farley Green while he sat on his own at Stephenson's. He had to concede that it made more sense to let his farm hand, George Hempstead, live there, and for Adrian to return to the maternal fold. He would not settle into Farley Green though. The family soon moved again, and he would move in with them.

They did not go far. Vic Savage had decided to leave Seabrooks Farm, the land of which backed on to Stephenson's. Victor would head across country to Cambridgeshire, to a village called Weston Colville, where he would rent an impressive Hall and a farm with nearly 1,000 acres of much lighter, sandier soil. The Savage family would keep the bulk of the land around Seabrooks, but Victor was to vacate the house, where he had cut down an apple tree every day before breakfast and thus made himself a tennis lawn out front. When he offered the place to the Bells, Fanny eyed the glorious cherry tree that was left standing outside the house, and the lean-to conservatory adjacent, where pot plants could be nurtured. Without doubt, it represented a better home than Farley Green Farm, and so it was purchased.

On 7th October 1922 Frances Hanbury Bell - Adrian's mother - became the new owner of Seabrooks Farm. A price of £620 shows in the farm accounts for the acquisition of the house and 15 acres of land. A further figure of £401 was paid to Vic Savage for 'Horses and implements.'

Adrian was now master of a farm totaling 50 acres, a cottage and a farm house, more buildings on the other side of the main road from Bury St Edmunds to Haverhill, and a whole raft of extra tackle. He would come to employ more men, use more horses, and expend a great deal more energy, in the pursuit of a living.

His first task was to organise the family's move and this time the operation was carried out in full daylight. For several days the farm wagons were commandeered for the work and the sight of Fanny's precious furniture and belongings trundling along the lane was poignant to her son. Robert's piano came too and by the time it reached Seabrooks it needed tuning. The piano tuner, brought down from London, was feted by the Bells who were desperately short of visitors, and they invited him to stay for lunch. It would become quite a regular habit.

Adrian's father Robert was still contributing a wage from the *Observer*, but he was home for less than two days a week, setting off for Suffolk after he had 'put the paper to bed' on Sunday mornings. Then he would quietly slip into the household, where he could play his piano, or go for a stroll, head tilted to the clouds, hands linked behind him. He might hum a snatch of Bach or Beethoven, and he would go for miles without realising it. There was no need to rush back to the house, except for meals: he had devolved all responsibility as head of the family to Adrian, who had just celebrated his twenty-first birthday.

Seabrooks Farm had plenty of room to accommodate all the Bells, with six bedrooms on the upper floor. It also had a water closet upstairs, which was positively modern by local standards, but for a time the bathroom would consist of a tin bath by the fire, with two screens made of 'scraps' - cut-out pictures of flush-faced Edwardian ladies, pasted on board. These were arranged around the bather to afford a modicum of privacy.

The drawing room, a long, low room with heavy beams and marble fire surround, was gradually filling with antiques for which Fanny had a passion. There was a separate dining room where her huge, brass-railed sideboard stood. Then there was a kitchen, dairy, housemaid's pantry, and scullery complete with sink and copper. In the garden was the old privy, a three-seater, poised over a brook.

In Adrian's memory the house smelled of pork, apples, baking, and, if the back window was opened, the muddy horse-pond.

The theory had been that Fanny could live simply in the country, with a maid to do all the housework, leaving her free to relax. In practice, it was just not in her nature to sit back and let her son get on with his job. In no time she knuckled down to being a farmer's mother and wife all in one, and she ran up several pairs of corduroy bloomers to wear, which in itself was unique. And just as she had made up her mind about what was the right thing to wear, so she re-invented herself in the process.

Forsaking her role of genteel lady she took on the maintenance of hens, cows and pigs with a fervent gusto. Adrian was worried that she was driving herself too hard but nothing would curtail her efforts to make a success of this farming business - his farming business, or so he had thought. Soon she would be telling him how to do that, too.

If he sat down for a minute, or seemed to be wasting his time even on a Sunday when Robert brought the London newspapers home, she would be there to chide him.

On Adrian's behalf, Fanny was constantly on guard against distractions. On the rare occasions that he went to a local dance, she would sniff around for signs that he had been close to a woman. Inspecting his jacket before his next sortie, she would make some acrid comment such as, 'I've cleaned the face-cream of your last lady-love off the lapels.' As if he had time for lady loves. As if he could have one and not tell her about it. She knew everything about him, inside and out and by keeping him busy, she could also keep him to herself. It worked for a while, at least.

The family had stayed in touch with their London friends and soon Adrian found himself with a regular list of orders for his fresh farm produce. First he went by motorcycle and sidecar, until he could not fit all the produce into it. That meant buying a van for the deliveries, and spending one day a week, sometimes stretching to two, doing the rounds. He had to confess, it was no hardship to stay overnight in a London house where he could enjoy a hot bath and an evening on the town. He could leap the gulf between country and town living, and then be off back to Suffolk the next morning.

It became necessary to take on extra staff to cope with the farm work while he was away, and more money was invested in fixed assets. Fanny wanted all the latest implements for making butter, she insisted on the most modern of hen houses, and she needed all the accoutrements for packing eggs, patting up butter or trussing up chickens. Each Friday the family worked on a production line well into the night before Adrian set off early next day on the long and arduous journey to the city.

Adrian saw less and less of his farm. His team of men, all older than him and married with families, were also considerably more experienced at farm work. He would give them their orders and leave them to get on with it while he tried to keep up with the paperwork and logistics of their venture. He might just as well have tried to run up an escalator that was going down.

In his book *Silver Ley*, Adrian wrote about this manic enterprise and posed the question, 'Did it pay?' A glance at his farm accounts for 1922-23 provides the answer: no, it didn't.

Against an income of £325, there in black and white are all the outgoings. First there's the men's wages: Coote, Bannister, the Hempstead brothers, the Kings. The bill for their pay came to £462 that year. Pigs were bought, and bullocks, plus feed for them, and extra manure for the fields. There is a figure of £156 for 'Sundries' and another of £171 for repairs to Stephenson's Farmhouse. That seems surprisingly high considering the whole farm had cost £850 to buy, but as one local person commented, 'Ah, but that was the price to Mr Bell.'

Times were harder than ever, and it was every man for himself. Vic Savage had always said there were two prices for everything - what it was worth and what you could get. Tradesmen clearly felt they could get more from Adrian Bell than from a near-bankrupt farmer. One look at the state-of-the-art hen-houses, the immaculate dairy and the house full of antiques and they knew they were onto a good thing. There is a suggestion too that, while Adrian thought his horseman was overfeeding his beasts, in fact others were coming and helping themselves to his supplies. Canny farmers had their names printed on their corn sacks. Adrian's anonymous ones could go anywhere.

In such a close community, nothing can be kept secret for long and word had it locally that the young Londoner was losing a thousand pounds a year. Nobody was surprised - it was as they had predicted, after all.

Still the frenetic activity went on, even though there were times when all the family looked at the figures and acknowledged that money was running through their fingers like sand. Robert, relatively happy in his bachelor existence in London, showed no interest in the accounts and made no complaint that all his hard-earned money was being frittered away. It was simply not his problem any more.

One might conclude that Adrian's mind must have been sorely troubled by all this. Not necessarily. By the spring of 1923, finance was not the foremost matter on the young man's mind.

# 7. Love and Friendship

Although Adrian had become house-trained again in many respects, he had to remonstrate against some things. It simply was not practical to wash and change before entering the house every time, he stated. He was a working man, and this was a working farm, so the others, having chosen to live there, must live with it. He did try his best not to be carting too much mud onto the carpet on his hobnail boots, stopping at the back door and using an old palette knife to peel the worst of it away. He could do little about his worn and dishevelled clothes, his permanently grimed hands or his hair, which had a tendency to wave wildly unless slicked down. He would remove his cap as he walked in, and if his hair wasn't stuck down with sweat, it would spring up in all directions.

And so it was that one day, late in 1922, he strode into Seabrooks farmhouse, collarless and unshaven, sweaty and aromatic from carting manure, to discover that they had visitors. One, his former Glengorse headmaster Mr Jones, he was surprised and pleased to see. The other, the sister of a former school mate, caused him to feel perplexed and embarrassed. Little Mary Graves - grown so pretty and stylish? Perched on a chair in his low, beamed sitting room, sipping tea and smiling at him through a trendy little black net attached to her pert hat. It was as though she had hit him with a brick; his mind reeled. What on earth...?

They explained that they had been out for a car trip in the country, it was not really far from her home in Cambridge, and she had suggested they might call on Adrian, who she'd heard was living in Stradishall. Mr Jones, who was clearly besotted by her, had readily agreed. And here they were.

Adrian, having hastily washed and changed, went through a mechanical business of making conversation but his eyes struggled to move away from those forget-me-not blue ones that held him firm. The pretty blonde hair, the smooth ankles in stockings that started in dainty shoes and drew the eyes upwards along twin gleaming tracks - by the time the visitors left, it was not only poor

Mr Jones who was besotted. But would Adrian ever see her again?

Mary Graves saw to that. In their final parting words, she sealed his fate: she ordered some potatoes. Could he deliver? Again those appealing blue eyes. Yes, he could. Would Saturday suit? Saturday would be fine. Perhaps he might stay for lunch - her parents would be delighted, she was sure.

Adrian later noted in his diary that in those days, 'I was very shy, diffident. I was always afraid that if I touched a girl she would slap my face. But I did not feel that way about Mary. I was soon at a dance with her in Cambridge: these things easily happen...'

They danced close he said, and it felt exciting, dangerous. He stayed in her parents' house that night, and somehow they met in the dark on the landing; not, he insisted, by any explicit design. They embraced, and he felt the contours of her body through her thin night-clothes. He was startled. The effect was like static electricity in his hair. He shivered and was on fire all at once. But they whispered good night and went back to their rooms. This would set the tone of their relationship, which, he would later comment, 'was all sweet fire and sighing.'

Mary was six months older than Adrian, who was still just twenty-one. She wore smart suits and matching accessories, with the latest style of hat. She worked and had money to spend, and she mixed with women of the world. At a dance, Adrian overheard one of her sophisticated friends saying, 'Why, he's just a babe!' and he did look very boyish. His hands were rough and his body lean, but he could not act like a man, not yet. His mother would never allow it.

But Mary didn't seem to mind. In the ensuing months they were to spend every spare moment together. Every Saturday Adrian would race through his chores and then motor to Cambridge, often with another half-hundredweight of potatoes in the back among his overnight things. He would stay with Mary and her parents, and go shopping with his girl, stopping for tea in a little cafe and expressing amazement at how much they had in common.

At some stage, Adrian says, they became engaged. Elsewhere he says they were engaged, 'or thought we were'. There is no sign of an announcement in *The Times* as one might expect if it were official. In any case, he bought Mary a ring and she wore it while she was with him. At that point in time, she vowed to spend the rest of her life with him.

To a girl in love, even farming can seem appealing, and Mary saw herself becoming part of the family. She could fit in, and be helpful to him, she said. For one week in April 1923 the farm accounts are entered in her big, round, curly writing. 'F. Hempstead finished ducksfoot-harrowing (field) no.12 second time about 12 o/c', she noted, 'then began drilling barley on no.12.' There was more detail, far more than Adrian could ever find time or be bothered to put down. Bannister had been hoeing, King had been doing the gardening, and G. Hempstead had carted middlings before breakfast. A bull calf had been born to the brindle cow, she put, and a fat sow had been taken to Haverhill market.

Everyone's workday is charted on that page, everyone except Adrian. Was he getting much work done?

In other weeks he had noted in his straightforward, slightly spidery handwriting that he and his brother Francis had worked alongside the men. He did not really need to keep track of his own work, because the purpose of the exercise was to make note of how many hours he would have to pay each man for. But now Adrian was busy elsewhere, renovating a cottage that was reached by crossing the road from Seabrooks, and taking a tiny green lane northwards. Tiny green lanes were generally called 'drifts' and consequently the cottage was called Drift Cottage.

Its heavy-beamed frame was in-filled with wattle-and-daub, and its foot-deep thatch overshadowed the ground floor windows. When the Bells had bought Seabrooks, this had been included in the sale description as a 'building' but in Adrian's new plans it was to be a love-nest for a new generation.

Arthur King, their farm hand and part-time gardener, was set to work in creating a proper little garden around the thatched cottage. The house itself was basic, but could be made comfortable. Its three small bedrooms ran one into another, and in the main bedroom, the middle one, a great cross-beam intersected it to form a stile.

Mary, accepting the water supply from the pond, and the lack of electricity, felt she could make a home there. The oil lamps and candles were delightful, she insisted, and she would not mind washing up in a bowl, for there was no sink. So, with the eagerness of idealistic romance, she and Adrian got to work on the decorating.

They were comfortable in each other's company, talking now and then in their special, baby-like language of love. Mary had a clipped Cambridge accent, which Adrian would mimic and they would laugh. Then one day, the laughing stopped.

Whenever he looked back, Adrian could not be sure what had actually sparked the argument. All he knew was that one minute they were painting in their bedroom - it was to be rose pink - and the next minute they were hurling invectives at each other. When the time came for Mary to board her train home, she left Adrian standing on the platform with the engagement ring in his hand. The dream of his own home, a wife, a family, a happy future, melted like ice as he looked at the scrap of diamond and gold in his callused palm. He went home, slowly, to tell his mother the news.

Mary did get in touch with Adrian again, two weeks later. He would say that she even tried to re-establish their engagement. But by then he was over the worst of his heartbreak, and wasn't taking any chances. He would not see her again for another twenty years. Eventually, he would write, Drift Cottage, neglected, would fall to rubble. The only souvenir of his engagement was Mary's handwriting in his accounts, like a signature in a guest book.

Somehow life went back to the old routine. It must have been a relief to Fanny that she was not about to lose her boy, because, as she so often said, he was all she'd got, or nearly all. When she had first arrived in Stradishall she'd sat back and waited for all the local gentry to come visiting, but she had waited in vain. She had asked one of the yeomen's wives, where were all the 'right' kind of people - 'our kind of people, don't y'know?' The woman had evaded the question and assured her that they would find her. But they didn't come looking.

The family were philosophical; they recognised that snobbery was rife in the area and as they were merely farmers who laughed and chatted with the tenantry, they were 'persona non grata' to the upper class. Fanny, with her music-hall humour and extrovert personality, was not invited to take tea with the honorable ladies and squires' wives, and would never get to see the inside of the beautiful houses of the district she so admired.

It was not just for herself that she was disappointed. Her daughter Stephanie was happy to make friends with the local lads and was forming an ambition to marry a farmer, but Fanny had at least hoped he would be a gentleman. Her advice as always was not to let emotion cloud one's judgement, for, she said, 'What matters is not the man you marry, but the life you marry into.'

Meanwhile the canyon between rich and poor everywhere was widening fast. The mid 1920s are noted for the desperation of workers all over Britain who, faced with unemployment and poverty, finally went on a General Strike in May 1926. The heroes of the trenches had been badly let down, it was said, and everyone rallied to show their disdain.

Robert, at the *Observer*, was in the thick of it, while his family in the country bought themselves a crystal-set wireless to keep abreast of the news. Farm workers could not afford to strike, but they too felt most disgruntled when their rate of pay was cut and cut again.

Adrian could really not afford to keep all his men on, but he could not bring himself to let them go and be destitute. Trying to apply the adage of 'up horn, down corn' he invested in more calves to make money where he could. This met with disapproval from Fanny, who would have to relinquish her butter-making activities, for the calves were drinking all the milk. To her son, that was a bonus in itself, as he had been unable to persuade her to take things easier. Now she had no choice.

But that year would become especially notable to Adrian for another reason. A woman he had met briefly some years before through a friend was looking for a cottage to rent in the country. Bobby Baker wrote to Adrian on her behalf, asking if he knew of anywhere suitable. Yes, came the reply, there was a little thatched place on Seabrooks Farm, for which he had no use. She was welcome to come and see it.

That she did, arriving with Bobby in the dark one evening in a hired car. They had lost their way, and been driving for ages. Ignoring his mother's sibilant questioning, Adrian fetched a lantern from the stable and guided his visitors along the green lane to Drift Cottage. When they stopped to talk there, the golden marigold glow of light held them in its circle of warmth, and, in that little house that was devoid of electricity, Adrian felt a current surge through him.

He had only seen this woman before when Bobby introduced her in the dim light of a cinema, and although he had experienced a brief frisson of interest, it had passed when the couple moved on. This was different.

Holding the lantern and rotating round the rooms to light up the features, he quivered, not because of the draughts, although there were plenty, but with excitement. Whenever the light fell on her face, her dark eyes appeared to be no more than deep, shadowy pockets with twin pinpricks of reflected gold, like sunflowers in a distant field. Adrian was finding it hard to concentrate on the tour.

He explained away the old paint pots that had remained there with brushes sticking out in frozen attitudes. His guest smoothed sympathy on his wounds. When finally they went back to Seabrooks, Adrian saw her in the full light for the first time, and was entranced. Slender and breastless as a boy, she had a grace that suggested she thought carefully before every step she took. With deep brown eyes and hair, and lips that are usually described as 'generous', she filled the room with a sultry aura. In a cherry-red hat, coat and shoes she might be considered the epitome of the scarlet woman. Adrian's mother hated her on sight.

A tense time followed, with Fanny putting on airs and graces that extended to a sudden change in her diction. 'Isn't it' was pronounced 'is it not' and 'don't y'know' came back into play. Would they take 'cawfee?' she enquired. But after the guests had gone, Adrian was left in no doubt as to his mother's reaction towards 'that woman.' She knew the type, she said, and reminded him of their time in Brighton when she had tried to arm him against gold diggers and heartbreakers. Again she warned him about all the kinds of women who spelled danger, and stated once more that love is a disease. He must concentrate on his work, she insisted.

Fanny was no fool, she would have sensed that her words were wasted, as her son's attention was elsewhere, his emotions held in a dam that was ready to burst. Her premonition was justified, for nothing would restrain Adrian from seeing Dolores again.

Dolores; oh, Dolores; what a woman she was. Beautiful, passionate, encouraging: all of these things, and also at times aloof, self-centred and manipulating. A widow, eight years his senior and aeons more worldly wise, Adrian fell for her like a boulder from a cliff top.

Dolores, real name Sybil Denison, had originally been introduced by Bobby Baker as his girlfriend, but Dolores belonged to nobody. She had been married, it's true, but her husband had died young and she would never give herself to another. And yet she needed men, and enjoyed their adoration. Even a tramp, seeing her approaching, would unconsciously straighten his jacket or brush a piece of grass from his sleeve. She was captivating, entertaining, irresistible, and to most, untouchable.

But she was drawn to Adrian and permitted him to pursue her. She did not move into Drift Cottage, but he went to visit her in London, and sat, clasping her hand, imagining what might be. She would not be the sort to marry him and come to feed the hens, he saw that. But she stirred the muse in him, and suggested they could write a book together, and make their fortune out of a tale of love.

In fact, Dolores didn't need the money herself. She had means even without the gifts that arrived in a constant stream from admirers. Adrian would later write that she had at one time got through £10,000 a year. She had been abroad, gathering admirers all the way, including many rich men, and some titled ones. She also liked to encourage ardent, arty young men who had no money at all. There was drama in her every move, in every sentence she spoke. The effect was hypnotic and Adrian was under her spell.

He spent weekends in her London home, an eighteenth century house with a theatrical interior, dimly lit and overly plush. Pine cones in the grate and fat candles sputtering their dancing light created an atmosphere of intense intimacy. They drank corn-coloured wine in almost sacramental reverence, and, picking up his pen for the first time in years other than for farm accounts, Adrian wrote a sonnet in celebration of that glass of intoxication.

### Sonnet

And in that fire-bathed hour when thought fulfills
    Youth's prophecy, how doth my spirit sigh
    To lift the glass and watch the wine's bright eye
And fancy what far light that flame distills.

From Time's dead rock a rainbow fountain spills
    Whose rich reflections round my fingers lie
    Painting my flesh with memories of the sky,
And footsteps of the dawn upon the hills.

So to lean forth and dare that spirit-touch
    And crush the giddy breath of lips that gleam
Deep in thy shadowy furnace, wine, and clutch
    The exquisite adventure of a dream.
    And so to ride the dark and downward stream
From Life's small moment conjuring so much.

His epithets were not particularly original, there was rather a conglomeration of styles of all those he had admired before, but to him, it was a new experience, this maturity and sensuality.

He may have lacked practical experience but Adrian had dreamed about such a love for so long that his instinct led him on to explore this new territory of a willing woman. That is to say, Dolores was willing to allow only so much. Their love was never consummated.

Adrian jotted down a description of her bedroom, with white carpet, mirrors on the walls and delicate white china; a lamp with cherubs frolicking with handfuls of grapes, vases overflowing with marigolds and an alabaster basket with glass grapes. He spent time in there, and remembered the sound of her sleeping, snoring slightly, as he leaned out of the window and marvelled that he could share the very air she breathed.

She worked at embroidery and sewing, making her own fashions and putting on 'shows' for her friends and fans. In her studio he saw flame-coloured fabrics cast over a deal table, and an old sewing-machine arching above her slender, expressive hands. A worn couch by the fireside was held in cosy embrace by a studded-leather screen and Adrian would perch here, or arrange himself in a pose, waiting for her to finish her work and put down her pink-rimmed spectacles.

Caressing her, he would seek to smooth away her worries, for she always seemed to have so many, and, when she relaxed, his hands would become more adventurous, more importuning. He adored her nimble fingers, and her toes, like a nursemaid with four pink babies, he said. He worshipped her ears, her neck, her face, every inch of her body...That was where she put a stop to it, sending him to fetch her a drink, or diverting him in some other way. Perhaps it was this very limitation that fired his passion even more.

Back at Seabrooks he would take her letters into the meadow to read, away from his mother's hawkish eyes. He could sit in the shade of a great oak, often with a crowd of inquisitive cows around him, standing like the spokes of a cartwheel. Oblivious to the bemused, munching faces he would absorb the words that had flowed from the envied pen which she had held in her beloved hand. In return he sent streams of amorous thoughts, and his emotion, buried for so long in the workaday and prosaic, soared like the skylark.

The effect of Dolores on Adrian was not restricted to his inner self. Suddenly his appearance mattered to him very much, even on the farm. He must have new, bespoke breeches to replace the old shapeless ones. Instead of bagging at the knees to allow room for bending and kneeling, these would taper gently from a buxom-cut hip, and his lower legs must be clasped in smart leather buskins that were polished to perfection. He bought hunting horses for himself and his sister Stephanie, an extravagance in such desperate times, but now he was beyond rational thought.

For transport, he spurned the old delivery van and bought a sportier car, which was hardly suitable for the haphazard surface of the country lanes, but it was far smarter for taking a woman about in. He could run Dolores home to her mother's house where they strolled under copper beech trees and shared the intimate tenderness of nature's beauty. She noticed the minutest detail, and they marvelled together at every new discovery. He wished he could take her to the ends of the earth, and see all the wonders of the world together.

But the fragility of the sporty car proved itself on a trip to the West Country, when its back axle broke and he was forced to seek help. Somehow the bill for repair fell into Fanny's hands and she accused him of being artful, using her when it suited him, and casting her aside for That Woman whenever he liked. He could hardly argue.

Adrian would say in his autobiography that it was an absurd, short-lived affair. It seems that Bobby Baker, their mutual friend, had to go away for a time and when he returned, he was surprised to be met by both Dolores and Adrian. He had brought her an orchid, but he kept it by his plate during dinner. Adrian could see that he was creating a crowd, and left.

But he was still writing ardent letters to Dolores in 1928 and beyond, promising among other things to get on with the book they were supposed to be co-writing. Addressing her as Juliet - the allusion is obvious - he wrote, 'Life is difficult, Juliet. There are a million wallflowers here, and that means a million thoughts of you, a million desires to be with you, and their scent is a millionfold ache for the touch of your hand, and you by my side walking in the places where we found wallflowers this time last year....And now there is lilac too, and to reach it down to smell it, is to remember how your hand reached to it upon a sunny day, your arm green-sleeved, and the courtly gesture of the plumed bough as it yielded and bowed to your hand.'

'The dazzling pain of gardens in the Spring - because one is alone... How strangely one is made, knowing that the acute sensitiveness of this love of ours is the one thing that matters really, and the world well lost for it, and at the same time being caught in the works of life and prisoned by one's own sense of - what is it? Responsibility?'

The next passage shows Adrian's frustration that the family was depending on him, and at the least sign of his going away, his mother would surely break down. It was like a tether he could not untie, however gently he might try. He was morally bound, he declared, and yet, 'Dear love, my heart cries like a nightingale all the while, to be with you in the heaven that is ours - you know that, as I know you are thinking of me, can feel you loving me.'

He added 'There is the consolation of our book, at which I have been working all this time.' In truth, he was still suffering those recurrent bouts of migraine, and he had written very little of the improbable, lush romance story that was to be their best-selling novel. Still, he was enjoying the research.

He wrote to Dolores, 'Need you? I should think I do and always shall. It was no dream, darling, my lips kissed you, and I held you in my arms, and we were tenderly close for hours in your room scented with old gardens. How beautiful the warmth and stir of limbs, the delicate harmonies of touch, in a love like ours, what peace.'

This was indeed a seminal time for Adrian, not entirely thanks to Dolores. Looking back, he would see that she had given him the courage to think for himself, and to prepare the way for his eventual flight from the family. But it would be another acquaintance, a man of greater depth and passion than anyone else he had met, who would direct him towards his future path in life.

## 8. The Girl Downstairs

In the midst of the Bells' social exclusion from the upper classes, Robert had heard about a newcomer to the district, a gentlemanly poet with no snobbish pretensions, and he urged his son to pay the man a visit. Adrian did, and, in the neighbouring village of Cowlinge he tracked down Edmund Blunden, who was renting a cottage called The Villa. It was a curiously unromantic house with a blank facade and rotting cabbage stalks in the garden. It was remarkable in being one of the few houses with a tiled roof instead of cosy thatch, but Adrian would eventually realise that this perverse choice of a prosaic home was typical of Blunden's character. The man was determined to deny himself too much beauty it seemed, for he felt he could not deserve it.

The place was easy enough to find as it stood opposite the grocery store where Adrian had bought supplies in his solo days. He would return that way frequently in the next two years, and similarly, Edmund Blunden would visit the Bells at Seabrooks.

To Fanny, he was a quenching cup of culture to her long-endured thirst for stimulation. He was charming, polite, graceful and sensitive. She worried about his gaunt frame, his bird-like appearance and his ill-fitting trousers. He suffered from asthma, it dogged his life as migraines blighted Adrian's, and Fanny felt sad for him. She wanted to mother him, to laugh with him, to draw him into her house and keep him there to amuse her and entertain her with stories from abroad, from London and from his youth in Kent.

He had no need to tell her about the torrid time he had been through lately, for Fanny had an intuition about people that was rarely wrong. From his beaky visage to his twitching limbs, a core of acute suffering could be glimpsed beneath the veneer.

The pain that was most evident in Blunden's restless eyes was often focused on images he could see, which others couldn't. He was haunted by the scenes he had witnessed at the Somme and Passchendaele, and on some days even the wind stirring the trees could transform itself into the rush of an enemy approach, or the howl of shellfire. The guilt of his survival weighed him down and he would later say that since 1918, hardly a day had passed without him losing the present and finding himself living in a ghost story. The dead, so many of them, followed him wherever he went. Why had he survived?

Marriage had not been his salvation. In 1919 his little daughter had died, and, like her name, Joy, his new-found happiness had faded away. He and his wife Mary had had two more children in the 1920s and Edmund had begun to find success in publishing books of his poetry with the aid of his friend, Richard Cobden-Sanderson. In 1924 he had moved abroad to take up a post as professor of English in Tokyo. Mary had refused to go, and he had whiled away his spare time with a Japanese mistress.

He had come back to England three years later, worn out and confused. Installing his mistress in a flat in London, he had agreed to try to patch things up with Mary, and so they had moved to Cowlinge, Suffolk.

When Adrian visited The Villa on that first day in November 1927 he was struck by the voluptuous, gipsy-like Mary, and intimidated by her forthright sexuality. But she intrigued him, too. In an unfinished book about Blunden, he wrote, '...Now Mary addressed me. "Mr Bell, what I want to know is, who are all these girls he writes to? That Corrie..Corinia.." "Corinna," Edmund corrected, smiling kindly. "And that Daphne whose hair he says he caressed - and that Flora? He seems sweet on a girl called Flora. Always writing poems to this Flora. Why don't he write one to me? Do you know any of these women, Mr Bell, I mean personally?" '

Adrian adds, 'I stared and looked at Edmund. He rocked his head slowly, smiling inwardly, and said nothing. I was puzzled and embarrassed. Could she really be serious?'

Mary was by no means a connoisseur of poetry, and it was hard to see what the couple had in common apart from their two young children. In spite of Edmund's kindly smile, he was still racked with angst and he was now working out his nightmares in verse, in a book that was to become one of his most celebrated, *Undertones of War*.

Embarrassment notwithstanding, Adrian enjoyed that visit immensely. He had spent time in the study, admiring the collection of leather-bound classics that Blunden picked up from market stalls, never paying more than sixpence a time. He restored them with boot polish, which lent a distinctive, almost clinical air to his narrow, shelf-lined room. He showed a comprehensive knowledge of all kinds of books, authors, and even their life stories. Adrian felt ignorant and illiterate in such a presence.

Only five years older than Adrian, Blunden had indeed lived a much fuller life, and yet he was pleased to hear about farming. For once, Adrian found himself opening up about his sense of the spirit of the land, and what his life in Suffolk had come to mean to him. He felt that Blunden understood.

Locals would later comment about the strange little fellow who cycled the lanes from Cowlinge to the railway station, waving to the trees and calling out compliments on their fine blossom or handsome foliage. When Adrian was working in his fields, he would first see the top of a hat gliding along, apparently by magic, just above the line of the hedgerows. Then Blunden would call out a salutation and be gone.

By this time, Edmund Blunden was already a celebrated figure and so he gained entry to that upper echelon of Suffolk society that had been denied to the Bells. Among his acquaintances was A.H. Fass, a wealthy man described by Canon A.J. Webling as 'the flamboyant and knickerbockered owner of Gifford's Hall at Denston', just a couple of miles away. The poet and the landed gent had known each other for several years, and Fass, full of 'antiquarian chat' according to the writer Siegfried Sassoon, was eccentric but well worthwhile, in Blunden's opinion. Fass seemed to look upon young Edmund as a surrogate nephew.

On one of his visits to Seabrooks, Edmund suggested to Fanny that he was sure Fass would be pleased to meet her and her family. He would mention it to the old man, he promised. Her anticipation was high, and her disappointment brought her correspondingly low when the old bachelor kept his distance. Fanny had to accept that they were simply not 'his sort of people'.

Adrian was more than satisfied with the friendship of Edmund Blunden. The poet lived and breathed his art, and even when he sat amongst the Bells in Seabrooks Farmhouse, he would be composing little complimentary poems about them. He introduced Adrian to the works of his favourites, like Robert Bloomfield, John Clare, and Wilfred Owen, and while they were out exploring

Edmund might point out a wisp of vaporous cloud and say, 'In former times they would have said that was an angel'. Then Adrian could see it, just as, guided by Blunden, he could hear the stream chuckling, or mark the flash of a darting fish.

In turn, Adrian started seeing the potential poetry of his own experiences. There was inspiration in the seasons all right, and in the sights, smells, sensations of his intimacy with the soil, with the animals, with the men in the fields. He was beginning to think that he might write a book one day after all, but it would not be the one on which Dolores had tried to collaborate. His craving for her had peaked, and, seeing her more objectively now, he had started to inch himself out of the all-engulfing longing he had felt, and consider the possibility of a real, two-way relationship with a woman who might genuinely return his love.

It was in May 1928 that Adrian had written so adoringly to Dolores, and it cannot have been long after that when he happened to be in London and was invited to a soiree at his Aunt Mabel's boarding house in Pimlico. Mabel was married to Uncle George Bell, the last refugee from the ironmongery business, who nowadays passed his time padding about the cellar in his carpet slippers, reciting Shakespeare and fixing wooden furniture. To earn their living, Aunt Mabel took in lodgers. A fair amount of money came in but it soon went out again, as Mabel enjoyed company so much that she spent all her profits on hosting dinner parties. She fancied herself as quite a matchmaker, and was happy to invite Adrian on an evening when several young ladies would be present.

His father Robert was still living at Mabel's, in a small back room on the upper floor. In the small back room below was a young man named Dennis Brogan, and in the larger front room were two girls, called Marjorie Gibson and Marjorie Parfitt. None of this had registered in Robert's mind as being of particular interest but they were all present at Mabel's little party. Before long Adrian was taking a very keen interest in Marjorie Gibson. In fact, he made up his mind he would marry her.

He described their meeting in his autobiography. 'I was introduced to a girl sitting on a sofa in the lounge drinking a cocktail, wearing a frock of cream silk with a gold fringe. She had a slightly one-sided smile, and her eyes were grey with flecks of brown in them, and she had a wide forehead from which the hair grew in a widow's peak.'

In photographs, Marjorie does not appear to have been a great beauty, but all who knew her agree that she had a calm and gentle nature that gave her a loveliness the camera could not capture. At dinner she hid her horror of oysters gracefully, and having only a small appetite, she picked delicately at the entrees. Adrian would say that when the roast meat and vegetables were being passed around at dizzying speed, he deftly fielded a stuffing-ball that was rolling across the table towards Marjorie's lap. She smiled her thanks, and their future compact was assured.

Adrian embarked on a courtship of Miss Gibson, but again his only free time was at weekends. It must be said, his former fervour in the pursuit of love had taken a battering, and there was at least one opportunity of which he failed to take advantage. He and the family decided to spend a few days' break in London, staying in a friend's flat, and Aunt Mabel passed this intelligence to her young boarder. So Marjorie waited for the call, happily anticipating the extra time she could spend with Adrian. But the call never came.

Marjorie was not to know then that Adrian was as a puppet in his mother's presence, and in London she kept a tight hold of him. He was sent back to Suffolk on some errand, and at all other times he had to accompany her around their old haunts, and also to any new ones she fancied. He was kept so busy that it didn't cross his mind to excuse himself and go to see Marjorie.

Her friend and room-mate consoled her - had she not warned her to be wary of that man? She had known he couldn't be trusted. But stoically, Marjorie didn't even mention her disappointment next time she met Adrian, and in fact she would keep it secret for another thirty-five years.

If Adrian thought he had some sense of his future unfolding, it would be necessary first to close the current chapter of his life. The family must finally admit defeat in their farming enterprise. They had been able to carry on longer than many of their bankrupt neighbours, but even Robert's well-spring of income could not continue to irrigate their revenue drought. It was time to sell up.

Francis, now a devil-may-care, fun-loving young man, had already been packed off. He wanted to be a farmer but there was no more money going spare and no point in setting him up with a farm in the depth of an agricultural depression. So it had been arranged that he should go out to Argentina, where Aunt Katie was living so comfortably. Work would be found for him.

His experiences over the next few years would fill a book of their own - working with the gauchos for two years, then his pioneering job testing crops and encouraging farming settlers to populate the barren land from Buenos Aires to Chile. How he lived in an old railway carriage alone, and with no English-speaking company for months on end, in wild country and blistering heat.

According to his cousin Carlos, even Aunt Katie had been disillusioned out there, in spite of her luxurious lifestyle. He said of his mother's second marriage, 'Like so many steps in her life it was idealistic and misjudged. In the Argentine she found herself exiled in an alien world where money was the ruling god.' For Francis, a lad whose chief experiences had been private school followed by rural Suffolk, that was highly alarming.

Francis kept a journal, but in later years he would rarely mention those days. He had been given only a one-way ticket, and it was unthinkable to ask Aunt Katie for the money to send him back. One day he would work his passage home.

For the rest of the family, Christmas 1928 was their last at Seabrooks and according to Adrian it was idyllic. They had all agreed that they should try to move out before Spring, when the beauty of the landscape might weaken their resolve. The idea was to find a small house near to London so Robert could commute to the *Observer* and Stephanie could try obtaining a little job. Adrian might also find some sort of employment, although his unpredictable health would always be a barrier.

Fanny put all these plans into disarray when she found by chance a house that she said she simply must have, and it was in Suffolk. In the old market town of Sudbury she had peered through the window of a large, empty house called The Gables in busy Stour Street, and she had fallen in love with it instantly. Even on closer inspection, the six bedrooms which would all have to be redecorated, the attics, the cellar, the freezing cold, stone-floored kitchen, none of these could put her off. This was where they were to live.

Their lovely home with the cherry tree in front, Seabrooks, changed owners on 7th June 1929 when its deeds were legally transferred to Thomas D'oyley Bulkeley of Chatsworth House in Sussex. It would be sold again the following year by his mortgagees, and once more, before being purchased by the Suffolk brewer Greene King, who turned it into a public house, The Cherry Tree.

Stephenson's Farm was sold too, along with Adrian's dream of farming. A local man by the name of Will Lunniss bought it and at least Adrian felt some small satisfaction in that he was very friendly with Will and his sister Cissie. One day he would go back and stay a while in his little farmhouse but in the meantime he would have to go to Sudbury and live with his parents again. He saw it only as a temporary measure, for he was determined to get back into farming and this time to do it properly, and make a living at it.

Meanwhile he was still courting Marjorie. She came to stay at the Gables, although it would be stretching the point to say she was made welcome. Fanny saw the way her son and his sweetheart seemed so very at ease in each other's company, and her intuition told her that her grip on him was slipping. The pair had much in common, not least that Marjorie had attended the Grammar School in Bournemouth where Adrian's Aunt Dorothy was English mistress, and they held a mutual admiration for her.

In fact, Marjorie rarely had a bad word to say about anybody. The girl never raised her voice in temper, never seemed to scold Adrian or make demands. When they laughed together it was gentle, relaxed, and intimate. Instead of leaving Adrian looking exhausted by the burden of passion as with former loves, this girl left him feeling content, and at peace. Her kisses were firm and cool, he noted, not burning, but reassuring. She didn't give him headaches like others had, she imbued him with confidence, like a sweet warmth inside. Yes, he was falling in love again, this time not hard and fast, but slowly, permanently.

Marjorie was a fairly complex girl, for all her calmness and mildness of manner. Her father was a military man, he was William James Gibson, originally of the Royal Horse Guards, then Bandmaster with the Royal Tank Corps, and latterly he was serving as Lieutenant and Director of Music in the Life Guard. But Marjorie had been born in Potchefstroom, South Africa, in 1908. She was the fourth and youngest child of William and his wife Alice, whose maiden name had been Bellringer.

Alice's father had been a publican and, having seen him die as a result of alcoholism, she was vehemently against drinking, so the life of an army wife suited her with its restrictive code of conduct. She had married young and had her first baby by the age of nineteen but it was difficult to settle anywhere as they were constantly on the move. She had followed William as his career took him around

Britain, then to India, and then to a corrugated iron bungalow on the edge of the veldt where the scenery consisted of hundreds of miles of parched grass with hardly a tree in sight.

Marjorie's sister Alice, nicknamed 'Lallie' later described the family's experience of life there. 'Majestic elephants and giraffes would pass close by and at night we could hear the animals calling. Leopards would do their hunting at night, often leaving their kill in the fork of a large Fever Tree to be eaten the following day. We were near a friendly farmer who was often a great help. Once a swarm of locusts descended on his farm and all his crops were stripped in a few hours. The swarm was heralded by a large buzzing noise and all the time they were near we heard it.'

On another occasion, the family had gone trekking in an ox-wagon to camp by the bank of the Vaal River. A forest fire broke out, roaring across the open plain and killing everything in its path. The Gibsons were safe on the other side of the river, but they mourned for all the creatures that were perishing in the voracious furnace.

The seasons were the opposite of those in England said Lallie, so they celebrated Christmas in the sunshine. They had no electricity or gas and did as little cooking as possible, but there was plenty of exotic fruit to enjoy. The exotic insects were less welcome and Lallie recalled seeing their dining-table cloth 'black with flies.'

However, the inhospitable conditions were more than just inconvenient, they could be deadly. It is thought they contributed to a great tragedy, when William and Alice's latest baby died of illness and lack of proper medical care. Alice's own health broke down and the family returned to England, where they resumed a nomadic lifestyle.

Marjorie herself suffered from nerves at times and as part of a military, undemonstrative family, she did her best to cope in silence. But she was taken out of school before finishing her education as her weight had dropped below seven stones and there was no hiding her state of distress. When she had recovered, she trained as a secretary and was working in London when Adrian met her, but her health still gave cause for concern. In the spring of 1930 it was arranged that she should go abroad for six months to stay with her mother's sister Florence in New Rochelle, just north of New York City, U.S.A.

Adrian was shocked when she told him the news; he had been thinking maybe it was time to propose. He asked, when would she marry him? She gave him the impression that she might consider such an offer, upon her return. Without intending to, she had effectively set him a challenge. He had just six months in which to prepare himself for the role of eligible bachelor. The latter part was easy enough because without doubt, he was a bachelor. But eligible? He hadn't held down a paid job in his life, and there was little hope of that changing all the while he kept being incapacitated by migraines. What on earth could he do to show her that he would make a good, dependable, and above all, solvent husband?

Young master Adrian, aged 18

Fanny Bell

Robert Bell

The Savage Family at the wedding of Tom to Christine Thomson 1919
Top row, from 3rd man: George, Amy (nee Collen), Herbert, Tammy. Next to bride: Fanny and Walter Savage
Seated in front: Martha in fur coat, and Victor Savage - 'Mr Colville' in *Corduroy*

Adrian with Bob, 1923

Adrian, Stephanie and Francis
with Fanny and Robert at rear

George Hempstead on the binder

Broken-dream homes: Stephenson's Farm

Drift Cottage

Seabrooks

## 9. Crosswords and Corduroy

Adrian had been in the doldrums since moving to Sudbury. There he was, living with his mother, broke, unemployed, and without prospects.

His sorrow at quitting the latitude of Stradishall was profound, and he moped around the town feeling hemmed in. At the shops everything seemed so measly to him in its tins, packets, pints, and pounds. Milk in sterile bottles instead of frothing in the pail. A paltry bag of apples - how could this equate to plucking one from the bending branch? A bag of flour - how far removed this seemed from the ghostly miller in his winged turret, standing amid eighteen-stone sacks of the finest wheat.

Pounds and ounces? Pah! This diminution of goods seemed to sum it all up - his life had been reduced, his hopes and dreams discounted.

He no longer received letters addressed to A.Bell Esq., Farmer. His conversations on farming were all in the past tense. In country inns he was a tourist among the corduroy-clad men of the land. He had time to sit and sip his beer while working men would down theirs in a gulp and, cuffing away the drips, clatter off back to work. No, he could stay on - he had all day to sit and contemplate.

With a rush, the old bitterness at parental interference returned. He could hardly claim to have proved himself, though he had stuck at it during that first year with Vic Savage at Hundon, against incredible odds. And for three months after that he had thrown himself into the work on his own farm; become manager, made decisions, seen the results as his crops had started to flourish. But then his mother had arrived, like a wind-borne disease. There was a horrible inevitability in the sequence of events that had followed, and recalling them brought him close to despair.

He could not take out his anger on his mother, for she could transcend any sulk or outburst and come back with an even greater counterblast of tragic drama. There was always the danger that she would turn back to the bottle, or lose her mind completely, and Adrian could not risk being the one to cause it. She had worked hard on the farm, he couldn't deny it, and he couldn't accuse her of deliberately sabotaging his business; why, almost every farmer in the county had been brought to the brink of bankruptcy, many had toppled over the edge.

Fanny had lost a great deal of her own money, and seven years of her life, thanks to him. And he had to admit to himself, in her sweeter moments she could be so compelling, so amusing, and so maddeningly nice. Her intentions were good, he was sure. That she adored him was beyond question. That she adored him too much for comfort was best left unsaid.

Now, living with her again at the Gables, he found some solace in being on his own, either in the garden where there was a quaint, mock ruin, or in his room. Sometimes he even crept out of a tiny door that led from the attic onto the leaded gully between the pitched roofs. There, he found, 'I was in a humane mountainscape. I could see the Essex and Suffolk fields all around the town. Smoke came up through the chimneys like messages. It was sheltered, sunny, between the twin slopes of mossy red tiles. The clouds went racing overhead.'

There was a soothing spirit about this house, which stood just a few yards down the road from Gainsborough's one-time home. It was three storeys high, half-timbered at the top and, as its name suggested, with a great protruding gable at one end. Standing on the corner of Stour Street it had two entrances, the doors straight onto the pavements of the two roads, which always led to confusion for callers, and tradesmen often knocked twice. Traffic chugged and rumbled past the front windows at an alarming proximity.

Once inside though, its atmosphere was one of coolness and serenity. It had an air of gentility that stretched back over the centuries; it had been the home of Gainsborough's niece at one time, but bones from Anglo-Saxon times would one day be found beneath the cellar floor. Its occupants never felt a malevolence, though. It would go on to become the home of artists, musicians, people of inspiration and creativity.

This house would not let Adrian sink into despondency. Gradually, it worked its charm on him, soothing his anger, restoring his composure. Like a kindly therapist, it encouraged him to put his thoughts and feelings down on paper.

As he sat at his desk overlooking Stour Street, the voices of women from the nearby weavers' cottages floated up to him, transporting him back to Vic Savage's Farm, and the scenes he had witnessed there. With the mentality of one who is taking an exam, he determined to recreate those scenes in a book.

It wasn't the romance that Dolores had proposed, it was a novel, a largely autobiographical one that told the tale of his apprenticeship to Vic Savage, whom he re-named 'Mr Colville'. That and other names he picked from the villages in the Stradishall area: Depden personified stood in for the name of Victor's in-laws, the Collen family, and Farley Hall, named after Farley Green, took the place of Great Lodge, Hundon.

It was Edmund Blunden who had suggested that he could write of his experiences. Seeing his first attempts at a manuscript - the fanciful romance that exposed his passion for Dolores - Blunden had tactfully offered that time-honoured advice to 'write about what you know'. Adrian had then had a short piece published in the *Manchester Guardian*, in which he described the winding length of an autumn lane, with the last leaves fluttering on the hedges. In evocative detail he portrayed a team of horses pausing to drink at a pond, and their masters, dressed in pale corduroy, and with pale, faraway eyes. He called the piece *A Mile of England*, and its acceptance and publication had spurred him on to greater things. But a whole book - that would be more like a marathon.

Adrian had not kept a diary during that year as a 'dunt' at Hundon but it was not difficult to close his eyes and see again the faces, to hear the voices, the chinks and clanks of working life, and to smell the myriad stinks and scents of the farm and countryside. He built characters from those with whom he had worked and played, changing their names and features enough to avoid upset or litigation, and then moulding them into shape until they were lifelike and credible.

He recalled scenarios, trimming away the duller moments and adding humour, pathos or commentary if any were needed to make the action flow or bounce along as appropriate. He took himself back into dusty barns and straw-littered yards, explored again in his mind the tracks, fields and byways in all the seasons. He populated his village, which he now called Benfield St George, with real characters in all their many-hued moods.

He poured in not only the pain but also the intense pleasure he had derived from learning his skills the hardest way possible, and finally he unveiled the tremendous pride he had felt when he could toil alongside a country-born labourer and believe himself to be useful. As narrator, he portrayed himself with wry hindsight and honesty. His early ignorance, arrogance, ineptitude and frustration all went in. Then his dawning recognition of the skill and power behind the labourer and the horse. He added his indignation that Thomas Hardy had written off the latter as a stumbling dreamer. Finally his burgeoning confidence, his tenacity, his plans, they were there too.

When he wrote the closing line, 'I lit my lamp and opened my new account book at the first page,' he had gone through the whole year again, and was spiritually back at his own first farm, with all the anticipation and optimism still intact. The effect was cathartic. He had reason to be proud of himself.

In September 1929 Adrian collected all the pages together, stood them on end and tapped them into order. He bound the manuscript in brown paper and string and carried it to the post office. The parcel was addressed to Edmund Blunden at Hawstead near Bury St Edmunds.

Adrian knew his friend was very busy, he had moved in with his brother in the midst of a messy divorce from Mary. Clearly he had plenty on his mind, and Adrian must have been grateful that Blunden had agreed to look at his work at all. So now there was nothing else to do but sit and wait. The suspense was excruciating.

Finally the reply came; 'My dear Adrian, Forgive me for taking so long over your m.s. I have been so out of sorts that even my usual delays are exceeded.'

It went on, 'There is no mistaking your book, it is excellent and various, with many curious and some powerful, imaginative passages. The wording is almost always choice, with some inclination to over-word, however, as it appears to me. I have noted on the card enclosed the few points where I would have you revise. I hope you will one day write an inquest on pastoral poets of this age, me among them, in continuance of the apt comment on (Thomas Hardy's) somnambulist, but your book breaks off at such a crisis as not only makes possible but even demands a sequel some day, and there you'll frolic. I would suggest that you do not let this manuscript go without pretty good terms for its publication.'

The publisher Edmund had in mind was Richard Cobden-Sanderson, with whom Blunden himself was working at the time.

Richard's father Thomas Cobden-Sanderson had been a bookbinder who took such care over the presentation of his authors' work that William Morris had patronised his work and encouraged him to set up the Doves Bindery. Thomas had endowed his son with the same sense of diligence and aestheticism, and Blunden was satisfied that his poetry was in good hands.

He had said to Adrian, 'I hope you will let Cobden have a chance to publish. He is probably not able to sell a winner as do the great firms, but wouldn't be amiss for a shy, good piece of writing with a fit audience! (Not too few I hope, all the same).' Later he qualified his advice by bidding Adrian not to feel limited to Cobden, because he was sure that others would 'jump at the book,' but at least he could effect an introduction to the former.

Edmund's recommendation would prove sound. Richard Cobden-Sanderson and his partner Kenneth Rae liked *Corduroy*, as Adrian's book was called, and agreed to publish it. The only snag was that there would not be much money in it, they said. People were mostly buying war books these days, so they did not expect to sell more than 500 copies. Adrian was too ecstatic to care. In six weeks of pleasurable writing he had achieved what ten years of hard grind had not - he was going to be in profit.

His father Robert did care though. He had just had a small book of his own work published, some of his poems collected together under the title *After-Thoughts* and he knew only too well it was not a lucrative business. He reminded his son, who was nearing his thirtieth birthday, that it was time to take responsibility for himself. Robert was not so forthright as to mention the possibility of Adrian thinking about marriage, but the message was received and understood. Adrian agreed to take on some reporting jobs for the *Observer*, and he went abroad for the first time in his life.

He was to cover the Stockholm exhibition in Sweden and see how this agricultural country was turning to innovation as a way out of the universal depression. It was an interesting experience for him, and a thought-provoking one. Adrian had begun to appreciate that the old ways could not be adhered to indefinitely, against all economic reason. And yet his loyalty to tradition left him regretful that he had glimpsed a mechanised future for mankind.

Travelling never really agreed with Adrian's delicate constitution, but he did enjoy some aspects of his adventure. He loved the crisp, clear air of Sweden and thought the people very pleasant, but he found their liberal attitude towards nakedness rather alarming. He would relate that in his hotel he'd had to make a hasty excuse in order to avoid being bathed by the chambermaid, sending her to fetch his razor and quickly locking the bathroom door.

So far from home, he was not feeling homesick at all; in fact, seeing a train with 'Istanbul' as its destination fired his imagination and he considered taking off to see more of the world. As if by telepathy, his mother seemed to sense his thoughts drifting, and jerked them back with a telegram. The parents were going to visit a friend in Switzerland, and they would need him to help them on the journey through France. They simply could not manage without him. And so it was that while Fanny and Robert stayed with Percy Scholes, music critic of the *Observer*, Adrian and his sister Stephanie were booked into a hotel in the beautiful lakeside town of Montreux.

From the Hotel Victoria, on 19th June 1930, he wrote to Dolores, who had moved to Bath; 'So, Julitta, I find myself, with an interval of hot frowsty travelling and wild mental arithmetic in currency values, to have leaped from your embrace in Ebury Street and the patter of the fountain on the white petals to the shores of Lake Geneva. I find that Montreux is one of the few places where a person of impractical temperament such as this child's might live in conscious felicity. Bath, of course, is another.

'I am writing to apologise that the book is not yet to hand - I presume it is chasing me across the continent: of course you could get it anywhere, but I am to write a message in it to you, am I not?...'

Adrian went on to say how much he was enjoying life there, and described it as 'A place where a young man might easily become involved were his sister not with him...' Depicting himself as bewitched by the music in the air, the cool twilight and the beautiful ladies strolling by, he added, 'Oh how I need looking after!!'

But he acknowledged that Dolores would not be the one to take on that commitment, asking rhetorically, 'What are you thinking about us now, I wonder, sitting in Bath? "Let us swear not at all" are you saying? Or "I am afraid because we may be pledging ourselves to the awful beauty of trust"? What are we thinking, Julitta?'

In fact, Adrian was thinking a great deal about Marjorie Gibson, and how he might win her hand. They were exchanging warm letters and he felt the closeness of their bond even at this great distance. Of course, he would not find out until much later that she received three other proposals of marriage during this time but each was politely rejected. She, it seems, had set her heart on marrying Adrian.

Miles away both in thought and reality, Robert Bell had given them a tremendous boost in this direction, for he had lined up a regular income for his son. It was in a career that nobody could have foretold and to which Adrian, had he become a wealthy author, would certainly never have aspired. In the coming years it would stretch his vocabulary and lateral humour to the utmost limit and bring a bitter-sweet pleasure to thousands of people from various walks of life. It would not bring him celebrity status: anonymity was part of the mystique. But now there is a minor legend to the way it came about.

Robert, in his position as Assistant Editor at the *Observer*, naturally came into contact with many colleagues and rivals in the newspaper industry. On one occasion in December 1929 he had been lunching with his friend from *The Times*, Robin Barrington-Ward, who was later to become editor. Ward was bemoaning to 'Robbie' as he called him, the fact that he had been ordered to find someone to put together a crossword puzzle; the wretched things had caught on in America and now the quality British papers were vying to get in on the craze. But hardly anyone he knew had ever tried to solve one, never mind compose one. What on earth was he to do?

Robert, unusually alert to the opportunity presenting itself, suggested that his son Adrian could do it. A deadline of ten days was agreed.

Adrian's first reaction was almost certainly in the negative. But a fee of three guineas for doing the job could not be turned down easily. So for the following ten days including Christmas, he sat in his room overlooking Stour Street and stared at the grid of black and white squares set out before him.

He would jot down a word to fit, and then turn its definition inside out and upside down, trying to figure out a way to set a convoluted clue to its solution. Pun, anagram, ambiguity - all helped him to keep the solver guessing. By the time he had filled in all the gaps his brain had not just been racked it felt hung, drawn and quartered. How else could he arrive at the clue 'Heraldic gold between mother and me' for Maori? Or, 'Only a contortionist could do this on a chair' for the inversion, 'Tis'?

That first crossword appeared on the Sports Page of *The Times* on 1<sup>st</sup> February 1930. Reaction was immediate. To his bemusement, Adrian found himself at the vanguard of a revolution.

While some people had felt it unworthy of *The Times* to take part in this fad, countless others were hooked instantly. Wherever Adrian went, on public transport, in libraries, cafeterias, waiting rooms, people seemed to have their paper folded over to that chequered square. Smiles, frowns, hoots of indignation, all of these emotions crossed the expressions of those absorbed in pitting their wits against the mild-faced, bespectacled young man who watched them covertly.

He would tell a tale (and that may be all it was, for at times fiction would creep into his reality just as his reality was present in so many of his novels) about one such occasion. His son Martin relates it thus; 'I cannot entirely swear by this story, but I wish it to be true. Once, on a train journey to London, he picked up a copy of *The Times* with one of his puzzles on the back page. Across the carriage he saw another passenger struggling with it. He whisked out a pen, completed his in 60 seconds, laid it on the seat beside him with the crossword uppermost, closed his eyes and smiled serenely.'

Adrian, who always described himself as virtually uneducated, finally had the beating of some of the finest brains around. Completing the puzzle was one feat, but then time became an important factor too. In 1934 Sir Josiah Stamp stirred up a hornets' nest by writing in to say that he had completed a puzzle in 50 minutes. Was this a record? In no time Sir Austen Chamberlain had pooh-poohed this assertion by knocking nine minutes off that figure, adding 'and I had wasted time badly over one of the anagrams.'

He went on; 'But, Sir, ask the Provost of Eton (M.R.James). I have been informed by a person whose veracity on other subjects I have no reason to doubt, that the Provost measures the time required for boiling his breakfast egg by that needed for the solution of your daily crossword - and he hates a hard-boiled egg.' The author P.G. Wodehouse, who said he had just spent 20 minutes 'beating his head against the wall' over a particularly tricky anagram, was outraged by such a suggestion.

Of course, eventually someone would come up with the idea of a 'Times Crossword Championship', and then, in 1970, Adrian was still compiling them. Ten years later his 4,520[th] puzzle would appear to celebrate the golden jubilee of the craze in *The Times*.

Each of the three guineas he earned, later increased to five, was hard won. There were no set rules to making up clues but the first crossword editor, Ronald Carton, let it be known to his team that biblical allusions, abbreviations, diseases and names of living persons should be avoided. Double entendres were taboo but still Adrian inadvertently upset his high-minded adversaries by his use of such words as 'bust' and 'sweet Fanny Adams'. Heaven help him if he got a fact wrong, such as when he put Cleopatra's barge on the Nile instead of the Cydnus, prompting an outpouring of anger and derision from those whose pleasure had been spoiled.

Adrian always took criticism to heart but his power of endurance had been proved before. Through pain of migraine, stress at looming deadlines, anguish at finding himself at stalemate on an incomplete grid, and having to go back and rewrite several words and clues, he kept going. And of course, he was not allowed to tell anyone outside the family what it was that kept him immured, so there was no kudos in it. One day all would be revealed, and his name would appear in the *Guiness Book of Records* alongside those with equal talents, but which were often being put to even stranger uses.

For his own part, Adrian could never really understand the appeal of the crossword, although he was grateful for the rewards it brought him. To him, mental exertion could never be defined as a leisure activity. It was at best a necessity of his life, at worst, Hell. A prolonged bout of intense thinking was enough to send him to bed for two or three days with a thunderous migraine. Then he would rise, refreshed, and start work again.

How he managed to keep going, to apply his pounding brain to the task of writing and compiling clues, to find time to sit and gather the raw sensations of life that he turned into words of beauty, that must surely be the greatest puzzle of all.

# 10. Cutting the Cord

*Corduroy* had gone on sale in May 1930, priced at seven shillings and sixpence. Its cover illustration of a portly gentleman careering along on a hunter, in turquoise and red and in the typically spare style of the time, was created by the artist Clifford Webb to convey the lyrical agricultural subject matter. The book sold out in weeks.

It seemed as if everybody was talking about this new writer. Some people would dub him a 'poet in prose' although he did not consciously count his syllables or arrange his feet in such a way as to conform to an accepted pattern. Without doubt, though, he had an inner sense for rhythm and balance that set his syntax apart from the blank or bland. That, along with his eye for detail and deft power of description, made his work come alive.

It was a cracking good story, too. This was 1930, a time of depression and despair, and yet here was a young man showing how he had triumphed by determination. In just a year he had gone from ignoramus to ambitious young farmer, answerable to everyone at first, and finally to no boss but himself. 'I was flying from the threat of an office life', he had written, and oh, how many others wished they could do the same, to escape to the fields where the sounds were gentle and the sights natural, where one need watch no time-clock but the great sundial of the seasons.

Adrian had written about pride, community spirit, hard-working men and women, and poor but devoted families. He talked of self-sufficiency, affinity with nature, the beauty of England. The stuff that dreams were made of in a period of such bleak distress.

Farmers did not read his book, it was too close to reality, but many hundreds who had ever aspired to farming, or wondered if there was happiness to be found in the world beyond their grimy factory or office windows, they bought it, or borrowed it, or talked about it. Perhaps Adrian encouraged them to stop once in a while to hear a bird sing, or examine a weed growing out of a crack in a wall and call it a wild flower.

People needed something positive to cling on to. Some of them had come from the country, or rather been driven out by poverty. Some had never been there but held on to a vision of it as an Eden far removed from all the smog and deprivation. *Corduroy* gave them a glimpse of English paradise.

A second edition came out in July 1930, and a third run would be needed six months later. A cheaper edition at three shillings and sixpence would come out after another six months, and two more print runs were ordered the following year. *Corduroy* simply sold and kept on selling.

So now Adrian was an author, and he might even go so far as to call himself a successful one. He also had a regular income from the crosswords - three guineas a week was a good enough salary, and it would be more when he increased his output.

By autumn 1930 he had also started working on the sequel to *Corduroy*, and he would have much to tell Marjorie when she came home. He had fifty pounds in the bank and slightly better prospects than before. Would it be enough?

Marjorie had written to say she would be sailing home from America, arriving back in London in November. The tone of her letters suggested she still cared for him, and even though he hadn't seen her for months, he had made up his mind he was going to marry her.

The day after Marjorie's return, he rushed to meet her in London, and they walked in the park on a harlequin carpet of leaves. She seemed calm, relaxed; she had put on a little weight and looked so much better for it. Her grey eyes, her warm smile, gave him all the confidence he needed. Finally he stopped and asked her the Big Question. Without hesitation, she assented.

Now they walked hand in hand, and smiled at each other, and walked on. Adrian, happy beyond measure, nevertheless had a tremor of unease inside him. Was that the difficult part over, or was the worst yet to come? He would have to present his plans to her parents and put his case in such a way as to seem worthy. He pictured their drawing room, with its wicked-looking artefacts from foreign lands, and her father, upright, correct, abrupt except when reminiscing about people and places he had known in the course of his military career. Could Adrian convince him that he, unfit for most kinds of service but writing books and compiling crosswords, was the right man for Lieutenant Gibson's daughter?

But still that was not his biggest worry. Even more dauntingly, he knew it was time for a son-to-mother chat.

Things had been much better at home of late. Rekindling their earlier amity, Adrian had often been out for walks around Sudbury with Fanny, and to a number of social events in the town. She had begun to regain her former joie-de vivre now that she had people around her and places to go to. She took more care about dressing up, and, although she had a theory about too much soap being bad for one, so she only washed her hair once a year, she kept it all in place with a daily application of Gloy gum. People say she always appeared immaculately groomed. Adrian, back in his role of escort, had not invested in any new clothes, and was less particular about the creases in his trousers than she, but they had been companionable enough as they strolled the streets of Sudbury.

Fanny's artistic imagination had been reborn. They would walk down Stour Street to the river or up past Gainsborough's house to the market square with its imposing church of St.Peter. They liked to explore the alleyways between the old, imperfect garden walls of the old, imperfect houses and now and then Fanny would stop, holding up her hands in a frame to show Adrian 'Look - that would make a picture.' He commented in his diary that when she did that, 'Then I would see, under her guidance, not dull Mill Lane, but a ravine, man-made, under flashing spring clouds.'

Today it was not spring, it was winter, and yet Adrian's mind was on thoughts of love, and his future with Marjorie. Now he must tell Fanny, his life-long oracle, that he had made his decision.

They sat on a bench by the river and it would be reasonable to assume that Fanny knew exactly what was on her son's mind, as she very often did. She would offer him no help at all in his difficult task of broaching the subject. He - awkward, shy, embarrassed - had to force out the words he had rehearsed.

He had been brought up with the doctrine that the Englishman does not demonstrate emotion in public. To talk about his feelings for a woman, to a woman who wanted all his feelings for herself, was anathema. Only the deepest love could have wrung those words from him, knowing as he did that each one was as a dagger to his mother's own heart.

What would be her reaction? How would she play it? She could rant, scold, accuse. Or wail, throw herself on him, and beg him to reconsider.

Fanny, quite to the contrary, took the news with aplomb. She was as usual dismissive of the idea of love, for she had long ago made up her mind that the word was a misnomer for the basic urge of nature. Who was there to love? 'God is dead' her idol Nietsche had declared, and the motivation of mankind was the Will to Power. Compassion was misplaced, as we all have to suffer in order to progress, so Nietsche reckoned, but then, he had ended his life mad and diseased with syphilis. Fanny chose to overlook the latter, and clung to the belief that true love was a lie. Having never found it herself, she concluded that it wasn't out there.

Adrian knew he would not change that view, but he felt he owed it to her to try and explain that he believed he did love someone, Marjorie, and he intended to make it last. He was doing his best to prepare her for his transition from son to husband, for she would not share him.

'You're no great catch,' Fanny observed. Even so, Marjorie was satisfied, he countered. And yes, he conceded, her background was different to theirs, and of course her family could not match the Hanburys' lineage but her parents were good people.

So Fanny had to agree that if he must marry, then the girl he had chosen would suffice; she was sensible and without drama. Adrian picked up the barb behind her choice of words - she found his fiancee dull. Well, so be it.

His parents' relationship now consisted almost entirely of sniping and public bickering, which was not an example he wanted to follow. While Robert had become increasingly dour and negative, Fanny herself liked nothing better than to burst into music-hall song or to come out with risque jokes in company. Frankly, Adrian found this quite embarrassing. He didn't want a woman who craved the limelight. He didn't want someone who dressed in outlandish clothes and flirted outrageously with every man in the room. There was no risk of Marjorie doing such things, and he was thankful for it.

Now the couple could set about making the arrangements. They agreed to keep it as simple as possible and made a short list of people they would invite. Adrian's brother Francis was still overseas, and Stephanie had gone abroad too, to visit a relative who was a Superintendent in the Indian Police force. With claims for independence and Gandhi's respectful request that the British go home, the country was increasingly witnessing scenes of unrest, but there was still a life of elegance and ease to be had out there for the time being. Knowing too what was on Adrian's mind, it might not seem the best time to have gone, but Fanny had known there was a chance that Roy Bell was interested in Stephanie as a potential wife, and counselled her daughter to go and see if she might like the life out there. Fanny disregarded the point of whether she might like the man. Roy Bell was seventeen years older than Stephanie and of serious disposition as those male Bells often were, but even so, even after her own experience of a stultifying marriage, Fanny had felt he was worth a try.

On the trip there would be many other young ladies hopeful of finding a husband, so that those liners were often dubbed 'the fishing fleet'. Miss Bell was duly invited to some very gracious receptions as guest of the Viceroy and the Governor, but also as partner of Superintendent Bell. They were photographed in groups of young people, first together, and then farther apart. Stephanie's album would contain pictures of another young man, a dashing officer who was the son of a titled lady, but eventually she would return home alone.

Meanwhile Adrian, having taken the plunge, was not going to waste any time in sorting out the formalities. They decided on a quiet wedding in Ealing church, London, near to the bride's home, and arranged the wedding for the earliest practical date, which would be 12ᵗʰ January 1931.

In preparing himself that morning at George and Mabel's boarding house, Adrian was at his mother's mercy for one last time. While she and his Aunt Mabel seemed to be vying to put on the most inappropriate outfits, he horned himself into his ten-year-old suit, made for him by the Army and Navy Stores before he ever set foot in Suffolk. It was a dark one, almost funereal, and it matched the mood around him. He was fighting off the threat of a migraine, and wished he and Marjorie could have just quietly slipped away and come back as man and wife. But the ceremony must be gone through.

No photographs were taken of the event, and there were no reports in any newspapers, so the only clue to the proceedings appears later, in a novel entitled *A Young Man's Fancy*. In the guise of the narrator Roland Pace, Adrian describes the preparations, during which his mother puts on a home-made hat she has created out of his old prep-school topper and his aunt, whom he re-names

Winnie, dresses in fake leopard skin. 'So we set off,' he writes, 'my mother and I looking like mourners, and Winnie like one of the Great Cats.'

After stopping for a gin in the local pub, they discuss catching a taxi to the church. Robert, ever the socialist, insists they go by bus. Adrian chooses to walk there alone.

The vows were made before a very sparse congregation, with the bride in a dark turquoise velvet dress and the groom in his dark 1920's suit. Outside, confetti was forbidden and nobody had brought any anyway.

The champagne reception was held at the Gibsons' house, amid African ju-ju's, spears and tom-toms, while the two families made polite conversation. They had virtually nothing in common at all. Fanny, consuming champagne morosely, found no quips for the occasion, and Robert, deaf, dyspeptic, detached, failed to see the joke when Marjorie's uncle, a wallpaper salesman, suggested they were in a similar line of business, both being involved in printed paper.

At last the young couple could make their escape by taxi. Adrian's final view was of his mother, waving, fixing a wan smile, which did nothing to conceal her look of utter desolation. He turned to Marjorie, his lovely, happy wife.

His life as a man could now begin.

## 11. Unsettled in Suffolk

A few pounds of Adrian's savings were spent on a short honeymoon in the Earls Court Hotel, Tunbridge Wells. It was an odd start to their life together. In his book *A Young Man's Fancy* he describes some of the characters who amused the fictional couple Roland and Naomi there, clearly drawing on his own experience. One man used to slap himself noisily in his room each morning. An elderly woman guest constantly harangued an obsequious waiter who bore a remarkable resemblance to Rudyard Kipling.

Adrian wrote about their days spent exploring the area, notably Toad Rock, a local beauty spot which they visited twice. There seemed to be little else to do in this town populated by the aged and infirm. They wondered, what had happened to this once-fashionable resort? Now there were swashbuckling films at the cinema and lectures on indigestion in the local hall. He noted, 'We had tea that day in a restaurant. On the wall before us was a large framed photograph of all the vehicles which the confectioner used for delivering his bread and cakes.' It was lucky that Adrian and Marjorie shared a similar sense of humour.

Adrian also describes his new bride, as the character 'Naomi.' She, he said, 'was but the bud of the person she is today. Sometimes we did not know quite what to say to each other. We discovered mutually how little experience we had of life.'

He said nothing in his book of the nights spent at the hotel, but at other times he would make brief reference to their compatibility, and his surprise that his demure bride was a far more welcoming lover than the siren Dolores could ever have been. Marjorie, sincere, dependable, generous of nature, would give herself entirely to being a good wife. Adrian, for so long the wistful dreamer, the hostage to imagination, could at last savour the reality, the flesh and blood, the loving gifts of a real woman. It was idyllic, but for three days only.

After that, the couple returned to Sudbury to live with Adrian's parents at the Gables. Or rather, with Adrian's mother, for Robert was still away during the week working at the *Observer*. He had kept his room at Mabel's house in London and effectively he was little more than a lodger at the Gables, with no special space allocated him for his books or desk. His big black piano was his salvation, and the house rang with the notes of Bach every Sunday and Monday morning as life went on, unnoticed, around him.

The newlyweds moved in and tried to fit themselves into this menage. Stephanie was away overseas, and Francis too. Adrian was effectively the head of the household, but there was no vacancy for Marjorie; the position of lady of the house was already taken. If this were not enough to take the shine off the new bride's enthusiasm, she discovered that her husband held an ambition she had somehow overlooked.

Adrian was writing another book, the sequel to *Corduroy*, and he took Marjorie back to Stradishall to see Will and Cissie Lunniss in Stephenson's Farm, his one-time bachelor home. He was writing about his venture there, calling the farm and the book *Silver Ley*. He still loved the place, and in his mind he saw it as an ideal little home for two. Perhaps one day, his chance would come again. They would find another Silver Ley, and start afresh.

As they walked around the farm, Marjorie began to get an inkling of the things that truly mattered to her husband, and it was an alien world to her. Cows, pigs, the muck and the smells that went with them - how could he enjoy all this? The sweat and toil, the rough hands and weathered skin - she could not see the eurhythmics behind all the effort, or separate the beauty from the beasts.

It was obvious that Adrian ached to get back into farming, and she was alarmed. Her parents had thought the country life would be good for her nerves, but the thought of squelching about in boots and pushing wet snouts aside gave her palpitations. In all honesty, she had been quite relieved when he gave up farming the first time and she had never had to consider how she might adapt to rudimentary plumbing and sanitation.

Sudbury, an industrious market town, was closer to her idea of civilisation but the atmosphere at the Gables was only just civilised. It was a big old house but at times it seemed crowded. Adrian could not be affectionate to his wife while Fanny was around, and Marjorie felt the burden of competition whenever the three were together. Conversations always seemed to be loaded and she felt her every move being assessed. Her mother-in-law was like a kestrel, hovering, watching a mouse.

It was a stressful time for all concerned and the arrangement lasted only two months. The couple soon went in search of an alternative and they found a small, one-up, one-down cottage three miles away in an unmade lane. It was priced at £120, which they could just about manage and there would be no bills for gas, electricity or water, because none was laid on. A hand-pump drew water from the pond, complete with all kinds of aquatic life. Candles and lamps would cast a warm glow over their evenings and they would be free to talk, to touch and love each other at will.

They moved in their few possessions and one day mounted their bicycles for the ride home to Gad's Cottage, near Great Waldingfield. Fanny had been so offended by their desertion that they hardly dared say goodbye, but the ride along primrose lanes and between confetti-blossom hedgerows served to put all that behind them. Next day they would wake to birdsong and eat their first breakfast alone together.

It was a new start for them and as for any couple, early married life was to be a series of awakenings. They still hardly knew each other as they sat facing across the small table in thoughtful silences punctuated by brief conversations. Marjorie had barely ever cooked a meal before and Adrian, feeling he could only truly love one woman at a time, was still struggling to shift the focus of his intimacy from mother to wife.

He tried hard not to make comparisons but the confidence-sapping shade of Fanny's oppression lingered about him. Had he done the right thing? Should he have taken on this responsibility for another person, who was virtually a stranger? He knew he had gone against his mother's wishes and perhaps she was right, perhaps animal instinct was behind it all, but he had been so sure of his feelings that no other course could have been contemplated. He was simply not used to making decisions for himself.

He even worried about the green carpet they had bought; his mother hadn't liked it, he could tell. Would it be all right? Or would it wear out in no time? Was it the right colour? Could Marjorie's taste and choice be trusted? This homemaking business was new territory altogether.

Gradually they settled in and found that beyond all else, their choice of partner had been sound. And Gad's Cottage: tiny, damp, low-roofed, leaky, and from a distance invisible in an ocean of wheat, with nightingales in the brushwood and tadpoles in the bath water, gave them the chance to get properly acquainted.

Looking back, Adrian would admit the conditions in that cottage would now be called 'scandalous.' Their sitting room needed only a rug to carpet it and two chairs, one easy, one not so easy, almost filled it. In the bedroom there was only a bed, and just enough space to get in the door and get into it. For a scullery it had a lean-to, with a deal table and two pails, one for clean water brought in, one for dirty going out. A basin served as a sink.

The bathroom was a screened-off portion of the lean-to, and hot water was put in from the big black kettle that hung in the chimney. Cold water came from the pond - hence the tadpoles, in season.

Marjorie, not long back from her trip to New York, adapted to it all. They were in love, and they were alone, that was all that mattered. They would sit out under the apple tree, sipping cider and watching moorhens nesting on the pond. Sometimes they ate upstairs on the five-plank landing, where a small fruitwood table and two chairs were positioned so they could look out of the little window over the waving corn.

Beyond their property their neighbour Clarke would be working in his fields, with his little pink-dressed daughter helping to drive a horse-drawn roller. Adrian was just starting to write a diary again and such observations would be stored away for future use in his books and articles, when they would be resurrected with affection and respect for a passing methodology. Meanwhile he could discuss crossword clues with Marjorie, for she was every bit as bright-minded as he and often she helped him fill in the grids with words for which he could then devise clues. It was a comfortable, companionable relationship.

They had bought a piano for Marjorie to pursue her love of music and she would play soothing tunes as evening fell and the light began to fade. Once, as Adrian leaned out of the bedroom window, the strains of Moonlight Sonata drifted up to him and mingled with the song of a blackbird bidding the world goodnight. He felt as if he was in heaven.

And yet his mother still managed to haunt them. On Stephanie's return home from India she was greeted with the gloomy pronouncement, 'He's gone'. The atmosphere was one of bereavement, and at every opportunity Adrian was summoned to visit, or to undertake some little chore. In between trying to write, and compile crosswords, and be a husband, he found himself pedalling back and forth along those leafy lanes, caught between his old world and the new. It was a situation that could not go on.

In July the couple moved right away, to Buckinghamshire, and a cottage in the market place of Princes Risborough. Adrian's publisher, Richard Cobden-Sanderson lived nearby in Long Crendon, and so did the writer John Massingham, who admired Bell and expressed the wish that he too could have practised farming as well as writing about it. To complete the coterie, Edmund Blunden was not far away at Merton College, Oxford.

Life around the picturesque Chiltern cottages seemed restful and appealing. They rented a little place called Market Cottage in the main street, where cows clattered past on the cobbles twice a day and life bustled all around. Inside their little home, which was as Adrian described it, 'piled on end - living room, bedroom, attic' they felt secure from interference.

At first Adrian felt an affinity with the stone buildings and country characters. There was no class snobbery here and he noted that one day in the local bar he had met a mole-catcher talking with a major, and a titled lady sitting alongside a professional economist. 'It was as nearly complete a rural community as you could wish for', he concluded.

Now, though, instead of relaxing and enjoying the freedom from Suffolk and all its ties, he found himself continually struck down by blinding headaches. Marjorie would later confide that she had been close to despair during that time. It seemed there was no hope of Adrian earning a proper living for them and she, a bride of less than a year, was in constant fear of the signs that another migraine was looming. In those days there were no drugs to combat the excruciating pain successfully and the only way through it was complete bed-rest in a darkened room.

They decided they must retreat to what Blunden called 'Darkest East Anglia'. On 25th January 1932 Edmund wrote to Adrian, requesting an article for the magazine *Queen's Quarterly*, and saying, 'I grieve in general that you are resuming Anglia, no I mean it has been a steady, happy thought that you are not far from here'.

But go they must. For a short time they rented a cottage in Weston Colville, near to Vic Savage but it was a temporary arrangement, for then they made up their minds to purchase a tumbledown heap of a house in Wissington, situated in the 'Constable Country' of the Stour Valley.

At first they had quailed at the thought of taking on the place. With a houseleek growing out of the roof and a sapling arching out of a hole in a wall, it seemed as if Nature had taken up occupation already, and eviction would prove difficult. The vast, higgledy-piggledy moss-covered roof offered little shelter to the dank, echoing rooms beneath and the wind whistled in through broken windows and rotten frames. Plaster had dropped away in fatigue and the whole building seemed to sag with resignation

The house was called Creems. It was a farmhouse with marvellous, forever views but the land had been sold away, and Adrian secretly hoped that one day he might be able to buy it back. He could farm and write: write about farming.

For the time being he was content to work on his fourth book, a rustic romance called *Folly Field*, and enjoy the relative security that was building around him. His last work, *The Cherry Tree,* had completed his farming trilogy and it had been very well received. It had been a complicated and idealised fabrication, in which he had placed himself and Marjorie back in Stephenson's Farm, or rather 'Silver Ley', with the great cherry tree uprooted from Seabrooks and replanted outside the cottage. With the tender craft of a bird weaving its nest, he had managed to include many scenes from his farming life with incidents from his marriage to date, and create a charming portrait of what might have been.

Adrian had become something of a celebrity and money was coming in more steadily. The £200 advance for *Folly Field* was a good deal from a small publisher like Cobden-Sanderson and there was high hope of royalties to follow. He still had to work hard at the writing though, and in a letter to his friend Edmund Blunden he complained that sometimes he struggled to find the right words. Edmund rebuked him in hyperbolic style. 'My dear Adrian,' he replied, '*You* are not the man to complain of not catching the very word, the identical, the sine qua non, the affidavit, the arrow in the white, the falling star, the mandrake, the Open Sesame, God Help the Sailors etc. Many thanks for your letter...'

Blunden himself was going through a thin patch, and was missing his country walks with Adrian. He wrote, 'How kind you are to forgive me all the absurd mistakes in *The Face of England* and my other rustical improvisations. I grow utterly ignorant of bird and beast, forget even fishes and know nowt of newts anymore. But still I will go out one day and find a lucky stone. Some few poems have I scribbled lately, all made out of the carver's brain as quick as horsehair turns into eels.'

Adrian could see that the enormous workload Blunden had undertaken in order to maintain his women and children was taking its toll on his inspiration and poetic talent. For Adrian too, the need to make a living would always take precedence over his most imaginative work, for which he needed time to sit and observe, or walk the fields and see, feel, breathe the countryside. Sometimes he would take his crossword grids out with him and try to compose clues while assimilating the sights and sounds of nature at the same time. It rarely worked. He would return home with a headache, or no clues done at all. Gradually he would develop a talent for mulling over clues almost subconsciously while doing another activity, but it would always be a hard slog to get them just right.

At least he could afford to pay local tradesmen to do the extensive renovations to their new home. Adrian had not dared tell Fanny where Creems was, because he knew she would be horrified by the sight of it. Of course, Fanny did find out where it was and commandeered a relative to drive her there. Apparently, upon seeing the place she declared, 'Adrian has always been mad, but this is the maddest thing he has done yet.' With hardly a care about this opinion, they took up occupation in August 1933.

In spite of their relative proximity to The Gables, this was a calmer time for Adrian and Marjorie. One of their near neighbours was the artist John Nash, whom Adrian accompanied on painting forays, and he noted with amusement how it irked Nash whenever he found that another artist had already moved in on an ideal spot. Their adventures together included a canoe trip from Sudbury along the River Bure, which in places was so choked with weeds that they seemed to spend as much time towing, pulling and pushing as paddling. They passed through some of Suffolk's most beautiful scenery, and on a cloudless day in July, with hardly another human being in sight, it was, as Bell described it, 'A fantastic journey.'

Adrian loved the gentle panoramic beauty of his adopted county, it was like living in a work of art, and he had no desire to be anywhere else in the world. This was one of the happiest times of his life; settled with his placid, loving wife, and the glory of Suffolk all around.

As often seems to happen, there were beginnings and endings coinciding in their lives at this point. Marjorie's family had been dealt a devastating blow by the sudden death of her younger brother Charles. He had been due to follow in the family tradition and go into the army, but instead had taken his own life. It was a tragedy from which Marjorie's mother, in particular, would never really recover. And Adrian was saddened too by the news that Victor's father, Walter Savage, had died, ending an era and evoking poignant memories of the stalwart old man who had represented a last link with the old farming traditions. Would those days ever return, and could Adrian be among those to welcome them?

Marjorie had help in the house now, and Adrian, in between his writing and exploring, started to collect some livestock - a pig, a heifer and some hens to provide them with home produce. Farming was in his blood it seemed, and he harboured a theory that his desire for the outdoor life could be partly genetic. For of all his relations, the one he admired and respected most of all was his reclusive great aunt who was living in a woodland hut near Brockweir, Gloucestershire. On a bleak November day, while on a fortnight's visit to his mother's West Country relations, he took Marjorie to meet the oft-mentioned Ada Hanbury.

Some might see Ada's life as a tragic one. She had been aged only seven when her father Thomas Hanbury was made bankrupt in 1862, but the repercussions had affected her whole life. The youngest of the six children, she had nevertheless taken some of the family responsibility upon her own slight shoulders, and as she grew up she saw that she must forget any hope of marriage and concentrate on earning a living. She had seen her elder sister Gertrude left with a broken heart after her fiancé ducked out of their engagement, and it seemed that the daughters of an impoverished businessman must become self-sufficient. It was suggested that Ada herself later fell in love with her art teacher, but no evidence of a romance remains. Only their sister Blanche would marry, she became the wife of the widowed Uppingham schoolmaster the Reverend Theophilus Rowe.

Both Ada and Blanche were very competent artists though, and they exhibited work in London between the years 1875 and '87. Two of Blanche's pictures were put on show at the Royal Academy, and five of Ada's were chosen, marking them out to be artists of some considerable repute when women were finding it hard to gain any recognition at all. Later Adrian saw one of her pictures, 'a great iridescent still-life of a mackerel and some apples and a cabbage, like the tipped-out contents of a shopping bag,' he said.

But Ada had had to turn her attention to finance, and spent much of her mid-life painting floral pictures for greetings cards. First she helped to support her parents in this way, and after Thomas' death in 1887 she continued to look after her mother and finally her sister. Only after Gertrude's death in 1927 could she be free. Casting off her hated mantle of domesticity she sold all the furniture to the first rag-and-bone man to come by, then headed for the hills.

She would tell Adrian that she was effectively born in that year, for that was when she truly began to live, in her ramshackle home called Rock Myrtle. Although aged 72 by then, she did in some people's eyes embark on a second childhood by moving into the remote, one-roomed ivy-drenched hovel and giving up any care for smart dresses or etiquette. In his autobiography, Adrian describes her with affection; 'Her clothes were mended with safety pins, since she could not be bothered to sew; and she wore hob-nailed boots, and had narrow, seafaring sort of eyes.' Ada, he commented, 'seemed content, even happy. She spoke to us, to rabbits, to birds, in the same tone, as though we were all part of a Victorian Sunday School.'

With that same matronly manner she entertained Adrian and Marjorie to tea, using an old wash-stand as a table with a dishcloth for a tablecloth. Marjorie's expression was no doubt a study of politeness as she tried not to let matters of hygiene steal into her mind while sipping tea from a brown-stained cup.

Ada's constitution was remarkable: she was never known to be ill. Younger relatives, Marjorie included, would worry about the doughty old dear in her woodland hut throughout the depths of winter, but she lived on in her blissful wonderland until she was 83, when she died quietly in Lydney Cottage Hospital. She was by no means penniless: she left nearly £650 to one of Blanche's daughters, enough to buy a large house in those days.

It was Ada's contentment with next to nothing that struck Adrian so much. 'Equipoise' was the word he used to describe her bearing. She was at ease with her world, wanting no finer jewels than the drops of dew on a spider's web, and no companions other than the mice who shared her food and her bed, or the rabbits and birds that gathered round for breakfast. One day she awoke to find it was getting dark outside, not light, and realised she had slept through the whole day. It was mildly intriguing to her, but not alarming: after all, she had no engagements.

Adrian was most impressed by all this. Perhaps he could not quite see himself and Marjorie in such a feral state, but he could compromise, surely, by having some land and getting back in touch with nature. He was still in contact with Vic Savage, and liked to walk the fields with him, talking about the old days, and also about current farming methods. On one occasion he learned that manure derived from whales had been spread on the land, its fetid dust making the air rank and unbreathable. It seemed a strange idea and a distasteful one, even before the questions of ecology and conservation came into it. Victor shrugged; that was the way to do it nowadays.

Times were changing and farmers were eager to find ways to grow food more efficiently, and increasingly more artificially. Adrian felt that he would rather do things his way, embracing some of the new technology, but not yet abandoning the old methods if they worked best. To him, farming was a precious secret, a craft, but also to him a desire, a need, a vision glimpsed before the curtains closed. He so wanted to have another go at it, to make use of his knowledge and prove that it had yet to become completely outdated. One day he voiced his thought that perhaps he might invest in a small farm. Marjorie's reaction was emphatic - 'No, no NO!' he quoted in his diary.

Perhaps there was more to the scheme than just a wish to get back to the land. Adrian felt that it took ten years of living to make one good book and he had used up all his experiences. Like Monet, who created a garden to paint, Adrian needed to get his hands dirty before he could pick up a pen and convey the genuine feel of the soil onto the blank tableau of the page. He had sent a book called *Summer Cloud* to Richard Cobden-Sanderson and his partner Kenneth Rae, but they had rejected it. Adrian was perplexed; 'Either I or they can't see straight,' he grumbled.

Now he was working on another semi-autobiographical novel, this time delving into his earliest days, and writing the story of the little child who had stood on the balcony of the London flat, and who had been governed by an overpowering mother. It was a risky route to take, and not always complimentary of his parents, but the finished book, entitled *The Balcony*, was published and very well received by the literary world. Congratulatory letters arrived from as far away as America, and before long the New York publishing house of Simon and Schuster were asking to take it on.

Buoyed by his success, Adrian offered a collection of his poems to the newly-formed Centaur Press for publication and they were accepted too, although in a very limited edition.

One of the features of Bell's writing which appealed to his readers was his sense of the spirituality of the countryside, while others enthused over his precise and apposite choice of words, saying that even when he wrote prose, his poetic phraseology brought glorious rhythm to every page. There were plenty of other country writers around now, some were clearly trying to emulate Bell's style, but few could achieve the same success when reaching for the *mot juste*. Describing a hopping frog 'like a flicked stone' or depicting a river 'paved with lily pads', he could conjure exactly the right image in his reader's mind and offer them a share in his every intimate interaction with Nature. He could paint in words every mood of the elements.

His eye for detail and memory for minutiae were unparalleled, but he could never explain why one scenario might wither from his mind while another would remain fresh for decades. In an article on the subject, he wrote, 'To me, any small daylight thing can become dreamlike by the chance of being remembered, stored like a shred of trefoil preserved, perfect and golden, in a bunch of hay dropped off the fork in being carried to the hayracks. There it lay as the mind's eye sees it, still dry, floating in a muddy puddle. All in the day's work, yet speaking something to the heart at that moment. I recall the gust which buffeted that shred of trefoil across the water in the hoofmark of a heavy horse. And that is all. Things so perishable, yet too delicate to perish from the mind.'

In that short passage, Adrian combines all the elements of the old farming scene. He never lost touch with the sentiments and the sensations of those dying years of a way of life that had lasted centuries. He seemed to retain the empathy that man had lost in those revolutionary times, the feeling of oneness with the earth and all the gods, goddesses, imps and fairies that inhabited it.

Now in rural Suffolk he was even dabbling in spiritualism of the supernatural kind. Two ladies in Wormingford used to hold seances and invited Adrian to attend. He was also persuaded to go along to a talk at the local sanatorium given by people who claimed to know they were re-incarnated. Explanations for the latter he found unsatisfactory, but his curiosity had been aroused and he tried to keep an open mind about contact with the dead.

At one table-tapping session he thought he had finally received evidence of an afterlife. The medium spoke of a lady in spirit who was asking for Robert, and wanting to show a house 'with many points'. Adrian leapt to the conclusion that here was his Great Aunt Blanche, who had lived in a gabled house at Bournemouth, and had made a pact with Robert Bell that whoever should die first would try to make contact from the grave. There was no more proof forthcoming.

Another time he had dreamed that they would hear from Marjorie's late brother Charles, and indeed the medium struggled to make contact with someone for her, but was unsuccessful. Later she said she could see someone, she described a man in a white suit, but his message was unclear. Eventually the Bells would drift away from this psychic circle.

This was not the first time Adrian had experimented with alternative ideas. He had previously visited a homeopath in search of a cure for his migraines, and more recently his father had financed a course of psychoanalysis with a certain Harley Street practitioner.

Dr. James Arthur Hadfield was already a celebrated name in psychological medicine when Adrian went to see him. Formerly an assistant neurologist in military hospitals, he had gained a broad experience in treating mental health problems and lately had set up a private practice to help cure the wealthy. He was an eminent lecturer in his field, he had published several books and papers on the workings of mind and body, and by the late 1920s he had been exploring hypnotism and regression as therapies for anxiety. Among his works were theories on 'Reliability of infantile memories', 'Anxiety States' and 'Sex Perversions'. He had published his findings on how some of the body's functions could be controlled by implanting suggestion, and he was convinced that many mental problems could be treated by hypnosis.

During a series of sessions he took Adrian back to his birth and tried to establish a link between that traumatic entry to the world and the ensuing agony of the migraines. Mostly Adrian found this all very boring, except on one occasion when, as the doctor's compelling voice urged him to imagine himself back in his mother's womb, Adrian felt sleepy. Floating in a strange daydream, a feeling of oppression and suffocation threatened to overcome him. Adrian felt panicky, trapped, and then at last came the release, and a light-headedness as his lungs sucked in the fresh air once again, and he awoke.

The therapy was set to continue and Dr. Hadfield said that now he had 'taken him to pieces' it was time to build him up again. The reconstruction never happened, as Robert felt that he'd wasted enough of his money. Adrian said he was none the worse for being left in pieces, adrift in his revisited childhood, although he was no better either. But ever after he would have strange recurring dreams, such as trying to climb a staircase that slid away and collapsed beneath him.

So much for the past. Perhaps his problems did stem from his birth, his troubled childhood, or his frustrated youth. But another contact Adrian made during this time would influence his future, and help to propagate the seeds of a new generation whose destinies lay far beyond Bell's beloved Suffolk.

# 12. Sowing Seeds

Adrian was now a celebrated author on country topics and as such he received a large postbag of letters from people who appreciated his books and the feelings they conveyed. Many of his readers were of the older generation but among those who were moved to contact him was a contemporary who thought he detected a kindred spirit behind the pastoral prose, a man named Rolf Gardiner.

Rolf was a farmer too, a naturalist, an author, and, he hoped, a saviour of mankind. This was not so arrogant as it may sound as mankind was in need of saving, but at that stage it took a man of vision and foresight to realise it. Too many people were feeling safe in the belief that the Great War had been the one to end all wars. But Rolf was one of a growing number who, alarmed by the events unfolding in the political arena, tried to find a solution to the growing tension by spreading a more peaceful message and was striving to divert attention towards positive goals.

Born in 1902, Rolf was the son of Sir Alan Gardiner the Egyptologist and his German-born wife Hedwig. In 1927 he had taken over the Dorset farm of his uncle, the composer H. Balfour Gardiner, and six years later he had added to it the adjoining Springhead Estate.

Here he was creating a rural university where young men from Britain and Germany came together at work camps to learn about farming, and also about music and folk-dancing. To Rolf, these controlled expressions of joy and vitality were fundamental to an appreciation of Mother Earth. In a community of comradeship, they would work on the farm or in his restored flax mill, then in the evening they sang and danced, bonding in spirit and purpose.

Rolf set out his aim for Rural Reconstruction in numerous papers on the subject, including one in H.J. Massingham's anthology *England and the Farmer: A Symposium*, published in 1941.

He wrote, 'Experiments in Land Service and work camps for men of student age have been developing during the past decade.

The time has come for a rapid expansion of these courses and camps. Their purpose is to give youth, reacting from an overbookish and games-ridden schooling, the experience of working on the soil in combination with the exercise of community self-government and cultural recreation.'

This last sentiment appealed to Adrian Bell, who himself had suffered from a 'overbookish and games-ridden schooling'. If boys could be given a taste of the outdoor life on English soil instead of being demoralised with Latin and Matriculation or drilled to die in foreign fields like his generation, then the scheme would have his vote. But Rolf wanted to spread his message about Anglo-Germanic accord far and wide, and his aim of teaching a new, or rather old, organic-based method of agriculture would take him way beyond the boundaries of his own considerable estate.

As well as organising work camps, in 1934 he had formed a group called The Springhead Ring, and invited sympathetic worthies to join. Lord Lymington, later Earl of Portsmouth, was one of the first on board. His family business included land dealings in Kenya, and he took an interest in what Rolf hoped to achieve worldwide which included such grand schemes as a proposal to reclaim the Sahara Desert. In a later letter, Rolf wrote to tell him that his European Working Party for Landscape Husbandry conference at Castle Fursteneck in Germany had been a joyous success; they had all sung a lot, danced a Greek chain-dance led by a former Balletmeister, and also built a monumental compost heap.

His ambition knew no limits, with world peace and prosperity at its heart. All these foreign matters were beyond the thoughts of Adrian Bell, but certainly he approved of Rolf's maxim that youths should be shown how to farm without chemicals, and respect the balance of Nature. It flattered him that lads might look to him for guidance, seeing him as an innovator, not a has-been. He was enthusiastic about turning men's thoughts away from conflict, and towards a more harmonious future.

In fact, the ethos of the Springhead Ring did more than gain Adrian's approval, it started him thinking seriously about his own future. Wouldn't it be wonderful to pass on all this knowledge to a new generation? It would really give him something to work for, if he thought that his achievements could live on, and be appreciated, and carried on by those who loved him. He, in consultation with Marjorie, decided it was time to start a family.

He would reflect in his diary, 'I can remember the moment of that resolve. It was part of the resolve to farm again, live by, with and on the land - a sort of island of the "good" organic life - at the climax of my "natural order" phase, when all the world was turning to ugliness and armaments. An idea of a new movement - a return to rural England, and a new social humanity to colonise it. The fact of headaches making travel an ordeal of apprehensiveness and often downright agony for me, rather clinched this idea to stay and make roots and found a rural dynasty.'

Now when he planted a tree, he could believe that there would be a child, and one day a grandchild, to take care of it. He could pick up an old tool, a billhook or a scythe maybe, and dream of showing his son how to wield it, get the swing right, and slice through the air. He would tell his boy about the old ways, explain how to read the seasons and the soil, to know when to sow seed, when it was time to harvest. And would the lad go back to ploughing with horses, those majestic companions of his own youthful enterprise? Adrian would one day admit that his motive for procreation at this time was ideological rather than paternal.

This, in 1935, when it was announced that an R.A.F. aerodrome was to be built at Stradishall and hundreds of acres of good farm land were to disappear under concrete. And Justin Brooke, apple entrepreneur of Hundon, was to build asbestos bungalows for the workers on his estate. Adrian was spending a great deal of time there, researching a book about the fruit-growing business, which he would call *By-Road*. His brother Francis was working there now, having come home from South America and putting his horticultural experience to use in growing apples, pears and roses.

Adrian's most recent book had been an anthology of country writings called *The Open Air* and although the reviews and sales would go well, the project had been far from satisfying. Adrian needed to put down his own thoughts and feelings, not just collect together those of other people.

He spent every opportunity talking to local farmers, among them Vic Savage of course, also a man named Green who was a distant descendant of Constable, and another named Batten with whom he went shooting and ratting, and helping at harvest. Adrian's sister Stephanie had married a well-off farmer, but one who enjoyed building barns and expanding his business with sheds full of pigs and bullocks. Adrian often visited and noted the operations going on there. And he went along to the county shows too, mingling with the men of the land, standing with his arms resting on the rails of the pens, discussing the finer points of the beasts on show.

As he walked or cycled around the countryside, nothing pleased him more than to stop and chat, delighted whenever he could guess correctly how much manure was needed to spread on a certain field, or what yield of crop was expected. Conversations on liver flukes in sheep and colic in horses were all stimulating subjects to one who craved the opportunity to get back into the action. His knowledge was like a trusty sword the old soldier might take out and polish occasionally. One day, it might be put to some use again.

Now Marjorie was pregnant, and his life was about to take on a very different focus. His diary takes a break in April 1936, a month before his daughter Anthea was born. He would not take up his pen again until the new year.

Of course, the events surrounding Anthea's birth would one day be re-lived in various articles and in Adrian's autobiography. He describes the horrified reaction of the monthly nurse who was expected to bed down in one of the beamed and plastered bedrooms, complete with bugs and mice that were all part of the character of Creems. She was critical of the swinging basket-weave crib he and his mother had chosen in a second-hand furniture shop. And she shooed him out of the room when it became apparent the baby was about to arrive.

As was customary, Adrian kept well away from the bedroom as his wife endured the agony that seemed never-ending. He knew he could not have helped in any way, not like on the farm, when they tied ropes to a calf's legs to pull it out. This was different, this was his darling wife, racked with the surges of pain that made her cry out with primeval fear and distress. No doubt his own birth must have been on his mind, and all the trouble it had caused. Would his child be all right? Would his wife survive, even?

All was well, although Adrian's new life as a family man was somewhat bewildering at first. Marjorie had far less time to sit companionably with him and talk about crossword puzzles and farming topics. Her mind was on bedding of the non-organic kind and she had milk production problems of her own to worry about. Adrian felt like an outsider for a time, there seemed to be nothing he could be trusted with - he could happily clear out a pig-pen, but nappy-changing was another matter altogether, and not one he was expected to undertake. On one of the rare occasions he was left in charge of the baby, his attention became distracted by something on the wireless and she rolled off the sofa with a sickening thump.

Such memories would remain with him for always but the happiest was when the baby was six weeks old, he had persuaded Marjorie to leave her in good care and come away to a seaside hotel in Southwold. There they would make love, and he could believe that she was still his and his alone, that soon he would be able to reclaim her affections and bask in her devotion once more.

The hotel itself would take a direct hit during the war, and his notion that he could still be king of Marjorie's affections was to meet a similar fate. It would take decades to rebuild their earlier harmony as a couple together. In fact, Adrian would come to recognise that a mother can never again be single-minded with her loving.

Adrian did not write a book in that year but when he restarted his diary in 1937, a new and inspiring friendship was about to open. The lengthy entry for January 20th gives an indication of the impression made on him by his introduction to the renowned artist Alfred J. Munnings.

'Last night at a very talkative party at the Parringtons. Met Munnings and his wife there; he's something of a young Vic Savage to look at, although actually no younger than Vic. A curious picture of him, as he talked of his early days, riding from one painting site to another followed by his gipsy retinue - caravan horses etc. Complaining that that was how his best work was done, and can't do that now - "too bloody respectable." His gusto such that he seemed to be talking as much though he looked towards the end of the evening half asleep. But at mention of something would start up wide-eyed, pricked awake, and go again.'

Adrian's observation continues, 'A great rider, not a lover of the hunt - "I can have a better hunt by myself". Always has a "point" - some little pork-butcher's where the sausages are wonderful, or a "bit of pig's face."'

Munnings, a man of massive ego and uncompromising opinion, was interested in the donnish-looking young writer. He approved of Bell's style, his sentiments, his views. That was a rarity indeed. A few days after their introduction, Munnings came over to Creems, but found that Adrian had gone out with an old friend.

Dolores had come to visit, and she had politely inspected the baby without any hint of maternal longing. Then while Marjorie and Anthea stayed home, Adrian had taken her to see some of Suffolk's attractions. Marjorie felt no alarm - she had met Dolores in Bath when they had been for a holiday there and the woman seemed to hold no threat to their cosy family life. Of course, her security of mind may be attributed partly to the fact that Adrian had omitted to mention many of the details of their past liaison.

To be honest, he was feeling a little foolish about the depth of his earlier passion. It would have been hard to explain that flight of wild fancy, the firework display of emotion and ecstasy, to his prosaic and down-to-earth wife. As Marjorie herself would say later, 'My job in life has been to tether his balloon,' and at times it had needed tight tethering, or they would have had no livelihood.

But he and Dolores were more than just good friends, there was a charge between them that could still generate sparks as they admired the views through two sets of eyes that saw as one. Driving through the Stour valley they stopped to look at a meadow on one of the farms Dolores jokingly referred to as 'bedsteads farms' because of the old bed-parts used to cover gaps in hedge or fence. She was not enamoured of the flat landscape and at first this seemed like another everyday scene of suspended work, an untidy litter of tools and equipment. But there was another element to it that formed a memory bond for them both, a snapshot in time which neither realised as being significant then, but which one day would seem like a monument to their deep understanding.

Adrian recalled it in an article entitled *The Red Ladder*, written after her death more than forty years later. He concealed Dolores' identity and changed her sex, but the story is poignant even when one is unaware of the history behind it. Part of it goes, 'In a broad level meadow stood a haystack. It had been carved into sharp angles by a stack knife. It stood blind and bright, black and silver-grey. A ladder leaned against it, a big stack ladder painted red, broadening towards its base. You would hardly see such a ladder today: it belonged to those days of stacking and thatching in which we lived.

'Our eyes took in that stack at a glance, with that ladder leaning up it and beyond. "Look at that ladder," I said.

"Yes, a big red ladder." Then we looked at something else, tree or church tower or barn.'

Adrian says that years later, at the end of a rare meeting, his friend suddenly said, 'D'you remember that red ladder up against a stack years ago? It seemed quite an ordinary ladder but I keep seeing it in my mind's eye'. Adrian said he did indeed remember it too, and then he realised that the shared vision and its duration in the memory represented more than just a photo-image imprinted on the brain. He wrote 'that ladder had meant something particular to both of us. But nothing you could put into words.'

Dolores' visit was short, but as always, her effect was like that of a sudden, stiff breeze on a gliding swan. She disturbed Adrian's equilibrium; she ruffled him, and blew him off course. He had come to terms with the fact that he had shared her with others. There was a sense of déjà vu to this, for had he not gone from being the focus of his mother's entire love to being merely at the front of the queue? That was bad enough, but now the hardest fact to face was that forever more he must share Marjorie too - with his own children, one day no doubt with grandchildren, ageing parents, a hundred other duties. Yes, he needed to keep working hard, to be sensible, to earn money and keep the family afloat but sometimes, surely, he could fly?

In a poem he later gave to his cousin Carlos Peacock, he seems to grasp again for that something unspoken.

## The Word

Truth: it is the rose tapping my door.
Come in, come in. Ah, no, come out to me;
This hour's the core of an eternity.
The gleam that lies along the valley floor
As a bird lit, yet with unease to soar
Again - therein halved stack and virgin tree
As by the inner eye of memory
Stand summoned out of shadow. There is more

Than light? A thought, encircling of a mind
Invisible as the weaving of the wind,
Yet by some sense as just-bared flesh aware,
Apprehensible? That sliced stack bright and blind,
Leaves leaden-shining 'neath their load of air,
Shall lift thy spirit yet from some despair.

Adrian's need for expression caused him to feel drawn to creative people and now that his craving had been aroused once more, who better to associate with than the quixotic Munnings? The artist raved about the beauty of the views around Creems, which he insisted were far superior to those of the Waveney Valley. In the Bells' sitting room he planted himself at the window and became excited at the sight of a flooded pasture and cattle standing in mud. He could paint that, with the light lying captured in the mirror of the sodden land, and the cows - good old Red Polls, not the 'unpaintable' Friesians he so despised.

The Bells were guests at Dedham too, where, as his placid wife looked on, Munnings would hold court to his dinner guests, expounding his theories and delivering them as unassailable facts. His colourful language, expansive gesturing, dramatic expressions, all served to make him a mercurial character with whom, at first, Bell was flattered to be acquainted.

He was invited out on excursions with Munnings and his chums. Piled into the back of the yellow, open-top, chauffeur-driven Buick like a gang from *Wind in the Willows*, they careered around the countryside enjoying jolly japes with Munnings as ringleader.

In an article entitled *Jaunts with 'A.J.'*, written after Munnings' death Adrian reminisced about these times. 'If a house took his fancy, he would tell the driver to stop, and lead me up the drive as though it were his own home, pointing out admirable features. On the point of leading me round to view the stables of the best Adam period, he would be intercepted by the owner, striding out of his portico. "You, there, what do you want?"

'Munnings would look at him, head cocked back, screwing up his one eye for all the world as though he were judging the irate squire's paintability. Just as the flash-point was reached, they would discover they had a Norfolk cousin in common, or grand-uncle, and the clenched fist would suddenly be extended in welcome. Or it might be a family of gipsies we chanced upon, as in an inn at Boxford in high summer. Munnings was the same to all men.'

To most, he was loud and bombastic, whether cursing a teapot for being a hideous colour, or preaching from the pulpit of a church to his captive congregation of friends. But Munnings could be sober too, and sometimes quite morose when he stopped to consider the decline of farming and the state of the countryside he loved with such tempestuous vigour. It all seemed so ephemeral; culture, tradition, life itself. On one occasion he became subdued, saying, 'How short life is. We sweat and toil at our art, and then we're gone. What is it all for, Bell?' He soon recovered his mood though, and off the group went again, singing ballads and cracking jokes.

Adrian could not help but be impressed by the artistry of Munnings at work. He was a genius: there was no doubt about it. In particular his knowledge of horses, their character and anatomy, could only be surpassed by their maker Himself. His portrayal of their different incarnations, among gipsies, at the race track, on the hunting field, or nobly posed, carrying some high-ranking military bod, captured the spirit of man's longest-serving mount. His pictures were poetry in paint.

Adrian's sense of propriety would soon cause him to question the friendship. Munnings collected people, he used them, yes he amused them, but his arrogance in commanding decent people to do his bidding or his buffoonery in playing practical jokes could be embarrassing. Munnings seemed to overpower everybody, and respect no-one. Even when he brought the keeper of the Royal Academy, Sir Walter Russell, on a visit to Creems, the man hardly got a word in. Adrian dearly wanted to talk to him, to discuss some of his favourite artists, works and theories, but their conversation was eclipsed by the antics of Munnings in fine humour.

Throughout his diary for 1937 and '38, Adrian notes his many outings with Munnings, and typically he jots down, 'M. objected to...' 'M. incensed by...' 'M. cursing...'. For every positive point, Munnings could find a negative. 'There's always a dragon round the corner with him,' Adrian concluded.

Sometimes the dragons would become too much for him and he would telephone Adrian and demand that they go out in search of something to cheer him up. Adrian recorded one such incident in his autobiography. 'A promising morning, and the telephone would ring. Through the receiver would come a vocal noise, articulation drowning in feeling: "Nowhere to ride my horse...barbed wire...bricks...must get out... move...back where I belong..."

"All right", I would reply, interpreting; "I'll be with you in half an hour."'

Adrian, abandoning his plans for quietly working on a book or crossword clues, would be off to Dedham for another day's adventuring. Munnings would often go about as if he was house-hunting, and, as if he could possibly remain anonymous, he would give Bell's name as the interested party. But Adrian said he felt that his impersonation of a man of means 'lacked conviction', and in any case, telling outright lies was against his nature.

While some people bristled at the treatment Munnings dealt them, it was clear he could create a rapport with others, such as the gipsies he had painted in earlier days. In his diary entry for 27th August 1937 Adrian wrote upon returning from a house-viewing excursion, '...Passed a pony cart on the way, M. shouting "Get off the road" and saluting and being saluted with great enthusiasm by a higgler. "That's old Darkie Barber, I gave him a caravan and pony after I'd done with them." This was many years ago.'

Munnings was a fascinating character indeed, but eventually the relationship began to pall. Adrian could not be at Munnings' beck and call indefinitely, he had work to do, and in 1937 he had started on another book. Richard Cobden-Sanderson and Kenneth Rae had tried to persuade Adrian to do a biography, as they felt the market for farming books was dwindling. But Adrian could see no pleasure in sniffing along the footprints of another. He wanted to stick to what he felt most comfortable with, what he felt he was best at: country writing.

*Men and the Fields* was to be a collection of anecdotes and observations, this time not confined to East Anglia. Adrian enjoyed writing it, as he explained in a letter to his cousin Carlos: 'I felt when I was writing it that it was good work; one knows inside oneself when one is on the right track somehow.' Adding that it was mostly written from memory aided by diary notes, he went on, 'Anyhow, I'm much happier not trying to write fiction! Though the public prefer turbulent stuff two pages long. Sometimes I have a go at something fresh, but the old theme is so inexhaustible, and it is just as though a current is turned on which fails when I turn to anything else, or throbs very weakly.'

The text of *Men and the Fields* would be amply complemented by the illustrations of John Nash, his artist neighbour. Unlike his friendship with Munnings, this one was on a more equal footing. Adrian felt at ease with Nash, with whom he had far more in common, as another of Nash's friends, the author Ronald Blythe, points out. 'They came from middle class backgrounds; they'd both been to public school. John was about eight years older than Adrian and he came to the Stour Valley almost by accident. He and his wife Christine found this cottage called the Thatch at Wissington. It was about the same year, I think, as Adrian and his wife moved to Wissington, to Creems.'

Blythe comments that the high fatalities of the First World War, coupled with the ensuing depression had left agriculture in a sorry state, and neither the author nor the artist could help but be moved by the atmosphere of tragedy and loss in the countryside. Farms had been left to fall into dereliction, and each in their own way felt the need to record it all.

He adds, 'You have to remember what the world was like in the 'thirties. It wasn't like it is now. One of the great things about both John Nash's paintings and Adrian Bell's books is their truthfulness. It is the great drama of their work that it is so truthful and accurate. They're not just seeing social history or anything like that, there's a profundity about it as well. As well as the details of what life was like there are thought processes going on at the same time.'

*Men and the Fields* was published in 1939 by B.T. Batsford Ltd. No doubt Adrian's friend and publisher Richard Cobden-Sanderson would have accepted it, but his business had closed down by then. The small, diligent firm that had given Adrian his first break was unable to compete with the bigger companies who regularly poached the talent they had previously nurtured. With reluctance, Adrian had had to look elsewhere for someone to put his work into print.

Meanwhile his own industry had been interrupted very briefly when somehow he found himself standing for election to the West Suffolk County Council. At first he had agreed almost absent-mindedly to the idea but he soon became caught up in the spate of canvassing. 'From consenting to stand in a semi-reluctant manner I have been edged into the position of being eager for the honour', Adrian noted in his diary. A natural gentleman, he felt guilty that his opposition to his keen rival was causing her to go to a great deal of trouble, producing circulars and hand-bills, sending open letters to the local Free Press and knocking on doors of the electorate. Adrian was not at all disappointed when he lost. Now he could get on with earning a living.

Throughout Bell's working life his peaceful existence would be upset by his rashly consenting to things he later regretted. In the midst of the election campaign he had agreed to give a speech to the Sudbury Horticultural Society, at a dinner held in the Four

Swans hotel. Adrian's parents had recently taken up permanent residence there, as Fanny had finally given up any pretence of wanting to be a housewife. She was enjoying her days in the bar, entertaining the customers with her old-time music hall renditions and jokes. Robert, now retired, still had a small cottage of his own in Stour Street, where he spent the day in bliss among his books and with his piano, until tea-time when he would make his way into town to the marital lodgings.

So Adrian was volunteered to address the Society meeting, where he found himself sitting next to Rudyard Kipling at high table. He notes little more of this encounter but his other neighbour at table began pressing him to write a tale to warn against another war. This was a premonition being voiced by many people and like the rumbling of an underground train approaching, the ominous sound was growing louder.

Adrian and Marjorie decided to move home again. The Stour Valley had started to change, and the country characters were being replaced by cocktail-drinking commuters and weekend holiday-makers. There was a benefit to this in that formerly derelict cottages were being bought and restored, and roses grown around the doors. But one day, as Adrian took a cooling dip in the river he found himself being observed by a group of onlookers as though he were a local tourist attraction.

Worse though, the newcomers were installing electricity in their homes by means of private generator and strenuously opposing any plans to provide power to everyone else by means of lines and pylons across the picturesque Stour Valley. So Creems remained lit by oil lamps and on one visit, Adrian's father Robert was in the sitting room with little Anthea when a lamp was overturned. Disaster in the oak-framed house was narrowly averted.

That was it. With Marjorie expecting again, they decided to head east in search of a modernised house, but in an area where genuine country folk could still be found.

# 13. From West to East

After much searching, they came upon a big red-brick box in a two acre garden and decided it was the place for them.

The Old Vicarage was by no means an attractive-looking house but it did have electricity and its situation in the village of Redisham near Beccles, Suffolk, seemed fine. Redisham was little more than a hamlet, a few houses strung along the road, the land around it was flat clay, the countryside 'wild' and the indigenous people were pleasant but diffident. It was everything Adrian was looking for.

From the start he felt settled here in spite of the prosaic, square-shaped rooms of the square-shaped house. He set about softening its angular exterior with shrubs and trees, while Marjorie made the inside homely and welcoming. The former occupant, an elderly spinster, had virtually lived in two rooms only, so Marjorie threw open the windows and let the brisk North Sea air blow away the mustiness. She adjusted curtains that had divided the cold corridors of Creems, and made them fit the square-paned windows of their new home. She was not one for 'knick-knacks' or ornaments that had no function but just by positioning their furniture in a pleasing array around the rooms and putting their possessions in place the Old Vicarage took on new life.

Of the four bedrooms, Adrian chose the smallest for his own. He was a bad sleeper and so as well as their marital bed he had another to which he could retire, restless, and sit reading or thinking, or writing. He might wake in the night or the early hours and look out of the little back window, past the slate roof of the old stable, to the garden with four ancient apple trees linking arms as if to keep themselves upright. He came to love that view.

Marjorie slept in their double bed, and it was here that the Bell twins were soon born: Sylvia and Martin, three weeks premature and an alarming shade of blue. They were small, only five pounds apiece, but nestled in their mother's embrace they soon throve.

Anthea, now aged two, was not so keen on the usurpers. She took one look into her mother's bed and stated 'No Babies.' From then on she would take it upon herself to keep them in order, to employ them in her fantasy games and give them a supporting role in her miniature adult world. For, as Anthea herself is first to admit, she was an unusual child. Precocious would be the wrong description, but she never felt comfortable as a minor. At a very early age she became convinced that she was an adult trapped in the wrong-sized body. Childhood would be a phase she must suffer until her intellect could be matched by her dimensions.

Perhaps the Bell household was a contributory factor to her advanced maturity. Adrian still suffered migraines and an air of hush had to be maintained when he was working, or when he needed to sit and reflect, or take a nap. Childish high jinks had to be kept low-key, and screeching or screaming was banned outright.

Marjorie was his first line of defence, ever attentive to his needs and ready to quash any uprising or disturbance. The children's natural exuberance was carefully controlled and channelled into more docile games. One of their nannies, Molly Pagan, went to teach Anthea when she was five and the twins were toddlers. She recalls, 'We weren't allowed to disturb Adrian in his study. In the winter he worked in his study. In summer he had a special corner of the garden where we weren't allowed to go in case we disturbed him.'

She adds, ' Marjorie was a very nice woman indeed, she ran the family. I was governess - I used to bath them, take them for walks. We had our meals together, but we didn't see Adrian, he was mostly in his own room with his own pursuits. We were expected to keep quiet.' Asked if that was difficult, she replies, 'Martin was probably naughty, I can't imagine the girls being naughty.'

The children themselves insist they were rarely smacked and nobody ever had the need to shout. Martin says they behaved themselves because they were expected to, and later on they would do their bit to help their industrious mother around the house. 'There was an expectation that you would sort of muck in', he says. 'Lay the table, wash up, keep your room tidy, and no shouting was necessary. I certainly never heard a voice raised in my family.'

On one occasion when Adrian did have to chastise a recalcitrant little Martin, it left him feeling mentally exhausted. He hated confrontation and when reasoning failed, he resorted to physical punishment. Sylvia remembers the slipper being applied to bottoms, not very hard, when the twins would not go to sleep at night. She says they saw it as all part of the fun, and would incite the ritual until the novelty wore off. Adrian would later write that his children had been smacked when little, and so by the time they were eight it was no longer necessary. In fact, the children would spend most of their formative years away at boarding school, and so the house would indeed be quiet during term time.

For Adrian, noise and stress were not just irritating or inconvenient; they could be the catalyst to a bout of incapacitating migraine. His headaches were a bane that lasted almost all his life, and it was early in 1938 that he tried one last 'alternative' cure.

The story starts with a famous mountaineer, Frank Smythe, a few months older than Bell, and a very different character. Smythe was a very logical and determined man who had made a name for himself by tackling some of the world's most gruelling climbs. He had been invited to attempt Everest three times by 1938.

Contrary to this image of the heroic explorer, Smythe had been a frail schoolboy diagnosed with a heart murmur, and as a man he was often full of self-doubt, and easily offended. But when he climbed he came alive, and colleagues said that at 20,000 feet he seemed to undergo an astonishing change, whereby he became self-confident, invigorated, almost unbeatable. What few people knew at the time was that he believed he was receiving spiritual guidance, and that had led to a physical transformation. Through a mutual friend, Robert Bell asked him to explain, and received a lengthy reply.

Smythe wrote that he had been in a 'serious motor smash' in 1932 and as a result had suffered bad headaches and internal pain for two years. Then a friend in the Alpine Club had told him that, during a seance he'd attended, a spirit guide called Abdul Latif had said Smythe had spinal problems, and should see a chiropractor. Smythe, after some deliberation, did so and was cured.

Smythe had been sceptical but after visiting the medium himself, discovered he too had psychic powers and communicated with Abdul Latif for some time after. He finally gave up the dialogue when he found it drained his energy too much, for he had a living to earn as an author as well as a mountaineer. He was not suggesting that the Bells should follow his path into spiritualism, but that they should visit his chiropractor to find out if Adrian's problem could also stem from a spinal problem.

Even so, Robert and Adrian did seek out the medium, as their relation Carlos Peacock noted in his diary for January 1938. 'Went down to Sudbury. Met by R. at the station, who asked me not to mention that I had seen Adrian in London....Discussed with R. the spirit message about A's headaches and their cause. Read to me part of Smythe's letter of his experience in the same field. R. very impressed. The experiment goes forward'.

Among Robert's papers is a transcript of that seance, in which Abdul, through the medium, discusses Adrian's astrological sign and says that, as a Libran, he has strength of purpose but a weak nervous system. He asked if Adrian had suffered a fall or had pleurisy at the age of about ten or twelve. Adrian said no. Abdul explained that Adrian's spine seemed congested and the poor blood flow was causing headaches - Robert notes here that nobody had mentioned the migraines so far.

Abdul suggested a particular therapist who could try manipulation. He gave the address as 29 Park Road. 'Is that Regent's Park?' Robert asked. The spirit guide said he didn't know, he had only been given 29 Park Road, but he would be there to direct the chiropractor's healing.

The medium placed his hand on the nape of Adrian's neck as Abdul continued to speak of the 'congestion', and how Adrian would feel freer when it was released, 'for though your inspiration is spiritual and mental, it is affected by the condition of the physical body. The freer the spine is the more open are all the psychic centres'.

He went on, 'You have a great understanding of humanity...You have great forces for good. You came to serve; you came with a message that people are waiting to receive, and you are going to do great work. You are one of the pioneers. I too was a pioneer - a pioneer for medicine, for astrology, for understanding, for the geographical. And when we are chosen we should be worthy, and I would ask you to prepare yourself every morning by deep breathing. Turn the face to the East and ask the blessing of Allah upon all actions and works, that they may be in harmony with the Divine Universe...'

Abdul added, 'All who have art are the real benefactors of the world. The world would never have reached the place it holds without them. Science gets you far, but it never gets you where art gets you... You have been tremendously blessed by Allah. In all you undertake, remember you are but a channel, and keep it worthy, beautiful and pure. Remember you are one of the whole and one with the universe, and have charity, understanding, love of humanity and tolerance for all'.

There would be times when Adrian would struggle to uphold this last exhortation, and if he did find his way to 29 Park Road, there is no record of what transpired. Adrian continued to suffer headaches for decades to come.

Of course, there was a great deal of additional stress about to trouble him. The twins were only a year old, in fact it was on their first birthday, 31st August 1939, when Hitler ordered the attack on Poland to begin, and the British government started evacuating children out of London. The Second World War was under way.

Only the day before, Adrian had been drinking with Munnings at a pub near Bungay, because Munnings was in a rage to get out of Dedham, where he said he felt hemmed in by little barbed-wire plots of land occupied by miners from Durham so they could make a living after the '20s slump.

The pub, called the Tumbledown Dick after Cromwell's puny son, was facing closure anyway, and the landlord had been growing flowers to sell, trying to make a living.

Adrian's poem, dedicated to that hostelry, is one of his most moving:

## At the Tumbledown Dick

That day before the whole world went to war
We stopped at the Tumbledown Dick, do you remember?
And sat out on the bench beside the door
And drank our ale and thought how that old timber
Had rested waggoners, farmers, men of yore,
When fellowship burned clear, whose dying ember
Was being trampled out this sweet September
Of flowers and swallows gathering to soar.
   Precious that hour, for this ensuing night
   Of love's eclipse; its sunlight calm and bright,
   And every flower and fruit and stone and tile
   Strikes to the heart - old England's russet smile.
   And all over a cloud of dazzling white
   Stood like an angel blessing us awhile.

What is our answer to the drum of death?
To know those things most fugitive most strong:
To miss no moment of the robin's song,
Nor to neglect the light wind's lightest breath.
Those gossip notes the homely redbreast throws
Among the orchard boughs for hours together,
While autumn kindles yet another rose,
And under one great cloud the swallows gather.
      At least thank God for these small ones that share
      Our world but not the folly of our fate.
      When one man haunts his brother to despair
      Thrice beautiful their freedom of the air
      That are too slight for guns, too delicate
      For all our vast machinery of hate.

Being so near to the East Coast the Bells felt very vulnerable. Soon the area was overrun with soldiers and the locals, afraid the newcomers might run amok if boredom turned them to drinking, tried to keep them occupied with games. But there was little trouble. The men were heading for France, and when the 'Phoney War' came to an end, news of dogfights and bombing raids, retreats and defeats brought fear of an invasion and capitulation. The British spirit might be indomitable, but its fighting forces were in serious difficulty.

Adrian noted in his diary of 14th November 1939, 'Met Canon S. as bewildered as ever. What with servants leaving, evacuees coming, evacuees going, the billeting officer having to arrange some to come, to go, to change billets - "I don't know when we shall have another game of croquet," he said.'

In their new village, the Bells had at first been treated with bemusement by the locals who thought that as 'townees' they would not settle. Adrian had disabused them, explaining about his farming, and the fact that their last house had only an Elsan toilet for some time. They were used to hardship, he said. Which was just as well.

Rationing was less of a problem in the countryside where extra provisions could be obtained without the paperwork, but at a cost. Animal feed was hard to come by, so many had to be slaughtered rather than let them starve, and Adrian was killing his own cockerels for meat and to save on their feed. He grew plenty of fruit and vegetables for the family, and Marjorie managed to turn them into all kinds of plain, tasty meals.

Later when petrol became too scarce, Adrian took to a pony and trap for transport, trotting out wearing a straw hat and a mild, faraway expression. Perhaps for this reason and also because of his address, he was often mistaken for a vicar.

As all the locals pooled their skills, Adrian was happy to help out on local farms, but each evening he was home before the blackout and listening for the latest news. Marjorie did her bit as well, helping to roll bandages at Redisham Hall and sewing new clothes from old.

On 2nd January 1940 Adrian noted in his diary, 'The policeman arrived with two terrible-looking appliances for keeping the babies alive in a gas attack.' But even as the clear winter skies kept clouding with dark, droning aircraft, the dormant camouflage of hedge and tree held the promise of continuity. Adrian would stand out in the garden in the evening and listen to the celebrating blackbird, envying its innocence. He stared into the gloaming until his eyes burned, watching for the first stars to prick the dusky sky. There - there and there; it was a timeless awakening that transcended the folly of man.

This land and its people had survived the centuries before and no doubt their descendants would be here for centuries to come. What about the Bell family? Was there a future for them? He struggled to find some kind of faith he could hold on to.

Adrian had become friends with another country writer, Henry Warren, one of the few men with whom Adrian would maintain a life-long rapport and friendship. Henry had sent him a picture of two grand plough horses at work; Adrian would gaze at this almost reverentially, as if in prayer for all it represented. 'I do thank God for those plough horses', he said, 'as a monument of affirmation'.

Then the time for contemplation ceased. The last week in May 1940 would go into the history books as the point at which the allied forces seemed most on the point of defeat, with the French having succumbed to invasion and the British fleeing from Dunkirk. It seemed as if nothing could stop Hitler's army from crossing the channel, and an onslaught of the East Coast of England was about to begin.

Marjorie's brother Laurence was involved in military intelligence and he warned his sister to clear out of Suffolk. Without hesitation she packed up the children and headed for Westmorland, where her sister Lallie and brother-in-law had a school at Moresdale Hall, and had arranged for the Bell family to take a farm cottage next to a recently-disused water mill at Grayrigg near Kendal.

Adrian was alone again for the first time in almost twenty years and he felt absolutely desolate. He had been left behind to pack the car with more belongings but he mooched around the house and garden, missing Marjorie and the children as though half his life - maybe more - had vanished.

And Marjorie was half his life, not just the cliched 'other half,' but certainly his equal in most spheres. She matched his mental workload with physical toil: cooking, cleaning, sewing, and nowadays of course, caring for their three children too. Still she found time to be his friend, lover, confidante, advisor, his minder and reminder. Without her he could barely function at all. It was not as if he hadn't appreciated her, he had; he counted himself lucky that she had become so adept at all the house-wifely duties, and furthermore she was his constant support in his own work. More than anything, she loved him unconditionally, and he felt she was the only one in the world with that capacity. And now she was gone.

Everything seemed to miss her - from the empty kitchen and the cold stove to the lonely garden, where the flowers Marjorie planted were peeping out of leafy sheaths. As Adrian stopped and gazed on them, he reflected that she would not be here when they bloomed.

He did manage to collect his thoughts and the belongings he was supposed to take and follow the family north a couple of weeks later. His diary stops, but he kept notes in a little red book and eventually wrote about their year in that unfamiliar land, a novel he called *Sunrise to Sunset*.

He described the change of scenery from heavily fortified Suffolk to the rocky water-splashed fells of the Lake District, where the war seemed to have gone virtually unnoticed. He wrote of the Blenkharn family on whose farm they lived, although he named them Rockfall. He told of their kindness, their odd accent, their easy-going, hard-working lifestyle. And he wrote of the farming operations with which he gladly mucked in and lent a hand.

Although it was by no means an ideal situation, this was a fruitful time for Adrian, back among the farming community, back in action. The style of farming was different to what he had known before, but now a whole new realm of impressions could be observed. The lapwing's nest that he came upon while harrowing, and set aside, returning it intact after he had finished. The harvest, with great golden sheaves which he described in his little red notebook as 'heavy to lift as a wardrobe of dresses.' The muck carting, turnip carting, swede carting; in bitter winds and finger-numbing frost. All these images would be stored for future use.

He wrote to Rolf Gardiner too, urging him to maintain the ideals of the Springhead Ring, and keep faith for a better future. Adrian had been to Dorset in April to give a talk to the lads on Rolf's farm, and although a number of the tired boys had nodded off during his speech he was impressed by the ethos and the camaraderie in all the work and the singing and dancing that went on. He sent a letter from the Lake District, from the cottage at Bye Mill which he described as being 'deep in a Westmorland valley, no road to it but a steep and stony track. A rocky stream dashes past the back windows.' He knew Rolf would appreciate reading about the Blenkharns' farm and their life. 'They have their own butter, cheese, bacon, eggs, bread - knit their own stockings - make beds and pillows of feathers - nothing wasted'. He said he felt privileged to work with these people.

Adrian returned to Suffolk alone in the following January and his life began again on 1st April 1941 when the family came home. The Battle of Britain was over but the war was still very much in evidence here with soldiers, guns, tanks, and barbed wire round every turn.

Things were not going well for Britain. In May the battle cruiser Hood was sunk with the loss of over 1,400 men. In return more than 2,000 German sailors died when the Bismarck went down. Anyone with a conscience could not wholeheartedly celebrate such slaughter. Adrian and Marjorie, like parents everywhere, feared most for the lives of their children, and worried that the threat of invasion might become an unthinkable reality. There was talk of the Americans coming to our aid but in the meantime Britain seemed to be a small and vulnerable island, in danger of succumbing to the monstrous enemy that might attack at any time by air or sea, or both. And all they could do was get on with life.

Adrian would later recall that he and others had practised standing beside farm wagons brandishing shotguns and pitchforks. They all knew it was an impotent gesture, but they called themselves Land Defence Volunteers and hoped if the time came they would delay the enemy long enough for their families to run. It wasn't much consolation. They might simply be bombed to oblivion, or machine-gunned by a swooping Messerschmit.

Adrian found some small comfort in the fact that the formerly derelict land that had been abandoned by bankrupt farmers was rapidly being brought back into cultivation. The Minister of Agriculture appealed for an extra two million acres of land to be brought into production and his vision would be surpassed, with an extra seven million acres eventually being ploughed up. It was not Adrian's ideal method of agriculture though, as every acre was being blitzed with machinery, fertiliser and other chemicals.

Rolf Gardiner was even more strongly opposed to this rape of the land, as he saw it. 'Our neglected countryside is being galvanised into an output that is beyond the load-limit of the soil' he warned. He proposed that a new group should be set up to draw together all those of a like mind who could prepare for the rural reconstruction that would be needed when the present 'shortsighted and unthrifty policies' were spent. He called the group A Kinship in Husbandry and invited his friends to join in, to keep in communication with each other and combine their talents to try to gain attention for their cause.

Adrian's name was on the top of the alphabetical list, with Edmund Blunden next. Henry Warren was there too, introduced recently by Bell, and a very keen supporter of Rolf's ideals. Henry, having just moved from an unhappy position in the Ministry of Information to one at the B.B.C., longed for the day when he could escape to the country and write. His chance was about to come, with a two-year contract that would lead to the publication of some of his finest work.

The plan was for the Kinsmen to share ideas and thoughts by means of a round-robin case-book system, and to try to meet occasionally in London or in Blunden's room at Merton College, Oxford. Adrian rarely attended, but he did make notes in the case-books. A typical entry in September 1941 sees Adrian complaining about local traffic problems and the menace of the motor car generally. At other times he would worry about the way the land was being drenched with chemicals, and the incursion of the tractor in the fields all around. He could see that their belief in the old ways of farming was leaving them out of step with the march of progress.

Later that year Adrian was to meet another renowned author, Henry Williamson, writer of the best selling novel *Tarka the Otter*. Williamson: thin, fidgety, with a wild-eyed passion, impressed Adrian immediately. On 10th October he wrote to Rolf Gardiner, 'Yesterday I met Williamson - intuitive, sensitive and true, a person of burning zeal, and though his views on the kind of action to be taken are not perhaps those of Springhead he has the great truth in him, consuming him, for which he is ready to suffer and does, outwardly and inwardly - and still remains essentially the artist in the finest and most vulnerable sense - for all of which he is to be respected.'

Bell added that he was to visit Williamson's farm. He did so, and did not enjoy the experience. One day, having seen the film *Look Back in Anger* he would reflect that Williamson had been a character of the same ilk, at odds with those around him. He told a friend that in his view, 'Poor Henry' had been affected badly by the First World War, and although his nature pieces were beautiful, he had lost his balance about other things.

Everyone who met Williamson was struck by the energy he exuded, but it was a destructive force at times. Professor Herbert Faulkner West, in an essay entitled *The Dreamer of Devon*, described Williamson thus: 'His mind turned too long upon itself, enjoying in its own solitude the inner landscape of the soul, the prey to imagined fears, dreaming of some Utopia...had woven for itself a set of ideals which clashed inevitably with the compromises the world of experience forces upon all men.'

Williamson and his wife would split, with Henry eventually moving back to Devon and Loetitia staying in Bungay, Suffolk, so the Bells easily remained on friendly terms with her. Their contact with Henry would remain cordial, but less frequent.

According to his family, Adrian did have some concerns that Williamson's commitment to peace with Germany was not necessarily on England's terms, and that his close involvement with the Fascist movement and Mosley's Blackshirts had led him to radical and unwholesome views. Henry had already been arrested in 1940, but no charges had been brought against him.

From Adrian's point of view, he admired the man's writings, especially his latest book *The Story of a Norfolk Farm*, but in this time of great paranoia, he had no desire to become embroiled in complicated politics. Williamson's daughter-in-law and biographer insists that Henry was attracted to Mosley's views on agricultural reform, and that he was simply naive. Indeed, his real cause in life was one Adrian could appreciate and agree with. In his biography, Williamson's daughter-in-law Anne writes, 'Henry Williamson was a man who drove himself unremittingly both in his writing and in his life. He believed himself to be a chosen one, destined to pass on the "ancient sunlight", and he never ceased in his task.'

Henry also knew Rolf Gardiner and they corresponded for many years, but does not seem to have taken an active part in the Kinship in Husbandry.

To some minds, Gardiner also seemed overly interested in the plight of Germany. In 1942 Henry Warren reacted to Rolf's articles by writing that he and Adrian were concerned as to whether the Kinsmen were supposed to be in favour of war or against it. He asked what other remedies there could be, and posed the question, if they were to believe Churchill was wrong, did this mean that Hitler must be right?

The following year, Rolf was incensed by the Dambusters raid, in which some 1,200 people were drowned as the Ruhr Valley was inundated. Warren agreed that it was a terrible loss of innocent life, but some of the kinsmen felt that Rolf's comments were becoming subversive, and probably illegal. Not until many years later would Adrian look back and see that Rolf's point about working with Germany rather than against could be put into practice in a common market, and that moves towards a united Europe could only be for the good. But by then, Hitler's plans had been thwarted and England could negotiate her own terms.

At the time of the Bouncing Bomb, Adrian had already declared his right to independent thought. Responding to Rolf's call to go out and spread the Springhead message, Adrian had written him a stern reply. In a letter dated 21st January 1943 he said: 'About the little part I am to play in the scheme of English things - I fully appreciate all you say. But you must allow me to have my own certainty of my own true destiny. Which is - to illumine, to give the glory of, - the humble earthly, earthy task, just that.'

Adrian's most recent book, Apple Acre, had sold 30,000 copies within the year, and Adrian pointed out, without wishing to boast, that this was where his strength lay. He had no intention of going out into the country to preach. As a postscript he added, 'The Kinship - I like the Kinship for its kinshipness - just that'. It was a tactful broadside to Rolf for trying to politicise their group, to make them more proactive, which Adrian thought was going too far.

Apple Acre was indeed a very popular book, full of cameos and essays on the nostalgic English country life, as played out in Suffolk. Ironically, its production had been done in something of a rush. Adrian promised his new publishers a book and they had duly ordered the scarce paper resources for printing. With nothing special on the go, he had sent them a pile of notes and they accepted it as a premise to be worked on. Surprised, he'd set about putting it all in order.

Then Adrian had suffered doubts about it, for a great deal of his personal life was in it. So he started on another book altogether, about the year in Westmorland. Two-thirds of the way through that he changed his mind again and returned to the first one. It seemed better now when he read it through, and feverishly he worked on getting it finished. It was really just a collection of notes he'd had stuffed in his drawer for ages, but he managed to build it into a flowing stream of anecdotes and stories. Its tone came across as though Adrian himself were sitting in a comfortable corner of a pub, talking about the strange, the funny and the moving incidents of his recent life. The result was *Apple Acre*, a delightful, intimate piece of work which many readers would call his best.

Only Adrian could bring together the wartime images of fear, discomfort and economy and yet also offer a potent peep at a cosy rural scene, as in this extract, in which he describes riding in a winter evening bus, its interior lights extinguished: 'In its darkness there is a stirring, as of poultry gone to roost, which tells me it is nearly full.'

And *Corduroy* was being reprinted too. Adrian's books were striking all the right chords in the hearts of those both at home and overseas. Letters were coming in from appreciative fans all over the world, on precious notepaper, on war-issue forms, even, poignantly, on prison-camp paper. One, from Mr Holland of Stalag VlllB, shows that this young man, originally from Stone in Staffordshire, had already written to Adrian and in return had received a letter of encouragement, adding that some cigarettes were on their way. Mr Holland had not yet had them. Now he wrote of his enjoyment of Adrian's books, and he told of his life before the war and his dreams for afterwards, when he hoped that one day they might meet.

Another letter, from a P.O.W. camp in Italy, came from a South African who had never been to England but felt drawn there in imagination as if to a spiritual home. 'The charm, the peace, the homeliness, the peace even in turmoil, the deep satisfying joy of your day to day experiences come to me and many others like circumstanced as a delight that refreshes and abides, and makes more bearable our own strange life here.'

He went on, 'To have met, even though in the pages of a book, you and your family, the company of your friends, to have been brought back to the simple, natural, intimate things of life has been a most grateful experience, though it has increased - oh! almost unendurably - the desire to see England with my own eyes.'

For a non-native to pine for Adrian Bell's England shows how deeply the author moved those with whom he shared his life and the gathered images of his surroundings. Another P.O.W. in Germany had lost his copy of *Corduroy* at Dunkirk, but had managed to obtain another. Marching for days on end, he'd had to ditch every other book, but *Corduroy* kept him going. He'd read every passage twice and now he was a prisoner he carried its imagery still, holding dear the mental picture of Home.

One final letter highlights the importance of Bell's work in providing solace for the displaced sensitive soul at this time. Percy Kelly of the Royal Signals wrote from Osnabruck in Germany, 'During long dreary months your writing came to me like a fresh breeze. So often have I been whisked away to an England of soft peaceful meadows and changing skies - where the discovery of the first snowdrop would bring wonderment and joy... perhaps 'ere long I will be sitting by my own fireside, stretching out my hand for the Cherry Tree - sincerely I could wish for nothing better.'

# 14. An Author Who Wants to Farm

A recurring theme in many of the letters from homesick soldiers, sailors and airmen was their thought that when they got home to England, they should like to become farmers. Adrian would write back, dispensing advice and encouragement, calling on his memory and the knowledge he gleaned from helping out on local farms and in Westmorland. In an open letter entitled *To a Soldier Who Wants to Farm*, printed in *Everybody's Weekly*, he gave fulsome advice, adding that determination was the key; 'I say, if you are set cn being a farmer, nothing in the world can stop you.'

But he longed to farm again too, and wondered if the high sales figures of his book *Apple Acre* might provide him with enough capital to buy something. His first book *Corduroy*, for all its popularity, had netted him about £500 in total while in the past year *Apple Acre* had brought him more than double that amount. Having the money was one thing, finding land to buy was another. Quite by chance an opportunity arose whereby one man's misfortune would be Adrian's dream come true.

With the drive to ensure maximum production from every acre, the government had set up War Agricultural Committees to oversee farming practice. They could advise, offer help, and in extreme circumstances, issue warnings to do better or they would take control of a farm themsleves.

In 1943 the local branch of the 'War Ag.' were on the case of a tenant farmer just outside Redisham, at Weston. Billy Godbold had been in bad health for years and Brick Kiln Farm had started to suffer. The freehold was up for sale as part of the ongoing dismemberment of the Redisham Hall Estate, which itself had been part of the great Henham Estate until it was divided by the coming of the railway. Goldbold's father had become tenant sometime in the 1890s and father had passed the land to son, who fought for his country in the First World War and was old before he reached middle age. Billy Godbold didn't want to leave this place, but he had no hope of raising the money to buy it.

By now it was spring. Of the eighty seven acres available, fifteen were thorny scrub and only three had been ploughed and drilled with corn, the rest was becoming wasteland. Any day now, Goldbold would lose his piece of England to the Committee.

In various articles and in his autobiography Adrian Bell describes how he became involved in Brick Kiln Farm. Having heard it was for sale he was one day passing in his spring cart, drawn erratically by Bubbles the effervescent pony, when he saw Godbold at his gate and managed to pull up. He heard the sorry tale of the farmer's plight, how the Committee were demanding that he undertake four hundred pounds' worth of ditching and draining work which he couldn't afford. How, in spite of the family's fifty-year association with the farm, he was to be reduced to farmhand, working for the Committee until a buyer was found. All of his stock, his horses and equipment were to be sold, except for one cow to supply milk for his family of eight children, the parents and aged grandmother. He was sure they would soon lose their home, a chilly old former pub that somehow housed them all.

Adrian suggested that he might buy the farm, and let the Godbolds stay on. A few phone calls, a visit to the agent and solicitor, and Adrian had parted with £800 for a farm which some said would 'break any man's heart.'

Brick Kiln Farm was certainly inhospitable land. As its name suggests, the clay was formerly used to make bricks, and as one local is quoted as saying, 'Heavy? That get together like cement on top and yet that'll be all of a pudden within.' But Adrian felt he could do a great deal to improve it, with hard work and help from the Committee. He would keep Billy Godbold on, and employ his boy John too, between school hours. Later he would take on one of the girls, Gladys, to help Marjorie in the house.

It was not the easiest of working relationships. Naturally, the older man had been used to running the place his way, and now Adrian wanted it all changed. John Godbold, in defence of his father, indicates that for a start he felt aggrieved that Bell was telling everyone how run down the farm was. 'It wasn't run down,' he insists, 'but a lot of people can't farm that sort of land, that's pure clay. That sort of land, you've got to live on it for a generation to know how to work it.'

For whatever reason, there clearly was a great deal of work to do. Adrian wrote to Rolf Gardiner in May that year that Marjorie was 'up with the lark' each day to get his breakfast for half past six, when he would then start his twelve-hour working day. She was helping in the fields too, while Molly Pagan looked after the children and Mrs Scarle came from the village to clean the house. Adrian was back on the horse hoe, and even more archaically, he came across an old man in one field breaking clods of clay with a coal hammer.

In writing to Rolf again he referred to the work of 'reclamation': fallowing, draining, hedging, ditching, 'trying', he said, 'to catch up with works of maintenance which should have been done in the last 20 years and have been left undone'. Henry Warren had written to a friend on the subject too, saying he had been staying with Adrian in the week he bought the 'derelict' farm. He marvelled at Adrian's courage, he declared, and said that he would retrieve a piece of England and save a small farmer's heart from breaking.

The War Agricultural Committee provided labour to help with ploughing and with gassing rabbits, and they sent a mechanical excavator to tackle the drainage. Adrian was impressed by its speed of work, but less so by the numerous breakdowns it suffered. What he described as a 'frightening looking gang' of Irish navvies came by coach each day to do the pipelaying.

Another team came, Italian soldiers captured in the African desert and brought over to help chop through the brambles and thistles of Suffolk. But soon the danger of unexploded butterfly bombs perching in the thickets caused work to cease until the army's disposal men gave the all-clear. Then a team of German captives arrived, and Adrian set them to work.

Going to check on their progress one day, he found them all stripped to the waist and glowing in the warm spring sunshine. The sight caused Adrian to stop and reflect seriously on the state of the world and the state of men's minds. He later wrote in his book *The Flower and the Wheel* about man in his nakedness, 'Class, creed, nationality are discarded and he becomes a creature straight from God. Nazis, Fascists, anti-Nazis, Communists - whatever those men were, they were simply mothers' sons to me, beautiful in the young manhood of the body.' Adrian knew that in theory he and they were supposed to hate each other, but seeing these young men 'stripped of everything save the grace and strength of their youth' his feeling was more of kinship, and an artistic admiration for the aesthetic glory of man in his prime. 'Seeing all that gleaming flesh among the greenwood', he said, he felt 'shame and pity at the wilderness inside us'. The bombers droning overhead, the armoured vehicles rumbling by, these were not just machines, they contained men, every bit as human and vulnerable as these lithe bodies he stared at.

Fortunately he had no such opportunity with his next farm workers. Two Land Girls, Doreen and Margaret, came from North London to work on the farm, kitted out in the regulation dungarees and green jerseys. For some time they did a good job of the tough manual labour until one of them, whom Adrian described as 'giddy', became pregnant by an American soldier 'and so faded from our view' he noted. The other girl carried on alone, going home each night to lodgings nearby.

As well as having various groups of labourers coming and going, and shortages of labour in between, it was taking Adrian a little while to get back into the swing of farming. It had been almost fifteen years since he had last been fully employed on the land and it seemed to him that every time something went wrong, Billy Godbold or one of the other local farmers happened to come along.

He made errors of judgement on the economical viability of some of the rusty old implements he found in the barns - a corn drill and an old wagon he paid to have restored lasted barely a year or two before falling to pieces with sheer age and fatigue. Similarly, his fondness for the good old Suffolk breed of Red Poll cattle led him to buy several animals which turned out to be 'rum 'uns'.

For basic mistakes like harrowing his beans before the danger of frost had passed, he knew he was derided by those who knew better. But sometimes, when the sun shone warmly on his acres of England, he just wanted to be out there, working rhythmically and letting his spirit sing. Billy, whose spirit had lost its voice in 1914 and had remained dumb ever since, merely shook his head and muttered about the folly of his actions.

In his book *The Budding Morrow* Adrian wrote down a mental conversation with 'Walter,' the pseudonym he had bestowed on Billy, in which the older man would caution against starting work too early in the year. Adrian would reply, '...you know by now that at certain seasons I am filled with impatience, in spring and in autumn; and am mad to break the stale crust of winter or of stubble, and see and smell the earth again. But for your irritating caution this would be a delight to me. Don't protest that you are always right: I know it...But the sun is bright, the hedges are green, the birds are singing; and I want to do something about it. I want to celebrate, and you don't: that is the difference between us.'

And what a difference it was - Adrian, with poetry and the golden music of life throbbing in him, urging him to frolic in the fields, and Billy, introspective, careful, unwell, with the burden of family and heritage on his back. By comparison Adrian was like a frisky colt that goes careering around the field and skids over in its exuberance. Now in his forties he might not have quite that kind of energy, but his heart could still swell with joy just from looking at the land around him. He would rest his hand on the crusty trunk of a great oak, and understand that, while he could not say he owned it, he could be its guardian and champion for the time being. Perhaps his children would take over one day and carry forth his resolve, playing their part in the great theatre of the fields.

Meanwhile he could look at a crop and say, 'Something of myself is buried in that earth, and has resurrected in that wheat.' Year on year he would follow Nature's script and his reward would be the tumultuous applause of harvest. Perhaps Adrian's timing was not always right, but even when prompted by Godbold to make his move, he would sometimes forget his lines, or, more precisely, his furrows.

Part of the problem was that nowadays Adrian's mind wasn't fully on the job. Although he had little time to write, he was still compiling the *Times* crosswords, and while his feet were trudging along behind a horse hoe, his thoughts would be floating away. John Godbold recalls, 'Mr Bell used to like to take part in his farm and he used to be a-going up the field and get about half way up and him and the horse'd be about four or five rows off. Father used to call "Whoa" and the horse'd stop and Mr Bell used to look round. "What's up?" And Father'd say "Ha' you noticed where you're a-goin? You should be in this row". "Oh", he'd say, "I was just thinking of an article" or something. And that was how he was, you know, he was vague. He was, when he'd got something on his mind he wasn't in this world, he was elsewhere.'

Adrian himself wrote that 'Crossword compiling was an ideal job for a chap with a vacant mind harrowing clods', and 'All good manual fieldwork consists in a man tuning his body as nearly as possible to the exactitude of a machine'. But every machine needs some degree of minding, and while Adrian's head was filled with words and images, his body, or the horse, or the tractor would be doing its own thing. The locals had a nickname for him, coined with more affection than originality: they called him Ding-Dong.

In his books, Adrian also changed the names of the people he portrayed, but of course the people still recognised themselves and were not always flattered. They might agree with some elements of the character that represented them, but would protest that they hadn't actually done exactly all the things Bell said, or hadn't said those precise words. Author's licence can construct a hall of mirrors, and the reader must be prepared for some surprises.

One such person, who gives a wry smile when he recalls the depiction of himself as a young man, is Martin Mottram, who is called John in the books. Was he really such a pain as he seems in the stories?

'No doubt I did try his patience at times' he accepts. 'I was twenty or twenty-one then, and like any twenty-one year-old, I suppose I was argumentative. Once I spent two and a half days hoeing beet, and when Adrian saw what I had done he went on and on because he said I had done it wrong. I had been working in Wiltshire previously, where you cut the soil underneath, with a slightly different blade. In Suffolk they scrabble the earth.' Somehow Martin managed to pull out the beet and leave the weeds to flourish. Adrian said it was because he was bored with the monotony, because he couldn't feel the art in it. Still, it made a good anecdote in *The Budding Morrow*.

But Mottram was surprised to read that Adrian had chosen to highlight his every mistake rather than show his positive aspects, although he appreciates that made a more humorous story. One injustice that irked him was when he and the land-army girl had been hedging and Adrian elected to burn the heap of rubbish himself. Later Adrian wrote about it as if he had had to clear up after the pair, as if they had simply left the mess, with no intention of finishing the job properly.

John Godbold expresses his indignation at some of the stories, too. 'He stood on a lot of people's toes', he says, 'and all what he writ under me is not all what I've done, it was all the boys, he made one character out of what all the boys did'. But John's resentment is mainly on behalf of his father, depicted as an old stick-in-the-mud. It is a hurt that can still rankle, like embedded shrapnel, almost 60 years on.

It is a hurt that Adrian did not inflict deliberately, but in writing about local events and characters, it was a risk he knew he was taking. He wrote to Rolf Gardiner about this 'common dilemma', saying that if one used real names of people and places one must emasculate the story and tread very carefully indeed, for had it not cost Laurie Lee about £1,000 for his mention of Kidderminster in *Cider with Rosie*? Even as the Savage generation of *Corduroy* was dying out he said he still used the name Colville for them, just in case. According to one of their descendants, only the wheeler dealer nature attached to the Arnold Colville character caused minor offence, although it was correct. The rest of the family were quite happy with their fame; but Adrian wasn't taking any chances.

Later when one or two of his articles caused anger through mistaken identity he would do his best to make amends, and the pain he felt himself at having unwittingly upset his friends gave him sleepless nights and restless days. But dozens more people were delighted to see themselves recorded in his light-hearted, fine-as-filigree prose, and of course, there were some who searched and were disappointed at being overlooked. Adrian couldn't win.

Martin Mottram, who in those days went by the name of Kay, joined the farm in 1943 after writing to Adrian and asking for a job. The son of a professor of physiology, he had followed his parents into the Quaker faith and had registered as a Conscientious Objector. Some saw such principles as cowardice, but he felt that Adrian understood his morals, and even allowed him time off in the midst of haymaking to attend a Quaker meeting in Beccles. He lived with the Bell family, ate with them and was treated as an equal, with a salary of three pounds and ten shillings a week.

Of course, even apparent equals can be ignored and Adrian might take Martin's advice in one aspect and not in another. Martin tells the tale of one such incident, which does not appear in a book.

'Typically the enthusiastic, young and would-be agriculturalist that I was, I read about all the new inventions and gadgets that were coming in; this included the electric fence. I remember commenting upon the necessity of introducing horses and cattle, on the first occasion they would meet the electric fence, in a controlled environment such as a yard, where its "sting" could be learnt more or less at the leisure of the animals.

'Anyway, I was away for a day and Adrian decided to set up the electric fence half way up across the home meadow, ready for when the animals were let out for the first time in spring. Billy Godbold told me that when Adrian let out the animals - horses, cows and a calf or two - they cantered off up the field with tails flying high, as they do when first let out. They went right through the fence and got all tangled up in the wire. They careered around the field trying to get away from this stinging wire until it was switched off'. Billy commented to his master that perhaps Martin had been right, the animals should have been 'trained' first.

Martin ends, 'I noticed that it was some while before I was "let loose" to set up the electric fence anywhere - but in time the job came my way.'

Overall, Martin remembers it as a happy time, although he says that once Marjorie exploded, saying 'I don't know how my husband puts up with you!' He adds that he probably deserved it, was probably arguing with her about something.

Marjorie had a lot to cope with, having three children and Adrian to care for, as well as the farm workers. Rationing was tight - civilians were allowed four ounces of ham or bacon a week, four ounces of butter and twelve ounces of sugar. Adults had to make do with two ounces of tea a week, and while there was no limit on tinned foods, little was available. She did the best she could with the meat and eggs from their farm, the plentiful fruit and vegetables they grew, supplemented by produce from the fields and hedgerows in the form of mushrooms, rose hips, damsons and blackberries. Martin Mottram says he never felt underfed.

As well as conjuring meals from morsels, Marjorie could create children's clothes out of all kinds of scraps. Several little outfits could be made from her own old dresses, and she eked out her remaining clothes with care. She would renovate tattered sheets and blankets by the 'sides-to-middle' method, cutting each one in half then joining the good sides together so it had a seamed centre and the worn sides could be tucked in round the bed.

Marjorie nearly always gave the impression of being capable and calm. She was kind too, and caring, and as generous as possible in those times, recognising that the Bells were better off than many others. Cycling round the village, she would call in on elderly neighbours to see if they were all right, pressing little gifts on them without hurting their pride.

Still, Marjorie's cool was sorely tested one summer when the house was overrun with fleas. It was a common enough occurrence

in rural households but that was no consolation at all. The sight of
her family itching and scratching, the bites red and throbbing on
her children's bare legs made her angry. It was as if her role as a
housewife and mother had been seriously undermined, as if her
children were under attack.

They had a lodger staying with them, a young lady vet who
was working at the Artificial Insemination Centre at Beccles, which
in itself shocked many locals. She offered Marjorie a quantity of
DDT to deal with the pests, but Marjorie declined, fearing for the
children's health. The creatures were hunted down, and every
crevice scrubbed and disinfected until they were exterminated. Her
pride would be restored, and she would be vigilant in future. Village
children never came round to play, and guests entering the house
would be eyed surreptitiously in case they were carrying livestock.

Throughout this time Adrian was still suffering his crippling
migraines and had to spend at least three days a month in bed.
Marjorie was his patient nursemaid and when he was well again
she would ease the load on his brain by taking care of the finances,
leaving notes on parcel tags to remind him of things, and checking
his waste-paper bin to make sure he didn't lose important papers.
At the breakfast table she would be happy to chat about his farming
problems. At the end of the day while she sat sewing, she would
listen to his news. While she was standing at the frothing sink or at
the kitchen table with floury arms, she would be helping him think
of crossword clues, or ideas for the new book he would one day
get round to writing.

She had help in the house from Mrs Scarle who did much of the
cleaning, and from Gladys Godbold who had left school at fourteen
and spent a year living with the Bells. She was paid seven shillings
and sixpence a week, and had to spend two and six of her first
week's wages on a uniform. She still remembers it. 'In the mornings
I had a checky dress and white apron and cap, and then in the
afternoon I had a brown dress with a little frilly apron and one of
those little things that went over your head - I used to hate it. I
used to wear the apron but I wouldn't wear the cap.'

By the end of 1944 the Bell twins were attending Molly Pagan's
school in Beccles which she had set up under the Parents National
Educational Union scheme. Anthea was away; at eight she had
been enrolled as a weekly boarder at an Anglican Convent school
in nearby Ditchingham. The children didn't mix with others in the

area, but played happily enough together. They liked to visit and help on the farm and Gladys would go too, trying her best to keep them out of the mud and out of trouble. Even so, she remembers a time when Martin managed to get a bean wedged up his nose. 'They had to take him to the hospital to have it out', she says. 'I can remember Mrs Bell saying "I'm mortally ashamed of you."'

A typical day for Gladys would consist of preparing breakfast, washing up, scrubbing floors and making beds. The stone-floored kitchen with its Aga cooker and stone sink remain clear images in her mind. For water they used a pump over the sink and the toilet was in an outhouse. At the end of the day she sat alone in the kitchen, knitting or doing odd jobs until it was time for bed.

To her mind, Adrian had some strange tastes, like kippers and jam for breakfast, or a custard-like dish made of 'the beastings' - the first, colostrum-rich milk from a cow that had just calved. But Marjorie did most of the cooking, says Gladys, and worked hard from morning until night.

'Mrs Bell seemed quite frail,' she considers. 'I don't think she was over-robust but I never heard her complain about being ill. She was very thin, but very smart. And she was the backbone of him, she done all the thinking, all the chivvying him along all the time. She did all the housekeeping, all the money side. That was a big house, but she was a very good organiser.'

Of Adrian, she says, 'He was very quiet, you'd never see him ruffled. He was always the same. In fact you couldn't have a good argument with him. He always wore that same old hat and a neckerchief, and he was always whistling 'You are my Sunshine.' He was always miles away, puzzling things out.'

In the final year of the war two new faces arrived at the Old Vicarage and took up residence in the refurbished stable and harness-room. Toni and Carlo, Italian prisoners of war, were allocated to Adrian for farm work, and the former horses' home was made habitable with furniture and curtains. They seemed to settle in as happily as could be expected, although at times they found the cuisine unpalatable.

'Mrs Bell used to feed them,' remembers Gladys, 'but they didn't like what we gave them, like sausages. One day they said cat was very nice with spaghetti - they said they'd eaten a kitten.' It might have been a wicked joke on the poor astonished girl: it might have been true.

Marjorie and Adrian with John Nash, 1934

Cumbria, 1940: Bye Mill, Grayrigg and Adrian (front) helping on the
Blenkharns ' Farm

Aunt Ada, 1930

Martin and Anthea

Bell cousins: clockwise from top left - Sally, Sylvia, Anthea, Martin, Peter,
Judy and a friend, Kate Leavis

Adrian at work on Brick Kiln Farm with Elmore Sayer and Bill Porter
circa 1948

*Photo: Eastern Daily Press*

Adrian and Marjorie, late 1960's

Meanwhile, one of the stables at the farm had become vacant too, because Adrian had been persuaded to do away with one of his horses and by permit had obtained a brand new Fordson tractor. One might expect him to have staunchly resisted the move, but he had seen with his own eyes the job a tractor could do without needing food or rest and, he admitted, 'In fact I see land a good deal better cultivated than it was twenty years ago.' Adrian appreciated the advantages of mechanical efficiency, but he also saw it on humanitarian grounds - better than seeing horses too tired even to stand at the end of a day, when a tractor could do the work easily and feel no pain, he reckoned. And he could curse a tractor without compunction, after it had ground itself into the mire or veered off into a ditch.

He did feel some remorse about selling Boxer, the young horse with an irritating mind of his own. In some ways Adrian was relieved to be rid of the problem animal. The biggest crisis of conscience came when he had to break the news to its former owner, Billy Godbold, who had always seemed soft on the creatures, making excuses for resting them on days when Bell thought they should be working. Adrian describes the day of the sale in *The Budding Morrow*. 'I felt like the perpetrator of some foul crime, and then angry that I should be made to feel like that about my own property.' He pictures Godbold, dressed as if for a funeral as he silently groomed the horse one last time. When he returned later in the day, it was to hang up the empty bridle.

So Adrian moved with the times, and his farming practice changed to embrace the new methods that were forced upon farmers in the necessity for mass production. People like Rolf Gardiner and his Kinship brethren hoped that moderation and sanity would be restored once peace was achieved.

But as the war drew to a close, it was clear that the old ways had gone for good. Now a new order must emerge from the rubble of tradition. There would be no going back.

Artificial manure, artificial insemination, mechanised labour and open-plan farmsteads were changing the face of the countryside and the fate of the countryman.

Adrian's team of farm workers gradually left, either repatriated or moving on to re-start their lives elsewhere. Billy Godbold stayed on for another two years but then he too, broken in health and spirit, moved on. A few years later he was dead.

# 15. End of Chapter One

Adrian wrote, 'I am constantly being told "You should let other people do the sheer spade-work, the machine-minding, the cow-keeping, while you give yourself to higher things". Creative literary work, and so forth. They will never understand that nothing good can come out of a man in that way unless it is squeezed; unless there is a pressure almost as physical as that of a hand crushing the juice out of an orange. And that pressure is only generated by actual frictional contact with life: that that is the very roughage and aliment of prose, of poetry too. And how much frictional encounter in my case with corn and ploughshare, with cow-byre and corn-bin is required to yield a drop here, a drop there, of honest expression? It really takes about ten years of hard living to produce a real book.'

This was in his book *The Flower and the Wheel*, published in 1949 and containing a large dose of philosophy on the state of British agriculture. It states the optimistic prediction that the black industrial cities would one day be replaced by happier communities, with adequate health services and education for all.

Adrian was in a reflective mood. The previous year's harvest had been awful, his oats and barley laid flat by storms. Two years earlier the harvest had been dogged by foul weather and Adrian had been lucky to sell his crops which, he observed, were better than most because he had resorted to cutting it with scythes. But the income merely matched the outlay: he had worked all year for no financial gain.

To cap it all he had also developed a case of chronic dermatitis which was aggravated by just about everything on the farm - straw, dust, cow-hair, everything. The children were all attending private schools, costing £600 a year in fees and it was becoming a struggle to manage. All in all he decided it was time to quit. In October 1949 he sold Brick Kiln Farm, reputedly for a handsome profit.

Looking back, Adrian would say that those wartime years, in spite of the fears and hardships, were happy times indeed when his young family were innocent and playful and he, the farmer, the writer, the man, provided for them all.

Now what? Had he finally got farming out of his system, at least physically? Could he hold on to all the thoughts and sensations, had he lived enough, gathered enough experiences, to write more books?

His famous trilogy of *Corduroy*, *Silver Ley* and *The Cherry Tree* had been republished with complementary illustrations by an artist who, unbeknown to each, had clearly shared Adrian's feeling for the countryside and the farm labourer. Sadly, they could never meet: Harry Becker had died in 1928.

Becker had never reaped the financial rewards of his genius. In fact during his life his talent was hardly recognised, partly because he refused to be drawn in to the elitist clique of the professional art world. But his energetic, almost manic style of banging down paint on paper appeared to capture the moment of toil in the blink of an eye. It was as if the figures were frozen for a millisecond and, when the viewer turned away, they would carry on with their work.

This was no product of a posturing Prima Donna, swanning around a studio and hanging out with the arty crowd. Becker had gone into the fields with the farm workers, spent all day observing, absorbing, their every movement and emotion. He would work up a sweat by proxy, caught up in the thrill of their mutual toil.

Becker's work spoke to Adrian as soon as he saw it. It drew him in, and at once he could hear, smell, feel every sensation the artist had experienced. Adrian had been there; those were his memories on the wall.

Gazing at a picture with Becker's daughter Janet, drinking in the scene, he was told, 'He painted that in about the time you have spent looking at it.' Adrian was enchanted, and Becker's family gladly granted permission for a number of his pictures to be reproduced for the most lavish edition yet of Bell's trilogy. More than seventy were selected, and as the art critic David Thompson wrote in his book on Harry Becker, 'it proved a remarkable marriage of image and text.'

Adrian received many appreciative letters for this venture, but also one that was heaving with invective from Munnings, who did not approve. Becker, said Munnings, 'can't draw horses for nuts.'

But Adrian had more sombre matters on his mind as the 1940s came to an end. His father Robert, now living with Fanny in a

Sudbury care home, was increasingly detaching himself from life. The *Observer* had dispensed with the last of his services during the war, and even though his old friend Garvin had written several letters expostulating on this outrage in the name of economy, Robert had been left with little to interest him or tax him. His deafness curtailed any attempt at conversation and Fanny could offer no companionship in his declining days. His greatest love, music, was reduced to an echo, for now he could hear it only in his head. He took to sitting out in the garden in his overcoat, reading Shakespeare and, said Adrian, 'waiting for death as though it were a bus'.

Robert's transport to the next world arrived to collect him on Friday 2nd December 1949. His obituary in *The Times* paid tribute to his career in journalism, adding that he might have made a name in literature, had he given himself the chance.

His widow Fanny adjusted to life alone among the elderly residents of the Ballingdon Grove home, and seemed to cope well at first. Her husband had gone out like a light, as far as she was concerned. There was no point in regret.

She carried on smoking and joking, reading Nietsche and singing her music-hall ditties. She would write to her favourite son on his birthday, and infrequently at other times, thanking him for his latest book which was doing the rounds of the residents' lounge. There was restraint in her writing, which was executed in pencil. Ever since Adrian had found he had the ability to walk away from her bondage, their relationship had become an uneasy truce.

In the following year when Adrian started writing his diary again, he noted that he was not missing farming as he had the first time in 1929. In a way he was glad to be out of the complexity of form filling, tax reckoning and office work that went with modern day practice. Now he could spend time with the children during their summer holiday, which he couldn't do in the past when the harvest was in full swing.

From what they'd heard locally, Adrian and Marjorie had concluded early on that their children must be sent away in order to gain the best possible education. For Martin that meant Taverham near Norwich, for the girls it was Talbot Heath School in Bournemouth where their mother had attended and Aunt Dorothy was still teaching. Anthea hated being away, and she says she 'wept buckets' every time they were put on the train. But she learned how to survive and be self-sufficient, and at last her older, inner self was being challenged. From Aunt Dorothy she would glean much about her family history, and also she would discover a talent for language that would set her ahead of all her peers.

Martin would suffer at school too, although not so much mentally as physically. In his thirteenth year he developed pneumonia and, as Marjorie spent many anxious weeks seeing to his recovery, she dissuaded Adrian from his notion that the boy should go on to Uppingham. Its spartan facilities could be the death of him, she insisted.

It was not that Martin was a sickly boy, by any means. Unlike his father he revelled in the rough-and-tumble games and sports of school. For many years the three children had been spending holidays with their Uncle Francis in Hundon, West Suffolk, and thoroughly enjoyed themselves. Francis and his wife Barbara were very relaxed about life, they were unconcerned when Martin came home black and stinking from having fallen in the horse pond yet again. Barbara just cleaned him up and sent him back out to play.

At Hundon, in their father's old stomping ground, Martin, Sylvia and Anthea had their three younger cousins to play with and they enjoyed this companionship and freedom. Nobody told them to keep the noise down, far from it - their Uncle Francis was the noisiest of them all, always joking and playing daft. Without a doubt, he inherited that side of his character from Fanny Bell.

Francis and his older brother Adrian were poles apart, and they knew it. During the war Rolf Gardiner had asked Adrian if he thought Francis might work at Springhead, as he was thinking of offering him a job. Adrian's reply was firmly negative, saying he was 'not the man for you. He is as different from me as can be: hard-headed, practical, with no ideas for agriculture but to get on with the job'. Adrian admitted that with his outgoing personality Francis was a good motivator of men, and also relevant to Rolf was the fact he could play the ukulele. 'He's an amusing chap,' Adrian concluded. Francis never got to hear about the job. Rolf was looking for someone who was more serious about the soil.

Sometimes it was a vexing question with Adrian how his brother and sister-in-law seemed to get so much out of life. They always had plenty of food, a bottle of wine now and then, even meals out at times and money to spare for a round of drinks down the pub. Francis would joke that they made do without an extra girl to help in the house and spent her wages instead; several times over, it seemed. In fact Francis was earning a good salary as manager of Justin Brooke's fruit farms, and put his own children through private school without appearing to scrimp and save. His house was well furnished, although Adrian could not work out why he hung on to their mother's old antiques and refused to have them renovated. He assumed it was a touch of Bell obstinacy, combined with a streak of Aunt Ada's eccentricity.

Money was a constant worry for Adrian, this he certainly inherited from the Bell side of the family. In 1950 he was still going strong with the *Times* crossword puzzles and by chance another source of income was presented to him. Lilias Rider Haggard, daughter of the great author and a talented writer herself, had been contributing a weekly article to the local paper the *Eastern Daily Press*. She had decided that it was time to move on, and another of their team, Eric Fowler, was dispatched to Redisham to ask if Adrian Bell might take up the vacant columns. He consented.

His first article, published on 1st April 1950 was entitled *Spring Storm*. He had been digging at dusk, he wrote, admiring the copper-coloured bonfire of the setting sun, when a brief shower stopped him. Emerging from his shelter in the cluttered shed he saw the now primrose-coloured sky and somewhere nearby a tractor spluttered into life. That sound - a tractor engine spluttering to life, damp on the magneto after the rain - his mind still associated that sound with a rainbow. And sure enough, there was one.

In the following weeks, months and years he would treat his readers to an increasingly neat package of anecdotes, thoughts, quotes and descriptions. He shared his experiences from the present day back to his childhood and often explored the work of other writers, from Bunyan to Keats, comparing their vision to the sights around him in his own time and considering their relevance in a fast-changing world.

His style would be expansive to start with, taking half a page to consider a topic from all angles. Gradually he honed it down until he might pick up three subjects and develop each in turn before deftly returning to his opening theme and delivering a parting thought, often with humour. It took days of effort to get it right, and while some weeks the words flowed, at others times they oozed sluggishly. The migraines dogged him still, but with Marjorie's help he met every single deadline.

In the early days Adrian found plenty to write about, with a store of observations from farming and local life in his diary and his head. The characters of the community were many-faceted and whether it was with a squire or a servant, a parson or a pig-man, Adrian could make conversation with equal pleasure. He might sometimes find it hard to put exactly the right words down on paper but he never, ever suffered from talker's block.

A new friendship had been forged during the war, when the Bells had been introduced to Dr Frank R. Leavis the eminent supervisor at Downing College, Cambridge and his more than equal wife Queenie. The two families had exchanged books and children's clothes during hard times, and Adrian had even sent chickens, killed and suitably prepared for the table. The two families had remained in touch since, whether at Cambridge or when the Leavis's were on their regular break at Southwold. Queenie, recorded as a formidable character, is remembered by the Bells as warm and kind, and she got on well with Marjorie. As a mother and wife as well as a scholar, Queenie had the ability to switch onto any subject, whether it be cookery, clothes, children or nineteenth century English novelists.

Talking to Frank Leavis stimulated and stretched Adrian's vocabulary and he enjoyed the feeling that he could be on a level with one so erudite and well versed in literature. Leavis had described Bell's work as naive but 'naive in the right kind of way,' which was a compliment from one of such classic taste.

Adrian recognised that most of the time Leavis's mind moved in a completely different orbit, at which non-alumni could only ever peer as if through a telescope. Leavis, veteran of the Somme, supporter of the great novelists as social commentators, and proponent of 'the novel as dramatic poem,' inhabited a star where logic and reason lived closely with supposition and philosophy. There, criticism was almost an art form, and devotion to the deconstruction of great works set these scholars apart from the everyday world. These people did not engage in small talk.

Leavis himself, idiosyncratic in his teaching methods, irascible and outspoken among his fellow dons, felt the establishment had it in for him because he did not receive all the gifts of recognition that should have been due to him.

Certainly his was a vulnerable world, soon to be overthrown in the populist coup that sought to provide paper qualifications for all rather than higher - some might say elitist - education for the privileged few.

Adrian had not been 'through the system' but he was bright and his knowledge far-reaching. His love of the classics, of the prose and poetry of the great and the minor writers too, gave him a vast store of topics to fall back on. With Leavis, he could take part in a debate on literature and delve into the realms of metaphysics almost as if his past had been different and he hadn't had his education truncated by migraines and a socialist father. So what if he was largely self-taught, that didn't stop him having valid opinions. In everyday life he might shy away from noisy confrontation, but now and again he relished a good bout of friendly, intellectual disputation.

It is said that nobody could beat Leavis in a discussion, but Adrian was nothing if not a trier. He always enjoyed the experience of reaching for that distant star, glittering in the firmament; it left him feeling quite exhausted, but elated too.

On one occasion, having dropped Martin off at his new school in Cambridge and visited Leavis there, Adrian and Marjorie called in to see Vic Savage on the way home. What a different man he was now to the Mr Colville of *Corduroy* days. There he sat, an old man of 70, recently widowed and living alone in the farmhouse he had had renovated for his retirement. Adrian studied him in his grey suit, swinging a pair of horn-rimmed glasses on his finger. He thought back to the man who had commanded a legion of men and who, at Seabrooks, had cut down an apple tree every day before breakfast to clear the old orchard for a tennis court.

The tennis parties he had held, the shooting parties, the days on the hunting field, all gone now. The Vic Savage of today was a peaceable man, he had turned his back on bloodsports and yet the memories of farm activity and sporting days put zest in his voice. Adrian jotted in his diary that night, 'From F.R. Leavis to Vic Savage: what a change. I changed my conversation to match. From T.S. Eliot and D.H. Lawrence to old Borham and the cows and memories of who rode Cantilever.'

One day, when Adrian's spirit of adventure for debate had waned, he would declare that his preferred topics were of the latter kind. But for now he could happily move from one context to another, up and down the social and intellectual scale.

His friendship with Leavis was one small consolation for the hardships of war but Adrian, as much as anyone, hoped never to see another conflict. He signed up to an organisation calling itself the Authors' World Peace Appeal, launched in 1951 with the stated aim of encouraging peace and tolerance. 'We condemn writing liable to sharpen existing dangers and hatred', they declared. 'As signatories we are associated with no political movement, parties or religious belief, but are solely concerned with trying to stop the drift to war'. Writers of every genre, from novels to children's comics, should avoid putting in unnecessary brutality and violence, they insisted. This was easy enough for Adrian, who had never wanted to.

Of course, Adrian was thinking a great deal about children and the future. He wanted to see his own children grow up in a safe world, a fair world, a prosperous one. He was not a great activist, although he did a stint on the local Wainford Rural District Council, mainly to try to push through plans for a water supply for the village. Fellow councillor John Hill recalls that the first time he attended a meeting he noticed Adrian Bell scribbling down notes that he guessed had nothing to do with the agenda. He was right. Councillor Bell was composing a crossword puzzle.

Adrian was also a school governor, first at Hundon where meetings involved a genial chat over sherry and decisions such as whether to allow the head teacher to buy a new brush for the fireplace. In later life he joined the board at the Leman School in Beccles, and finally at Ilketshall St Lawrence, where he greatly admired the headteacher, Brian Patrick.

Adrian was happy to be a part of the Redisham community, he even attended the little church there on a regular basis, and often read the lesson. He never did work out in his own mind what faith he should adhere to, but he had a feeling that there was more to the universe than his mother's atheist view. When he touched the cool stone of an ancient church, he could feel a deep spiritual sensation, as if the energy created by generations of belief were recorded there. On a golden spring day, or on a near-clear night when the illuminated clouds teased the moon, or when storm clouds gathered and jostled overhead, how could he look up at the sky and declare 'there's no such thing as God'?

During the war he had stood in the pulpit and addressed the congregation with a speech on Rogation-tide, which was also known as Farm Sunday. Unfortunately, because the service was being broadcast on B.B.C. Radio there had been hardly any room for locals and regulars to get a pew, they were all taken up by the massed ranks of strangers, but his message went down well with those who could hear.

In his popular days Adrian would be invited to give a number of talks on air, but he always found the studio situation claustrophobic and the microphone an off-putting obstacle to his flow of speech. Similarly he found public speaking a trial, and for preference would rather sit quietly with a companion or two, chatting at length about anything that came to mind.

Adrian's mind was like an erratic car journey, taken without the aid of a map. A few trunk roads were the main highways but a thought could so easily be diverted onto a minor route, twisting and turning through unfamiliar territory in the hope of getting to its final destination. Sometimes it would discover a new view, a pleasant thought hereto unconsidered. Sometimes it would find itself in a dead end. Sometimes it would, without indicating, stop and change direction, even do a u-turn mid-carriageway. Rarely did it follow anyone else's lead. Adrian's driving force was a belief in his own opinion and those around him, his passengers, must trust in his judgement.

In his articles, one follows the circuitous route his thoughts have taken, and, as with any mystery tour, finds to one's delighted surprise that he has brought his reader back to the starting point. His charming style was as intimate as a little vintage car driven in unhurried fashion, a comfortable two-seater, with an all-pervading smell of leather and wood.

Now, with a heavy workload on his mind, Adrian was finding it hard to maintain the Old Vicarage and its two-acre garden. The drains were a constant worry, the roof kept leaking and the sense of isolation was getting his family down. He and Marjorie had bought Anthea her first teenage party dress at Christmas but she had had nowhere to wear it to. When the youngsters did get invited to their first party at nearby Raveningham Hall, the girls were due to decline because it coincided with their return to school. Such had been the dearth of social opportunity that Anthea was inconsolable and after much racking of conscience, her parents resolved to tell her headmistress a lie. Sylvia, laden with baggage and guilt, was sent on alone with the story that her sister was unwell. It was a heavy responsibility for the erstwhile honest girl, and her father was pained to inflict it on her. It was no good, if the family were to have any sort of social life, they must move.

Perhaps their sombre mood was connected to the national grief over the recent death of King George Vl, but generally their conversation was becoming negative and depressing. Wondering what became of the young soldiers who had wanted to farm, Marjorie voiced the opinion that perhaps they had decided against 'burying themselves in the country'. Even she had had enough.

While looking around the nearby towns for a suitable place to establish themselves, Adrian was also being urged to try a new direction in his writing. His publishers, The Bodley Head who were based in London were bringing out a collection of his *Eastern Daily Press* articles in a book entitled *The Path by the Window*, but it only received local reviews and was not given window-space in the big bookshops. Warning him not to expect more than his £125 advance the publishers explained that really, the subject of old-time farming was exhausted.

His gentle observations of life and the countryside no longer appealed to city-dwelling readers so much, this was the 1950s, and people wanted to look forward. Nowadays they were buying plastic goods instead of the old wood and metal, they wanted holidays by the sea, they wanted to watch television, listen to records, write with a biro pen. They wanted to see their lives moving quicker, not harp on about the days when the pace of life was slow and the people were too. This generation had seen the world almost destroyed and now they wanted to live for today. So, said the publishers, could Adrian come up with something more - er - modern?

The word was anathema to him. Frustrated, he paced around the little market town of Beccles, assimilating himself into the bustle of ordinary folk going about their business: shopping, chatting, catching the bus. What did he care about television or the square-eyed masses that worshipped it? What did he have in common with townspeople, who went everywhere in buses and trams, on motorbikes and in sidecars, and increasingly in cars? They never stopped to smell the breeze, or look at a wild flower. They were losing touch with the soil, with their agricultural heritage. And they didn't care.

Here in Beccles, it was another world, still rural, still caring. These were the people he identified with: simple, honest folk, country folk. Look at their faces - there was a man who had served his country, seen his comrades die, come back crippled in body and soul - did he want modern things? The women, brows permanently knitted, an expression they couldn't change after they had lost sons or husbands in battle, or given birth while bombers rumbled over head, and made meals out of nothing. There was pride and nobility in their movements, some shuffling, some limping, some striding out with purpose. He loved to watch their hands, diving into purses, fluttering at the bank counter. Caressing hands, clasping hands, shaking hands, trembling hands. He wanted to live among these people, get to know them, write about them.

Beccles itself was a splendid town. A fellow writer on the *Eastern Daily Press*, Eric Fowler, whose pen-name was Jonathon Mardle, had written about Beccles at length, describing how its red walls and roofs with orange tint gave an impression 'like the reflection of a sunset'. He said the 'fine old Georgian houses that look out over the marshes from the cliff top' stood gracefully alongside the imposing church that served 7,000 souls. Many Beccles houses were populated now, said Fowler, by 'retired business people, and old soldiers and sailors, who have come to Beccles as to a pleasant place in which to rusticate, and cherish its antiques as a hobby.' But there was no faded gentility about the place, he insisted; it was thriving, industrious, with its print works and maltings, and branches of Boots and Woolworths in the New Market. 'Beccles lives in the present' he commented 'but has due respect for its past.' This was the place for Adrian Bell, surely.

Back in Redisham he had been working on an idea for a book that would combine humour and pathos in equal measure. It featured a sweet, slightly dotty little man, some potty spiritualist types, a temperamental woman, her adored son....admittedly it was mostly drawn from his life and family, but heavily disguised. And it wasn't about farming.

He included some passages already used in his *Eastern Daily Press* articles, weaving them in to a story that revolved around Bertram Bee, the shy Scotsman who wrote poetry and loved to play his piano as dawn crept in to his room. It was an intimate portrayal, with detailed descriptions of the man's every belief, his every mannerism. The story begins on an upbeat note but gradually the tempo eases as Bertram grows old, and in the final chapter he dies, leaving behind his music, his books, and a little store of apples.

In writing *Music in the Morning* Adrian had finally dealt with the loss of his father in the best way an author can.

Now he was planning to move away from Redisham and the landscape he had loved almost on sight. He had felt a deep sense of peace in those flat, wind-whipped fields. He had grappled with its soil and shared comradeship with it. He had been a farmer again, a father, a provider. He had spent a lot of time alone, and it had suited him. Now he wanted to be gregarious, to have people pop in for tea and a chat, to do some popping in on others. Yes, he thought as he eased his aching back after an hour's digging in the vegetable plot, it was time for a change.

He and Marjorie eventually found a place that met their requirements. It was in Beccles, a tall house on the busy thoroughfare called Northgate. The back garden ran steeply down to the River Waveney and Adrian could picture himself relaxing by the waterside, composing his crosswords, his articles and a new book.

Only last month he had been confined to bed for a few days with chest pains and he had resolved to live a simpler life, with less physical strain. As he lay there he had grumbled that he would be glad to leave behind their two-acre vicarage with its burden of maintenance and its isolation. Marjorie observed that he must be feeling better if he'd started to complain again.

The others were sad to see their childhood home go, but as Anthea had said philosophically, 'Well, it's *your* eventide home.' And with that cheering thought they signed the papers.

They would have the house completely renovated and in fact had not yet sold the Old Vicarage, so there was much worrying to be done yet. They were also taking on Marjorie's aged parents, and would have them move in with them. That merely added to their long list of concerns.

By the close of 1953 Adrian had heard that school fees were going up, and he mulled over the whole future of education. He hoped the state system would improve soon, and spare parents this agonising decision over whether to entrust their children to an uncertain standard of education as at some local schools he'd seen, or harness themselves to the private system, a headstrong creature which could drag parents through the mire of penury.

Last year Martin had moved on to The Leys School in Cambridge, and adopted a whole new persona. Gone was the little boy in shorts and grey open-necked shirt, in his place ambled a young man in a white, studded collar and smart tweed jacket, his shoes shiny black and his hair matching, slicked down with brilliantine. But the boy inside the smart suit had soon managed to spill ink over the lot, and his parents had had to forget their ideas of new clothes for themselves as they forked out for replacements. The news put Marjorie off her breakfast egg, and Adrian teetered for a while on the brink of a migraine at the thought of the expense.

The Bells were not poor, but they had to be careful. Their meals were home-cooked, frugal and filling. Not for them the candlelit restaurant or even the gingham-check linen of the tea room. When they went shopping in Norwich they would stop in a lane on the way home and get out the canvas camp chairs, and drink tea from a flask.

Yes, he had bought an old car, partly because he could no longer bear to see Marjorie pedalling up the road in all weathers to post off a parcel of the girls' clothes she had washed to save the ten shillings a week the school laundry would charge. The car had been handy went she had gone into hospital for an operation, because then he had been able to drive over to Norwich to see her, and take roses from the garden. He was, as ever, completely lost without her, and if he hadn't been able to visit her his life would have been frozen, and he, spending too much time sitting motionless and numb, might have taken root like the trees that so absorbed him.

Recently he had changed the car for a brand new one, having had to place an order for it five years previously. Such was the scarcity of vehicles now that one needed a permit to buy one and had to sign a pledge not to sell it for two years, when it could still fetch double the original price.

At £750 the new Ford Consul seemed luxurious and grand, or as Martin said, 'Wizard.' He had been embarrassed by his father's old jalopy at school, where his friends' fathers were much better off. Wizard? As Adrian stared at the bewildering array of knobs and dials, it might well have been a magician's car. Radio? What did he want a radio for? Defrost - choke - wipers - he hadn't needed all that on his old Model T Ford in the 1920s. One knob, a steering wheel and two pedals had been enough.

So the Bells were joining the modern world after all. But Adrian's mind was constantly backing up the road to afford him another look at his past. Sometimes an event made him jam on the brakes. One day he heard that Mary Graves, his first fiancee, had died. She had remained unmarried and had died virtually friendless, a few years before.

For a time Adrian's whole life since 1925 was replayed before his mental eye. That day when he had gone into Seabrooks, mucky and sweaty, and been met by those forget-me-not blue eyes shaded under that little netted hat. Her visits to the farm, and his trips to Cambridge where they had tea and cherry-picked their characters to find things they had in common. The engagement, such as it was, and the tempestuous break-up over the pink paint pots in Drift Cottage. What a different world, what a different man he was then.

And now here he was, happily married to a calm and loving wife, with three bright, healthy children. He loved to hear their discussions, maturing from childish topics to adolescent views. It gave him a thrill to take part, to put in his pennyworth and more, even if one of them might point out, 'Father has just read that somewhere.'

No, of course he didn't begrudge the money for their school fees, and they did receive scholarships to help out.

He reminded himself that he had chosen boarding school because it taught self-reliance, leadership and social conscience. Lately they had been worried about Anthea losing weight, especially as one of Marjorie's nieces had died recently as a result of anorexia. Marjorie herself had been taken out of school as a teenager when her weight dropped below seven stones. They insisted Anthea must eat, must look after herself, or there would be no higher education for her. For such an intently studious girl there could have been no greater threat.

At Christmas they were delighted to hear that Anthea, ahead of her time, had gained a place at Somerville College, Oxford. Aunt Dorothy had nurtured her protegee's flair for language well, and she was to be a philologist.

Adrian had always treated his daughter as an adult, they had enjoyed reading the same books and talking about them afterwards. Now he could look forward to some fascinating discussions with his eldest girl, he anticipated. And still they could be equals. Had he not danced the samba with her friend at 1a.m. at New Year? Surely that meant he *was* as young as his daughter at least in mind and spirit. This was the real Adrian Bell, he affirmed: the fun-loving, energetic, confident man, great in company and flirtatious with the girls. He might be fifty-two, but he was mature, not old. To Hell with the headaches, from now on he was going to enjoy himself, starting now, this day, 14th January 1954.

His mother, Fanny Bell, died on January 26th. It was not really sudden, she had been ill for some time, and her nerves had been bad for years. In spite of her bravado she had not taken well to widowhood, and Adrian had not been around to fill the gap. He had kept his distance physically and mentally, he who confessed to himself that in his youth he had only come alive when he was with her. He had felt that bond break when he told her he was to be married. It had been almost tangible, the stretching and snapping of an umbilical thread as they sat by the river in Sudbury.

Now she was truly gone. How would he remember her: as the laughing good-time girl or the vulnerable old woman? She had a habit of smoking rolled-up cigarettes to the very last drag, for which she employed a hatpin to hold them. It was one of the eccentricities the family would always recall, but it also meant her breathing had been laboured and painful for years. It turned out she had cancer too; she must have suffered a great deal. Finally, perhaps mercifully, her heart had failed.

On the evening of her funeral Adrian sat down and wrote page after page in his diary. From the state of the weather to the irony of the three Bell siblings praying together for the soul of a staunch atheist, he missed nothing out of his account. His feelings: morbid ones about the body in the coffin, regretful ones, placating ones. Lately he felt he had been getting on better with her, almost regained some of their old intimacy, but there had been a forlorn, wistful look in her eyes each time they said goodbye.

What was it all about, he pondered, if one so full of fiery passion could end so still in a box? Once he had been a tiny life inside her. Then she had become a force inside him, even when he was far away from her. He had truly been a part of her, and she him.

When Francis had seen her for the last time she had said to him, to her second son, 'We've always been good pals, haven't we?' She had never said it before in all his life. Adrian had always come first. They all knew that.

But Adrian had not got round to visiting her recently, so he had been spared the distress of seeing her last days' fight for breath, as

Stephanie and Francis had. He could remember her in happier times. He could remember how much she loved him, which was too much.

'I have today a curious sense of being alone at last...' Adrian concluded, 'now for the first time I am really cut loose on the sea of time.'

Was he happy or sad about that? He couldn't be sure. But he hoped she would be waiting at the gate when one day he went to join her.

# 16. Riverside Retreat

The Bells moved to Beccles and took with them Marjorie's parents, the Gibsons. Alice Gibson was always called Baba, perhaps a grandchild's variation on Grandma;William was nicknamed Pum for no obvious reason.

It was a big house so there was plenty of room for all, even when the children came home for school holidays. Marjorie's capacity for love and caring seemed to stretch out ever further to embrace everyone who needed it.

One morning Adrian stayed in bed until breakfast-time, thinking about his married life. He had read somewhere that a family is an island of life and to some extent he agreed, although for much of the time he preferred his island to be populated by just the two of them: him and Marjorie. His security in her love made life 'daring and delightful', he considered.

Perhaps it was selfishness, he acknowledged, but she gave meaning to his life, and he needed no others, no community or village commitments to pull him in all directions. He loved his family of course, but he and Marjorie - they were an island of magic, and the sea of life lapped on their shore.

The metaphor was by no means inappropriate. It was not long before Adrian realised that, residing on the bank of the River Waveney, a great deal of life and noise would flow past him, and his dream of placid contemplation by the burbling water would be shattered frequently by the angry buzz of motorboats laden with holdiaymakers. A recent invention, the transistor radio, seemed to be the essential appendage of every young person these days, and many of the hire-boats had one stationed on deck, broadcasting pop music to the nation. Even the floating parade of scantily-clad girls soon palled, and what with the neighbour's dog barking, and the traffic roaring by on the road outside, he was better off indoors.

Only in the summer evenings and in the winter months could he safely emerge and enjoy the golden light on the marshes, the gentle rustle of the reeds and the lonesome cries of the birds. He kept thinking back to the peace and solitude of Redisham - had he made a dreadful mistake?

But the Bells had moved to find company, and they'd found it in plentiful supply. They were constantly in demand for drinks parties, for lunch, tea, or dinner. In the holidays the children were always out and about, and even dear old Pum, Marjorie's father, enjoyed a march around the town by the gasworks.

A favourite haunt of Adrian's was just two doors away from his house in Northgate, at a one-room pub called The Cambridge. It was an idiosyncratic little ale-house with a regular clientele of rum old boys and rare visitors who stumbled in by mistake, never to return.

The landlord, Harry Young, should have been a gift to an author with a humorous bent, but in some ways he was too eccentric to be used as a fictional character. Formerly a circus acrobat, he had gone to sea as a marine engineer and somehow lost a leg in an accident. Still he was a performer on his own little stage, with fearsomely grotty trousers, wild grey hair and a talent for pulling his rubbery face into all manner of expressions in mimicry. Dramatically he would salute Adrian in mock respect, and roar with laughter at his own jokes.

In his diary, Adrian described the lounge-cum-saloon bar of the Cambridge as a dismal, dirty room with overflowing ashtrays and soggy bar towels. Only the most stalwart old customers kept coming back, and one day in July 1960 Adrian would note that he had sat alone with his half pint while Harry bemoaned the death of another regular. 'Rouse gone, Baxendale gone,' he wrote. They were diminishing fast.

In the days of the old wherrymen, Adrian contemplated, this place was no doubt bustling with doughty characters straight from the quay at the end of the road. They hadn't worried about the decor of the place, or the fact that it could only serve beer, for that was all they wanted. Now the wherries were nothing more than ribs sticking out of the mud at low tide and the ale-swilling, story-telling fellows who had quaffed and quanted with equal gusto were gone too. Today's discerning customer wanted more than a warm beer in a dingy room, they wanted short drinks and long chats about the latest cars and gadgets. As Harry was quick to point out, they would find no spirit in the Cambridge.

But among the regulars was an older man with whom Adrian struck up an unlikely friendship, for at first impression one would have said they had little in common.

Field Marshall Sir Claude Auchinleck, born in 1884, had been in the thick of the action during the Second World War as Commander in Chief of the Middle East, although historians would look back critically on some of his decisions. Sometimes it was pure bad luck that had seen him in positions of authority when the Allied forces were too weak or ill-trained to succeed.

All across North Africa the men in his command had performed a terrible dance of death with Rommel's mighty army, and countless thousands had been killed or captured. Auchinleck could be as stubborn as his colleague Montgomery in resisting Churchill's orders to attack before he felt ready; like 'Monty' he felt the responsibility for keeping his men alive, and twice they had gained the advantage at El Alamein. Later as Commander in Chief in India Auchinleck had been responsible for troop training those who would drive the Japanese out of Burma, and throughout his time in Beccles Adrian noticed that almost every old soldier seemed to have served under him, or at least had met him during the war.

In private Adrian always referred to Auchinleck as The Auk, and his sister, Mrs Fay Chevenix-Baldwin was called Goose by her own family.

The Auk's formative years were as different from Adrian's as could be imagined, but the two did find plenty to talk about in the bar of The Cambridge, where they set the world to rights. Despite at first being a little overawed by this renowned military figure, Adrian felt compassion for the great old warrior, whose wife had left him and so he would usually be going home to an empty house and having fish fingers for dinner.

In 1957 Adrian's son Martin would become a military man too, of sorts, when his period of National Service with the Suffolk Regiment would take him away to Nicosia in Cyprus. Martin admits that the greatest shock for him was being shouted at by the sergeant majors - he had been brought up in a placid household, and he wasn't at all used to being ordered about.

He wrote home to his mother every week, although he later destroyed all the letters when he re-read them and could hardly recognise the 'stuck-up Tory youth' with intolerant views on the locals. His parents needn't have worried about him facing dreadful dangers, he was in the intelligence section which mostly required writing up log-books or plotting on maps or, as he puts it, 'going on gentle little patrols and having coffee in Turkish villages'. Still, the training in self-preservation would come in handy one day.

In the same year Adrian and Marjorie saw their daughter Anthea married. She had phoned them at eleven o'clock one night from college and told them she was engaged. They didn't see how they could argue, she was a determined girl, but they weren't overjoyed at the news. She had always shown a horror of domesticity and had once insisted that if she ever had babies she would have to employ a nanny so she could get on with her reading.

The hoped-for conversations by the fire had not materialised for Adrian and his daughter, she had proved far too brainy for him and, with customary teenage disdain, far too scornful of his contributions. He had written an article about how she and a college friend had quashed his attempt to join in one of their discussions about the origins of words. First they had ignored him. When he repeated his point, Anthea had said, 'We heard you, Father'. It had been like a body-blow to his ego, a karate-chop to his illusion that he and his daughter had common ground in their love of language.

Well now at nineteen she felt grown-up enough to be a wife. Her chosen partner was very nice and very clever, but he was also Jewish, so to her parents' disappointment the couple exchanged vows in Lowestoft Register Office with the shouts and smells of the nearby fish market competing with the service until they shut all the windows. Adrian wrote an article about that, too.

They still had Sylvia who, having decided that she did not want to undergo a similar metamorphosis from adoring daughter to self-sufficient stranger, had opted not to go to university and chosen instead a secretarial career in London. She was a dutiful girl, a caring person who naturally took her father's arm to see him across busy roads, and walked straight into the kitchen to offer help when she arrived for a visit.

Adrian's diary breaks off soon after the death of his mother, and resumes in 1956. Another symbolic event not recorded therefore was the death of Victor Savage on 15th July 1954. One can imagine the effect this would have had on Adrian, whose life to date had been influenced to such a large extent by his year with 'Mr Colville.' His tribute to his late friend appeared within an article in the *Eastern Daily Press* entitled *A Late Harvest*, on 7th August 1954.

He wrote, 'This summer between the earing of the wheat and harvest, he died. It seems like the end of a chapter...'

After pondering in print over the changes in farming, he concluded, 'While fields are sown and reaped, I shall remember him.'

In spite of all the diversions, those Beccles years were productive ones for Adrian. He followed up the largely autobiographical novel *The Balcony* with the next phase of Roland Pace's life, and the title *A Young Man's Fancy* gives a good clue to its content. Dolores was exorcised between the pages, portrayed as Miranda the drama queen on whom Roland had a ridiculous crush. Adrian, with the benefit of a middle-aged man's hindsight, was feeling now that the whole affair had been rather foolish. He left Roland Pace happily married to Naomi, and trying his hand at farming again.

His next book, *A Suffolk Harvest*, was an edited collection of his articles from the *Eastern Daily Press*, and in the meantime he wrote the last part of the Roland Pace life-story. In *The Mill House*, Roland and Naomi go through some very testing times including a separation. The author's note at the front of the book emphasises that this is a work of fiction, and that the events in it are not those of Adrian's own life. Of course, many of them were, but it was certainly a tangled web of truth and fiction, and Adrian was well advised to make sure people didn't mistake Naomi for Marjorie, who would certainly never leave him.

As if to set the record straight, Adrian then produced his official autobiography, *My Own Master*, published in 1961. Many of the people and places were given their real names this time, but Adrian felt he should still protect certain identities, or couldn't contradict a previous book. Of course, he still couldn't resist telling a good story, and so, aided by his natural tendency to meander or go off at a tangent, he presented to his readers a delightful work of selective honesty. By the end of the year it had sold 6,000 copies.

If Adrian had lain to rest in print his former days of farming, he could at least keep them alive in conversation. His children had long ago grown bored of his stories of 'Old Coote and the stacks he built' or 'When I ploughed my very first furrow'. But Adrian would find, especially in new company, a kind of desperate shyness would engulf him and a torrent of reminiscence would flow forth. There was just no stopping him, and afterwards he would feel embarrassed.

He found himself becoming increasingly uneasy. Yes, they had wanted company, and there was no doubting the change in Marjorie since she had been enjoying such an active social life. But it seemed that Adrian had swapped the burden of household and acreage for a burden of popularity. He was really not a gregarious person. All the heat, chatter and standing up involved in a social occasion made his head spin. He much preferred to slip away up the River Waveney in his little rowing boat and burrow into the reeds, where he could compose his crosswords or just collect his thoughts in peace.

During this period his closest friend Henry was a frequent visitor. As a fellow author of country topics who had similarly seen the public's taste for the subject wane, C. Henry Warren could commiserate with Adrian on the difficulties he faced.

Henry's home was in the Essex village of Finchingfield, seen by many as the epitome of the picturesque, with its duck pond and bridge, its quaint cottages, and its fine church. But Finchingfield was blighted by U.S. Air Force jets that roared overhead, shuddering the thatched cottages and upsetting Henry's nerves. The trouble was, he couldn't find a buyer for his house for the same reason.

After a visit to Beccles in 1958 Henry wrote to their mutual friend and Kinsman in Husbandry, Rolf Gardiner. The kinship had petered out by then, although Rolf still kept the torch burning in the hope of one day re-igniting wider interest. Henry wrote of his impression that Adrian was suffering from his suburban life: he said he felt Adrian was pining, if not for farming, at least for the countryside, where the well-spring of his inspiration lie. But Marjorie was refusing to move again, and in a way there were benefits for Adrian too, in that small town community. Adrian fitted in, and managed to conceal his grief at being cut off from his beloved landscape, except to his closest friend.

Henry added that Adrian had been talking about finding an old shed in a field, a hovel of some kind, to which he could retreat. This is borne out by Adrian's diaries, but he never did find anything suitable. In fact, he wrote an article in which he grumbled about going house-hunting with his friend, and as they drove around he found they had less in common than before in terms of taste in music and books. Henry had suggested he was a fossil, and Adrian had begun to wonder if he might be right.

Of course, one of the reasons why Marjorie said they couldn't move again was because they now had her mother to consider. For Adrian, this added responsibility was becoming another prickle to his sensitive skin. His father-in-law Pum, mild-looking old man, set in his pedantic, military ways, had not been Adrian's ideal house-mate. He could begin a conversation at breakfast about band music, or people he knew in South Africa, or about the fact that all journalists incorrectly wrote about the Life Guard in the plural, and he could pick up the subject from where he left off at intervals throughout the day. Adrian, whose mind had driven off and was far away over the hills, was constantly wondering what on earth his father-in-law was talking about.

But after the death of Pum in 1957 he wrote with retrospective affection about the old man, whose army habits had never been broken. In the article *A Lick and a Promise* he described his shoe-shining ritual. 'In his day the scullery table became an altar to the rite, with last week's Sunday paper spread as cloth, and the whole apparatus from the brush box first carefully laid out on it - three sorts of brushes, cloths, a bone, and an ancient, stump-bladed dinner knife, its handle as yellow as an old tooth...By the time every process had been gone through, and the bone had done mysterious work, they shone like good deeds in a naughty world.'

Adrian's widowed mother-in-law, Baba, was a different prospect altogether. The loss of her husband merely added to her heap of sorrows, accumulated over the decades. As a young girl she had been lively and bright, but her publican father, to her life-long shame, had drunk himself into an early grave. Married before she was really a woman, she had had her first baby at the age of nineteen while they were living in South Africa. The loss of her youngest child, later the suicide of her son, the death of her anorexic granddaughter - she had had more than her fair share of tragedy. Such was her resentment of Pum's army life that she destroyed every document and photograph relating to it, including those he was most proud of, from when he took part in the Trooping of the Colour. That purging of the past did nothing to release her from her memories and regrets. She retreated into her room and waited for her own time to come.

Marjorie became almost completely tied to the house. She could not go out for long anywhere, because she had to get meals ready, make beds, do the washing and a hundred other tasks. And they never knew what Baba might do next. She had taken to rummaging in drawers and pattering about the house before collapsing, exhausted, in her bed. Also they had a cleaning lady who was scared of spiders and frequently the quiet of the house would be rent by a shriek. It was becoming a house of challenging behaviour.

Adrian was trying to keep up with a commitment to produce three or four crossword puzzles a week as well as his articles for the *Eastern Daily Press*, book reviews for the *Sunday Telegraph* and, when he could, another novel. The pressure was weighing him down and he walked a tightrope above the abyss of migraine, slipping into it sometimes twice a month. Still he was managing to inject humour and warmth into his work, but he must try to cut down, he resolved.

Of course he was not getting any younger, either. In 1960 Adrian had attended a reunion of the old boys of Glengorse School and found he was the oldest one there bar one: Sir Hugh Beaver, Managing Director of Arthur Guinness and Co. Ltd, who was ten years his senior. It was a sobering experience.

But these years were not all gloom by any means. Beccles out of season was a delightful place for Adrian, with its narrow streets of old houses to explore, and the river, when quiet, was a source of such peace and beauty, he could sit up in his boathouse and watch the panorama, or walk the open common land, muffled up against the blustering wind. The great church of St Michael would call out to the congregation to come and worship, and its peal reverberated around the old town, bouncing off the narrow street walls and jumbled red roofs. Adrian would stop and enjoy the rousing sound, but rarely responded to the call.

Even the dreadful traffic problems gave him some inspiration. The street he lived in, Northgate, was only designed for horse-drawn carts to pass and yet it was open to two-way motor vehicles, causing frequent mayhem when two lorries tried to negotiate it from either end. On one occasion there was the not-unusual bang outside, followed by a tinkling cascade as a milk float shed its load into the street. Adrian made a good story out of that one, stretching the point to depict the scene as one where the street flowed with milk and honey.

Adrian was a charmer, an amusing raconteur to those who hadn't heard the stories too often already, and above all he was a gentleman. Not in the sense his mother had hoped perhaps, but his manners were exemplary, he always treated women with respect, and that quality in itself had a magnetic effect. At any social gathering he would feel more at ease chatting to women than to men, and he had a large circle of female friends. In turn he admired each for their own attributes.

There was Mary Treadgold, rich daughter of a rich man, globe-trotting, fur-toting, scent-trailing, she wafted in and out of his newspaper articles as 'Louise', whose visits could be tense at times but gave him plenty to write about how the other half lived. There was the author Lilias Rider Haggard, her sister Angie and friend Margaret at Ditchingham near Bungay. Phyllis Nicholls was another friend, a widow who gave him meals when Marjorie was away, and chatted with him about her fifty acre apple orchard. At the other end of the spectrum were Jill and Tess, who had both given up good jobs in London and taken to the land and were now living hand-to-mouth in a hovel, a crumbling mill cottage in the nearby village of Westhall.

In between was a host of middle-aged ladies who were blossoming with the new 'permissive' society - or rather, the permissiveness had been there all along, but society had been more discreet about it - and sometimes the conversation would become personal, even sexual, with no harm done at all. If Adrian complimented a woman on her figure, even told her she had marvellous breasts, she accepted it with pleasure, recognising it as the judgement of a connoisseur.

Adrian was no voyeur. He saw no appeal in ogling at beauty pageants, preferring instead to admire the female form in a becoming frock, going about its normal duties, stretching up to dust a picture-rail, bending to pick up a sock. Hands arranging flowers or turning out a cake, all of these movements were like poetry to an old-fashioned romantic heart.

Were all the pill-protected youngsters of today sleeping around? 'Well brought up ones don't' he and a friend agreed. And yet Adrian had suggested to Mary Treadgold that only one in a hundred women was naturally passionless, the others were so by the man's fault. Mary had responded that she didn't think there was even one who was passionless, or didn't have the potential for passion. All it needed was the right man.

Thank God he and Marjorie were still passionate, he thought. His father's old friend, the author S.L. Bensusan had once said that physical love tended to turn into affection in later life, which was just as good. Adrian had had his doubts at the time and was still in no hurry to find out. In fact, he sometimes had a sneaking regret that he had 'saved himself' for his life partner.

Adrian's own children were certainly 'well brought up,' and in August 1961 Sylvia married a young curate, Colin, whom she had known for some time but had courted formally for only a matter of weeks. Although she told her parents that she had accepted his proposal, Colin had then followed traditional procedure by coming over to ask her father's permission.

Adrian, stressed to the point of another migraine by the time they arrived, had been concerned that the couple would be poor when Sylvia gave up her job but he could see they were right for each other. Again, his daughter could be very determined, but he went through the formality of giving his approval. At the ceremony in Beccles church, he felt the swelled emotions of every father who walks his beautiful, white-gowned daughter up the aisle.

As a mark of Colin's sense of humour, it would become a family joke that, Sylvia and Martin being twins, she would always refer to Adrian as 'Our Father.' Thankfully, he would not be in Heaven for some years yet. But he found it ironic that whenever he suffered a migraine, his atheist mother Fanny used to chant 'And on the third day he rose again...'

That was where Adrian's omnipotence ended. Certainly Martin's view of his father's almighty wisdom had faded many years earlier. Martin was a lad of his time, whizzing around on his Lambretta when he wasn't studying at Cambridge and hanging out with the 'Footlights' crowd including David Frost, the son of the Beccles Methodist minister. Adrian felt uncomfortable in young Frost's company, wondering if he was being watched and if he might see a caricature of himself on *That Was The Week That Was*. The lad seemed very sure of himself, telling Adrian that he could now get a 'David Frost haircut'. On one occasion over late-night coffee at Adrian's house, David and his girlfriend made up a crossword puzzle for *The Tiimes*, starting with David Frost as one answer, and gonad as another. Adrian did not use it.

Adrian was now greatly troubled by the shadow of imminent nuclear obliteration. All the world seemed to be holding its breath as Khruschev and Kennedy postured and threatened, and in October 1962 news of the Cuban missile crisis left everyone shocked by the narrow escape from all-out war. As Adrian bent to pull out a weed from his garden, he wondered if that move might be his last. The end could come at any time; he was completely powerless, just like every other innocent citizen of the planet.

He wanted to voice these fears, to vent his outrage at this idiocy but any discussion on politics or world affairs with his son left him dazed and frustrated. Martin's conversation these days went beyond metaphysics, it bordered on quantum mechanics. What was real and what was abstract patriotism? What was real and abstract anything? He wasn't sure at times.

Adrian's form of defence was to change tack, even to contradict the stance he had just taken, and Marjorie suggested that he should try to avoid conflict with his son. He saw it as censure, a taking of sides.

Retreating to his room in curmudgeonly mood he wrote in his diary of Saturday 16th December 1961, 'Sometimes I feel that discussion of ideas is forbidden me. After a first eager questioning regarding what the young are thinking about this and that - Communism, Religion, Morals, the Common Market, during which I put forward ideas that have been fermenting in my own mind, new syntheses, further questionings of basic assumptions - I relapse, feeling rather like a boxer who was glad to hear the bell go at the end of the round - dazed, head humming with reverberations.'

He concluded that if he were not to muddy the waters of family harmony, he would have to stick to casual comments about the passing day... 'To be the old man, pater, in the chimney-corner, chiefly the friend of nature, suits me best, is without strain, nourishing not depleting. So I once more resolved today!' This was a dudgeon of the highest order.

Like any young man, Martin was finding his feet in the world. He had ideas of becoming a teacher and was also very active in Liberal politics, but he was starting to write articles for the local press too, and, encouraged by Kenneth Matthews of the B.B.C., was becoming involved in television reportage. He had numerous female friends and his parents watched with interest to see if anything permanent might develop, but the young man was too occupied with his ambitions to consider settling down. Adrian, grumbling to himself, reckoned Martin had the right idea, staying free of emotional bondage.

When Martin was home his mother was only too pleased to be doing his washing and mending his clothes. She was proud of her boy, she went along to hear his political speeches, and she had argued that Adrian really should buy a T.V. set so that Martin could see what was being shown, and so help his career. But last year another new interest had been born for her - a baby son for Anthea and her husband Anthony. Straight away, Marjorie had packed her case and sped off to London to help.

More than anything else, Adrian hated being without Marjorie. A lot of the time he felt niggled that she had so many diversions from her husband's needs, but at least she was with him physically. When she was out of the house, he was completely at sea. Now his walks on the common were undertaken in 'furious loneliness', he said. He could hardly be bothered to eat, he couldn't find the energy or the will to work, he could barely see any point in anything. It was only when all the food and milk went off that he realised how Marjorie had to cope without modern conveniences. He went out and bought a fridge.

The worst part about it all was that it didn't seem to bother Marjorie to be separated half as much as it did him. And when she came back full of talk of baby milk, baby temperatures, baby this and baby that, he wondered if she had really missed him at all.

Throughout these years of the early 60's Adrian's emotions were riding on a stormy sea. They lifted high on the news that *Apple Acre* was to be reprinted by Brockhampton Press for whom his son-in-law worked, and came crashing down again when he heard that his last book *A Street in Suffolk* had been remaindered as sales had fallen off. The problem was that people were reluctant to buy a book that was a compilation of newspaper articles they had already read.

His 60th birthday had been a tough one to take too, 'The last stop before the terminus', as he called it. Ominous too was an exhibition in 1961 of old farm tools in which most of the exhibits were artefacts from Adrian's past. Adrian was invited to give the opening speech and he stated, 'Time goes very fast these days'. He called upon those gathered to spare a thought for those who had handled the worn old implements; he could have been saying 'and spare a thought for me...' But worse was to come.

Ron Carton, who had been editor of the *Times* crossword puzzles since the start, did not live to see Adrian compile the

10,000[th] puzzle in 1962. Harry Young, the eccentric publican was taken quite suddenly, and The Cambridge pub was closed for good. And, to Adrian's immense sadness, his brother Francis passed away.

The happy, larking 'ne'er-do-well' younger brother, the man so full of sunshine, succumbed to lung cancer even as he was planning one last party. If ever there could be a reminder of Adrian's own mortality, it was surely the loss of his younger sibling. Francis was only fifty seven. The last few years of his life had been hard, he had lost his job and struggled to make a go of turkey farming, but at the end his widow was left in a tied house with only £30 to live on. She, Barbara, would be helped by her father to buy a small boarding house and Adrian would lend a hand too.

His mother Fanny had left all her money to Francis, perhaps it had been her way of saying sorry for never having loved him as much as Adrian, and never having given him the same opportunities. But Francis, typically, had divided up the money and given the others their share. Adrian had been very grateful for the cash at the time, but now he was better off, he returned it to Barbara. He could do no more for the man who had always felt second best.

In his grief, Adrian might have turned naturally to Marjorie, and she would certainly have sympathised, but still she had other distractions. So instead he turned his thoughts inward, where a special relationship had been rekindled and, by the embers of that old flame, he could warm himself.

Perhaps, forty years ago, he had been foolish to love Dolores. Now, in the depths of his misery, a touch of foolishness was just what he needed.

On a rare holiday with Marjorie in Bath in the spring of 1963, Adrian had looked in the local phone book and by chance found Mrs D. Denison listed as living in Daniel Street. While his wife took an afternoon nap, Adrian had gone to find out if Mrs Denison would welcome a visitor from her past.

# 17.  A Bobbing Balloon

Even at the age of sixty-nine Dolores was still one heck of a woman. When Adrian's tentative knock at the door was answered, the voluptuous figure in tight black trousers and sweater was unmistakable. Her face, he registered, looked just the same as it had thirty years ago, when they had last met.

But Dolores didn't recognise him at first.

'Dolores,' Adrian said. 'Do you remember - Arcady, the two stone greyhounds in Drayton Gardens?' Her expression remained blank.

He leaned in and kissed her on the cheek, startling her. 'Adrian' he added. And then she remembered.

It was not the great reunion he might have hoped for, as they sat in her sumptuous room and talked. Dolores had read *A Young Man's Fancy* containing the dismissal of their affair as a boy's calf-love for a flamboyant older mistress. She was not pleased. In fact, she had been hurt terribly, she said.

Only after Adrian's abject apologies and excuses did she consent to forgive, and then her light shone on him again, driving out the dark shadows and bringing colour back into his world. She had always lived in the poem of those past days, she declared, and he agreed that he had too. She traced a groove beside his cheek that time had etched and told him 'I rather love that' and in turn he loved the blue vein on her wrist.

The restoration of their gallant affection was a cosy rug of relief wrapped around Adrian's weary shoulders. He relaxed and smiled, and his balloon floated high on a cloud of promise. He would come again next day and bring Marjorie, and Bobby Baker would be there too, and Adrian would gather together his past and present in a happy circle of friendship.

They came for coffee, and Adrian was delighted to see that Dolores had lit a fire of pine cones, as she had in the old days. Instantly he could picture again the glowing glasses of wine, the ravishing colours of the fabrics she sewed, the brown tulips - the latest fashion flowers - in a vase.

Her hair, still so thick and black, her eyes so full of passion and challenge, her artistic gesturing, all of these things had caused his mother to call her a dangerous woman. Yes, she was, to a young shaver, but what might she be now, to a man of sixty-one?

On the way back to the hotel he tried to tell Marjorie about the way it had been, about the secret language they'd shared and the unspoken knowledge of each other's understanding. Nature has a message for those who can hear it and they had listened together, clasping each other. Those pine cones she'd burned were special, he said; like old love letters, flaming in the grate. 'What sillies you were', smiled Marjorie, tucking her scarf around her neck.

But Adrian would not have his feelings so easily tied down this time. Back in Beccles he retreated into a world of his own, and his diary became a dispatch to Dolores, telling her of his day's activities, his thoughts and emotions. They wrote to each other in reality too, and she sent him a scrap of green-gold fabric from her dress. She wished she could be with him she said, and he wished it too, heartily and quite amusingly; 'I'd gladly put my feet down off the sofa and move over' he noted, 'so you could have the best end of it, where the springs are still springy.' Such is the sacrifice for love.

All of those past days returned to his mind again and again. Even as he prayed for his brother's soul in church at the funeral, he could not make sense of the incantations. He couldn't help feeling they were all missing the point. Surely the answer to the Great Secret wasn't here inside these stone walls, or bound up in dogma and cant? Outside in the air, in the soil, the plants and creatures, that was where the truth lay, unspoken but tangible.

If death was waiting to step out from behind a tree and hold up its hand to him, he must choose his route carefully and enjoy all the gifts of life and nature while he still could.

So he bought a bike, and went in search of wilderness. He would pedal away from the town, from his family responsibilities, from his popularity, and go and sit on a verge among the weeds and be himself once more. He would go out to Redisham and try to re-invoke the spirit of those days. He could hear again all the chinks and clanks, thuds and grunts of the farming scene, and feel again the tingle in his sinews that told him there was more to man than just flesh and blood.

It pained him to think of how his family life had been, and compare it to the way they lived now. Freed from his own maternal domination, he was still constrained by Marjorie's mother and also he had to share his wife with the younger generations and their own brood too. He loved them all, of course. But every time he saw that thoughtful look on her face, and knew she would soon say 'I think I ought to go,' his morale would crumble.

He had torturing memories of what had been said of an uncle and aunt, that 'he follows her about everywhere - can't bear to let her out of his sight: it's quite embarrassing for her.'

'So what' thought Adrian. 'A man's romantic mind continues in him as when he was young, while a woman in middle age changes to, at best, a maternal emotion for the man - he's another "son" - unless it is indifference as in our mothers to our fathers. So what is one to do? How to face these further partings and still retain one's dignity?'

He knew that when she returned from her mercy missions she always brushed aside his fears and made him feel secure again. But would they ever be as close as they were in those early years? Could they resurrect their love? Did she even want to?

Sometimes it seemed as if she had lost patience with him and all his little peccadilloes. When he clumsily spilled his coffee, she had scolded him. 'You are behaving like a child' she had exclaimed. Adrian had been utterly hurt and bewildered.

Perhaps Marjorie was overdoing it, he considered. Sylvia had recently had a baby too, and in the final stage of her pregnancy Adrian had been afraid of seeing his lovely daughter so distended. It was a relief to find her still smart and cheerful as ever. But she had a bad time of it giving birth and Adrian wondered if the baby would suffer in later life as a result of its trauma, as Dr Hadfield said Adrian had. Would baby Mark be prone to headaches and night terrors, as he had been?

Memory was such a strange thing. Climbing a ladder to prune a tree, he recalled how, in Bath, he and Dolores had talked about the minutiae of the scenes they had witnessed together in their shared past. He recalled a ladder propped against a stack, seen in 1936 in Suffolk. 'A red ladder' Dolores had added. It was in her mind's eye too, cherished for all those years as something they had seen together.

The metaphors flowed through his mind once again - she was the seed pearl in the gracious old shell of the city, he had been a chrysalis for the past few years, now the butterfly was emerging.

With the Muse upon him, Adrian tried to put some of his feelings down on paper, but failed time and time again. 'There is something gnawing at me - something sensuous, lyrical as in youth, a sense of the eternal moment, full of eternal energy,' he noted. But he just couldn't get a book out of it.

He wondered if his family could see the light in his countenance or the wings on his heels as he tried to hold himself remote in spirit and yet play the role of husband and father as required. A neighbour did comment that he appeared to be looking younger and more bouncy of late, and he replied that he was enjoying a new feeling of freedom now that his family had grown up.  To Marjorie he quoted Virginia Woolf, 'I don't believe in ageing: I believe in ever altering my aspect to the sun.' And Marjorie replied, 'All the same, she ended in the river.'

Lucky he had not let on that he was feeling so elated because he had found his love again after a gap of 35 years. It was the 'need to adore' that the Christian mystic Chardin had warned about - 'the more man becomes man, the more will he become a prey to this need.' Yes indeed, and moreover, it was the naughtiness of playing truant, if only mentally, from his marital fidelity that was providing the frisson just now.

He did still try to adore Marjorie. On her birthday he slipped out and bought flowers, but when she came to the door and saw them, her pleasure was brief. She was in the middle of putting ointment on her mother's bottom, she said. It rained all day that day, and Adrian worked on his crossword puzzles.

He still adored his children too, of course. His relationship with each of them had matured and he enjoyed his status as grandfather, at arm's length. The antics of the little ones would give him plenty of material for articles over the years.

Dolores now cancelled a planned trip to Beccles, so Adrian determined to go and visit her in Bath. Having made arrangements for Baba, 'the old lady' as Adrian now referred to her, he and Marjorie escaped for a few days in the West Country. His intention was to see Dolores' world and bask in her exotic friendship one more time.

The snag was, in the meantime she had read his autobiography *My Own Master* and his description of the 'absurd, short-lived affair' with the mustachioed temptress. He had really done it this time. A great deal more grovelling was needed before she would forgive him again. He could hardly tell her that he'd thought she must be dead when he wrote it.

Anyway, after nearly an hour's tirade Dolores' anger was spent and soon she was regaling him with tales of young men who adored her, including the son of friends. Adrian considered it possible, but his view was becoming increasingly objective as she continued with a tale of how the male shoe-shop assistant had fallen in love with her feet.

In the final day of their holiday, he and Marjorie were to be found strolling together in the sunshine and loving each other in the intimacy of their hotel room. Adrian had come back down to earth, and found that his own heaven was still there, in his marriage. Dolores was a woman who could never be satisfied, he concluded.

But now he resolved that they must move from Beccles and get back into the countryside where he belonged. He would later write that his heart had grown small and hard and shrivelled as a prune-stone in the town; that it took him ten years to extricate himself from the mistake he had made. Indeed it was late in 1964 that the Bells, minus mother-in-law, moved to Barsham, which was little more than a hamlet just outside the town.

The move had not been easy, with Baba threatening to finish herself in the river, but Marjorie had arranged for a local woman to take her on. Martin had already moved out by then. First he had been working as a reporter for the B.B.C. in Norwich and now he was transferring to London, from where he would soon be travelling all over the world.

So they were alone again, if one excludes the procession of builders and decorators that were necessary to make the place comfortable. For Crake's Hall as their new home was called was another wreck, uninhabited for some time, but Adrian said its windows 'gazed at me with the appealing patience of an old horse's dusked eyes' and he fell in love with it. Marjorie, although doubtful, stuck to her promise that she would live anywhere so long as it made him happy.

And he was happy at Barsham, truly happy again. Except for the odd occasion when Marjorie would take off to help one of their offspring, and he would be left alone to eat cold chicken and huddle miserably in his empty bed.

Soon he settled down to absorbing all the glory of the countryside that he could now find right on his doorstep. Their detached house was surrounded by fields and common land, there were great open skies offering a wide screen of moving scenery, and hedgerows of tangled twigs, nests, webs and creeping flowers. The electricity pylons marching across his view didn't bother him, he was willing to accept them as a necessity for the benefits of warmth and light.

Adrian had space in which to stroll, and gaze, and think. He thought about his parents, and their strange relationship. He recalled his youth, and his youthful resurrection in 1963 when he had projected love onto a whitewashed image of Dolores. He should like to re-capture that afflatus, but wondered if he could manage it without the impetus of one such as she. Certainly no real woman could maintain that fantasy for him.

Even so, he could look at Marjorie and see her as still beautiful. His love for her was not the euphoric kind that inspired him to gush words on to the page, but it was deep-rooted and genuine. So what did he really want? Who was the 'real' Adrian Bell?

When Adrian looked in the mirror he saw a thin-faced, ageing man with a droopy eye and uncertain smile. Surely *that* wasn't the real Adrian Bell? His father Robert had written a poem on the subject when he was at a similar age, published in his book *Afterthoughts* in 1929.

## We Two

If I, whose head the signs of winter show,
Met you, my Self of forty years ago
    (A ghostly sort of tete-a-tete
      In the dim corridors of Fate),
However distance may enchantment lend,
I wonder if I'd like you, O my friend!

I am not sure: I fear that I can find
No traces of the philosophic mind:
      You're ignorant and rather vain;
      Your views are crude, your talk inane
(Mostly of girls and dances you've been at):
I do not like your morals, or your hat.

Yet here we are together, hopeless twins,
And shall be judged for one another's sins
  (I for your errors of the start,
  You for my deeds of harder heart);
Since in so many things we disagree,
Which one of the two of us is really Me?


By coincidence an old acquaintance of his father now wrote to
him after a silence of thirty five years. Adrian would insist that Ivy
Litvinov had been in his mind all that time, because she had written
in response to his famous trilogy 'What's eating him?' and Adrian
had felt that she alone had insight to the frustration behind the
jolly prose. 'My most severe critic' he later called her, and certainly
she pulled no punches.

Ivy Litvinov was ten years older than Adrian and her life had
been very different to his. An Englishwoman with Jewish ancestry,
she had married the respected Bolshevik Maxim Litvinov in 1916,
and tried to contain her regal but explosive demeanour as she
followed him in his political duties. During the Revolution she was
based in London from where her husband could distribute
propaganda, and after visiting a hypnotist to help unlock her own
writing talent, Ivy had submitted poetry to Robert Bell at the
*Observer* in the hope of getting it published. Like Robert her father
had been a Fabian, but he had died young.

Ivy had loved the glamour of the Russian diplomatic scene but
from 1934 onwards, as Stalin ordered the imprisonment or
execution of countless colleagues, the Litvinovs had lived in fear
for their lives. They survived the rout and spent time in America
which suited Ivy, but after Maxim's death in 1951 Ivy had taken a
younger, lesbian lover.

After modest success with a detective novel her writing had
never amounted to much, although now she was regularly having
short stories published in the New Yorker. When she made contact
with Adrian she was living in Moscow again and while he was
mainly attracted to the idea that someone really understood him,
at the same time he enjoyed having a window on the outside world,
and a view into a life that had been through danger and intrigue.

Over the ensuing years Ivy would accuse him of being avuncular,
would tell him to 'come off the sweet old gentleman touch' and

stop preaching. He retorted in kind, told her to 'stick that up your samovar' and agreed when she laughingly wrote back 'Well! Well! There is life in the old dogs yet!' It was a tonic to be so rude to someone who enjoyed it. As for Ivy, her biographer John Carswell would say in his book *The Exile* that she 'worshipped' Adrian Bell.

But it seemed that for every friend Adrian gained these days, he lost two. His first publisher and ever-since friend Richard Cobden-Sanderson died in 1964 and in 1966 his most treasured friend Henry Warren passed away.

Henry had been aged seventy, not much older than Adrian, but closer to him in thought and temperament than any other man. Placid, deep of thought, a bachelor who preferred music and poetry to socialising, Henry nevertheless had several close friends and took many holidays abroad at their invitation. His obituary in *The Times* would describe him as having 'a happy nature, accepting rather than questioning, enjoying rather than criticising. His attitude to life and art was inclusive and not exclusive'. Even so, he sent a rocket of a letter to Rolf Gardiner when Rolf dared to criticise 'Dylan Thomas and his Beatnik crew' in 1960.

Born in Kent, Henry's talents had taken him through grammar school and on to Goldsmith's Teacher Training College, where his musicianship might have seemed to point to a career in that direction. Instead he specialised in English, until his career was stalled by a spell of soldiering in the First World War. His experiences there gave rise to a book of poetry and he tried to make a living as a writer, with some success in the 1920s. Finally settling in Essex, his books reflecting country life became immensely popular during the second war.

At that time Henry was working for the B.B.C. but he was not at all happy in his task of churning out propaganda. A two-year publishing contract offered him the freedom he craved in 1941; a miracle had happened, he told Rolf.

Henry's style was even more intimate than Adrian's: perhaps it was down to his roots in land labour, although his father had run a successful village store and had been active in local societies. Certainly Henry could talk to the countryman and write with clear insight on his hard-graft life, adding verbatim quotes that never seemed trite.

He and Adrian maintained a mutual regard, and when their country-tales genre declined in popularity they held a mutual sympathy. Henry's health troubled him and several times he had to cancel planned visits to Adrian. It would be a source of regret for Adrian that Henry couldn't visit him at Barsham, for he knew he would have liked it.

Adrian wrote to Rolf Gardiner two years later, still expressing his sadness at the loss of 'Dear old Henry.' He added, 'All I have of him is a rose he recommended to me in his last letter - a Zephyrin Dronhin. It climbs my stable wall, has scented pink blooms, and I talk to him as I stand and look at it.'

Adrian had not kept any of Henry's letters, he hadn't seen any need to, so when Henry's great nephew Geoffrey Warren came calling many years later, Adrian was unable to help much with his planned biography. Luckily Geoffrey did find enough about Henry's life from other sources, and used it as an introduction to a collection of Henry's work, entitled *The Contented Countryman*.

Despite this shrinkage of his circle of friends, Adrian was enjoying the isolation of Barsham, and vowed that, apart from friends such as Edmund Blunden, people would have to come to him, as he had done with long-distance driving. His headaches were gradually abating just as a specialist had once predicted, and now that the family had all grown up and gone, he could afford to cut down his output of crosswords and even enjoy a glass of sherry in the evening. Life was toddling along nicely.

In fact, his children had gone far and wide - Anthea was in Leicester, Martin was now a B.B.C. correspondent in various dangerous locations, so mostly they kept track of his movements by watching the television, and Sylvia had emigrated to Canada. Having made his pledge of non-displacement, it is confirmation of Adrian's great love for his daughter that he consented to go with Marjorie to visit her in 1967.

In his articles sent back to the *Eastern Daily Press* and in his diary Adrian would write his impressions of that frozen land where children and fish could be found in abundance. 'Children are everywhere' he noted, 'often grubby, always grinning, playing across the streets among American cars that are like floating three-piece suites.' He added that horses and moose seemed to wander about at will, and his abiding impression was that 'It is a country of rocks and dead cars.'

He enjoyed his experience though, especially the sight of icebergs floating in the bay while the pounding sea threw up foam, 'like great white chrysanthemums.' And he found the way of life intriguing; his son-in-law Colin would travel over 100 miles in a day to take services in remote churches and return late at night with a gift of trout.

But Adrian found the centrally heated houses a little stifling and was surprised that people who contended with such bitter cold outside should toast themselves so thoroughly in their homes. He was glad to get back to his draughty old farmhouse on High Common, Barsham.

In 1970 they visited Sylvia again but she was taken ill and admitted to hospital, so Adrian found himself trying to cope with babysitting her children Mark and Clare while Colin was away working and Marjorie was visiting. It was not a great success.

Finally he returned home on his own as Marjorie insisted she must stay to help, and that was not a success either. His mind's tendency to wander away led to various minor domestic catastrophes like burnt toast and boiled-over milk. When one ring of the cooker became choked with blackened gunge he simply moved on to another.

Martin smiles when he recalls the 'song and dance' his father used to make when he was left alone. 'You'd have thought he'd been totally abandoned,' he says. 'It wasn't that he was incapable of looking after himself, he merely didn't want to.'

Martin himself was a frequent visitor to his parents, although his reporting jobs often took him overseas. In November of that same year he had brought a girlfriend to meet them but supper was cut short when he was called to fly off to Pakistan. Adrian wrote about it in an article, describing the preparations they had made for the girl's stay, which all went to waste. The girl, Helene, would have to get used to Martin's kind of life, for she would marry him.

Apart from those regular articles for the *Eastern Daily Press*, Adrian's fame as an author had all but gone. Increasingly he was becoming known as 'The father of Martin Bell' and even at family gatherings he twigged that Martin was the guest they most hoped to see.

As a compiler of *Times* Crosswords, Adrian had to remain anonymous and could not get any kudos for all his efforts in that direction. It bothered him less as time went on. He began to accept that he would never achieve the pinnacle of eloquence he had striven for, the real essence of what he was trying to say. He resolutely refused to go back to his former style and drag out again those old farm stereotypes. 'Old Walter Wombat could neither read nor write, yet he had an instinctive wisdom...' he jotted down jokingly. But he was finding that people from his past, like Coote the farm labourer who died penniless, were nearer the forefront of his mind than ever before.

Unfortunately, when he did send a book of reminiscences and reflections called *As I See It* to his publisher, Faber's Rosemary Goad returned it with a rejection, describing it as 'altogether too minor and mild'. Adrian, miffed, considered that that might be a fitting epitaph for his grave one day. He kept her letter though, admiring that phrase for its almost poetic quality. The letter also contains placatory passages, adding that Ms Goad was looking forward to his next submission, but it is unclear whether he even bothered to send them the other book he was working on, a complicated saga connected with Dolores and called *Love and Friendship*. Certainly it was never published.

In spite of this feeling of failure, Adrian was now more at ease with his own life and he was also more at ease with the world in general. He had written, 'I was not prepared to find that growing old could be so pleasant. I can say sincerely that my sixty-sixth year is the best year of my life, and this summer is the best summer I have known. The world is in a terrible state. It has always been, during my life-time. But now I don't feel responsible for it. I hand it, metaphorically, to my son. "Here you are, my boy, the world is all yours - see what you can do with it." He is willing to accept the responsibility.'

The world, however, did not go away quietly. And if Marjorie had once declared that her job in life was to tether Adrian's balloon, she would soon find that it could bob up again when least expected, and this time she would find it hard to hold on to the string.

# 18. Faire Games

There was a move afoot in Barsham and the surrounding area to bring back an old tradition, the May Fair. In 1971 a group of unconventional friends met and agreed that there was a great seam of untapped skill and energy in the area. If the will was there, they said, perhaps they could bring it all together for the good. In the following year they formed themselves into a group called the East Anglian Arts Trust and after raising an initial sum they launched their first Barsham Faire, actually at Beccles.

Having made a profit, the Trust then was able to make contributions to other events such as a folk festival and a travelling circus but they had their sights set on another fair, a bigger one, at Barsham itself.

One of the founder members of the Trust, Rob Parfitt, who was then in his twenties, recalls how Adrian Bell came to his attention. 'He just looked so interesting. One of the first things I remember about him was the clothes he wore - a bottle-green corduroy jacket like a French peasant's cord jacket, and he wore a little straw knot which someone had made. He wore quite jaunty scarves, a gold or stagshorn ring he pulled them through and a kind of racy trilby that was battered. His hair was quite long ; wiry, sort of wire wool, like Brillo. I thought he looked quite elegant, an interesting mixture between a gentleman and a peasant really.'

The East Anglian Arts Trust stood for no particular cause and this was before somebody coined the term 'Green' for those with concern for the environment. They were decidedly 'not anti-anything', says Rob. They simply liked to have a good time; many had art and handicraft skills, and several were musicians, so meetings might be held in a hall or they might be in a field, where one of their number played gentle Irish music under an oak tree. It was their empathy with Nature that drew Adrian to them.

'It was almost like he was excited by what was happening,' agrees Rob. 'He always had his own point of view but he fitted in. The Faire included all the locals, it wasn't hippies imposing themselves. I don't think Adrian tried to influence the group. Many people probably didn't know who he was.'

Ley lines and telluric forces were all matters of importance to them and Rob and fellow Trust member Tim spent a great deal of time finding the right site for their next fair. The Barsham Rectory paddock seemed ideal. According to a book about the fairs, *The Sun in the East* compiled by Richard Barnes, the Barsham Faire of 1973 was attended by 22,000 people.

Adrian was busy that year. First Martin had been to stay. Two years earlier he had married his charming French girlfriend and now they had a baby daughter. Marjorie would be a help to Helene during Martin's many absences on reporting assignments but Adrian would find that his own deprecatory stories about Old Scottish Granny Bell did not appeal to the kind, convent-educated daughter-in-law. In fact she made him feel quite ashamed that he had sold his granny's portrait, simply by her reaction of 'Oh!'

Anthea had been with them next but again Adrian had found himself completely at sea when she suddenly opened up to her parents about marriage problems she was having. He knew he had failed miserably to give counsel or comfort, but then, his own marriage had been rock-solid, so what did he know about complicated relationships? Anthea would go on to work it out for herself, and later Adrian would feel flattered, albeit sadly, that she would choose to be a Bell again. She rediscovered herself, he would say, and they celebrated with champagne.

Glad was he to be living a steady life, close once more to his beloved Marjorie, comfortably off, free of parental responsibility, and free to pursue a life of idleness or hedonism, if he wished. Most of the subjects for his newspaper articles could be found close at hand - he wrote about his garden, his pond, the birds and wildlife, even the various smells that came to him, depending on the wind direction. There was no need to go far, and few people to travel anywhere for anyway.

Marjorie did go away again, to Canada to help while Sylvia was ill, and while she was away Adrian stayed with Anthea.One evening as she was clearing away his papers she was touched to see he had been composing a love-letter to her mother. Perhaps he didn't need many friends, but he needed Marjorie with all his soul.

If Adrian needed convincing about the fragility of friendship, he had it when his erstwhile pen-pal Ivy Litvinov having moved to lodgings in Hove, Sussex, managed a visit to Suffolk. Over the years he had been relishing her chastisements and jibes; 'I am tired of your cats, I am tired of your pond' she had scolded recently. 'And what aren't you tired of?' he had queried. 'Your magic' she'd retorted. 'But you often let me down.'

Marjorie, she had once said, sounded like 'the stern daughter of the Voice of God' because he had described one of her attempts to keep his feet on the ground. Ivy would not be told what to do by anyone.

Ivy's handwriting had been wild at times, as had her mood - the highs and lows of her temperament speak out from the pages of her letters with the terms 'manic' one day, 'depressed', another. But Adrian admired her zest and naughtiness, chuckled at her curmudgeonly grumbles. He even suggested that they could make a book out of their correspondence.

He wrote long letters to both Ivy and her daughter Tanya in affectionate terms and she would write in return with love and kisses too. They were all on the same wavelength, he felt. It would be a tragedy if they never met, never had a chance to share the rapport he so enjoyed on paper. But then the chance came, and Ivy in the flesh was not so much fun.

At first sight Adrian was alarmed by this bulky, masculine, wild-haired woman in baggy clothing. He was taken aback by her forceful, sex-charged personality and her rudeness face-to face he no longer found stimulating or funny. Within a day he had collapsed in a complete funk.

Throughout her stay he cowered in his room, leaving Marjorie to cope, to excuse, to entertain, to get Ivy on her train on the Monday, and give her money when she hunted in vain for her purse. The thought of it would make him cringe with shame afterwards, even though Marjorie forgave him time after time.

A scribbled postcard followed Ivy's departure, saying it had been lovely to be with them, and asking if Adrian was better. She had found her purse with not a penny in it - how much did she owe them?

Following that dreadful disillusionment Adrian wrote to Ivy's daughter Tanya, saying he had so wanted to show Ivy around Suffolk. Tanya responded 'Ha! Nobody can do that'. She explained that Ivy's married life had involved a great deal of moving around and she was done with travel now. It seems she had made a special exception to go to Barsham and meet the man she 'worshipped'.

Ivy suffered a stroke soon after her visit and her health declined steadily until her death in 1977, just before her eighty-eighth birthday. There was no funeral to attend - she had bequeathed her body to University College Hospital.

In 1974 Adrian would again lose two long-treasured friends: Edmund Blunden died in January, and Dolores in September.

The enchanting Dolores, his former love, had been released from her near-blind, crippled body and her glorious spirit could live on in his memory. Later he wrote a tribute to her, keeping it platonic, mentioning that Bobby Baker, her faithful boyfriend of fifty-seven years had died before her, 'by the expedient simply of not waking up one morning.' Adrian had visited her on her eightieth birthday at Marjorie's insistence, and she had received him in her boudoir, where she lay propped up on pillows. He had been surprised at how young and pretty she still seemed in repose. 'Almost I coined an axiom: every woman is beautiful if only she believes she is'.

He continued in his article, 'After my last visit I used to ring Dolores at intervals to find out how she was. She could no longer write because of her hands. Her voice sounded wistful, and her thoughts dreamlike. "When shall I see you again?" The "you" a little slurred. The last time I rang, her woman did not immediately hand me over to her. There was a long long pause, then the woman's voice came again. "I am afraid she has forgotten who you are."'

Adrian said he was not fit enough to return to Bath for the funeral, on Friday the thirteenth. He stayed home and wrote, had friends over for lunch, and did not mention the void that Dolores' passing had left in his world of dreams.

Then, as had happened before, as two friends were lost to him, another had been found.

A local woman had invited him and Marjorie to supper a few times and they had chatted about general things in her impressively neat and tidy home. They learned that she liked gardening and baking, and making things with dried flowers. It was all very civilised.

Then one day Adrian saw her in a different light. Marjorie had been to a meeting of the local Women's Institute which had included a judo demonstration, but she had left before the end as she 'couldn't bear all that throwing about.' Their new friend had followed to see if she was all right and Adrian spent time with her in his garden, discussing his passion flower vine, the problem with moles, a dormouse that visited her, the bluetits that were nesting in her postbox. As well as sharing a compulsion to chatter, they found they had a great deal more in common.

On 27th July the *Eastern Daily Press* carried an article entitled *The Fairy Ring*, in which Adrian introduced his friend to the public with the name Sighile, which was not her real name he said, but an Irish form of it. He had attended a W.I. function at her home, where the guests had played games and tried their hand at basket-making under her tutelage. He had admired her garden, her tomatoes, her pond, her hens and her duck, and she had shown him her circle of toadstools; a fairy ring. In his diary he also noted that when his identity had been revealed to guests there, he felt flattered at the respect it commanded and he was glad it seemed to boost Sighile's party too. At least in Barsham, Adrian Bell was still something of a celebrity.

In fact it had been a few days after the party that Sighile had shown him the fairy ring in her garden and urged him to stand in it and make a wish. He wrote in his diary of 7th July 'I have a stange feeling I may have wished for something in myself I shall not want when it is fulfilled'.

In the coming days he went on to list Sighile's attributes, from her puppet-making to her blackcurrant wine-making, from the flush on her cheeks as she greeted him in the midst of picking raspberries, to her shyness at her less-than-perfect bread. He savoured it all.

'She opened the door to her pantry' he observed, 'and everything was in beautiful neatness and order...I loved the thrift and housewifeliness of it all, in her brave effort to support herself without having at fifty to go back to teaching.' Afterwards, Marjorie wondered if Sighile would marry again, there was a man they had heard about who seemed keen. Adrian hoped not, as Sighile had told him of her enjoyment of a good book in bed, and her own little paradise home, of which she was mistress.

Not for the first time, Dolores came to his mind, who had also earned money from handicrafts. But he felt pity that Sighile did not have adoring men around her to bail her out of financial trouble. One day it occurred to him that he was sure she had never been truly loved, properly, every inch of her adored. Sighile picked up the signals of his sympathy and she challenged him that he was just being friendly because he felt sorry for her. He assured her that was not the case.

Sighile became a frequent visitor to the Bell home; the women often swapped gifts of jam, eggs, fruit and other produce and Adrian would look out for pine cones to give her for her craftwork. As she lived within walking distance, Adrian found it convenient to call at her bungalow on his way to or from the postbox. He liked to settle into a special chair, a big chair with two cushions by the window, or on the verandah and drink a cup of tea, and chat. He felt peaceful there, he felt at home.

Sighile told him she thought the newspaper article had been lovely, and he in turn found himself blurting out that 'A flower is as good as a word', and then wondering if she, or indeed he, had a clue what he meant. But in private he added 'Thus a lovely relationship of prose-poetry and potatoes and flowers develops.'

Inspired by the youngsters of the East Anglian Arts Trust, Adrian had been pondering. Perhaps the world was not lost after all. Mother Nature had a way of fighting back and through people with a sensitivity for her message, there could be a return of some of the old values. At the Barsham Faire in August 1974 he sat on a chair by Sighile's stall, or 'piccage' where she was selling her wares and he watched the proceedings in her companionship.

His resulting newspaper article told readers of the wonderful, gaudy, sometimes manic, but overall organic nature of the spectacle. The peasantry had risen and taken control for three days of harmless mayhem, adorning themselves in nature's garlands and dancing in their gay abandonment of materialism. He had been quite taken by it all.

On 1st September his diary entry started 'There is a place where one is secure from agitation, uncertainty, a small corner of one self on account of a certain light in the sky, a certain ripple of the wind across grass, or nuts grasped secure under hazel leaves, toughly adhering, green sheathed but slightly autumn-toasted. There must be someone else who but for such things is afflicted by self doubts and fears. There should be a green bond a little out of this world, but inviolable, such as nature is to natural people: that is my thought for today.'

In his newspaper articles, Sighile was now appearing frequently. '"Come round the oak tree," she said, "where we can step into the

field and pick primroses." So he wrote of one encounter. She may
not have said those exact words but Adrian wanted to portray her
as his ideal friend of Nature. In another article she stoops to tie his
shoelace for him, remembering a little boy she used to teach. Then
she says he looks like a sage, standing with both hands resting on
his walking stick. 'Sage of Suffolk' she names him. But it was Rolf
Gardiner who had dubbed him that, decades earlier.

And so it went on. If Sighile wasn't named, readers soon knew
who 'the lady down the lane' meant, or 'a lady friend,' but Adrian
was putting many more anecdotes in, which he hoped Sighile
would appreciate as a continuation of private jokes.

A section of Adrian's personal papers is full of jottings about
these little moments, like when they had laughed about runner
beans that entwine their way up their poles then wave about in
the air saying 'Where shall we go from here?' He wrote of  the
make-believe world they had invented after a visit to their favourite
craft shop in Bungay, where a patchwork counterpane that looked
like a landscape led them to a whole raft of stories about the boy
from Counterpane Land and Thumbelina, the little girl he loved.

There are poems featuring events and thoughts they had shared,
including the runner beans, and looking back on a visit to a local
churchyard, when she had given him a handful of wild mint. An
article about it had changed the mint-picker's identity to a young
girl, and dubbed her Thumbelina, but in his poem he wrote:

> And thus the heart will break
> Yet brokenly live on
> Showing no visible sign
> For such things are untold.
> This sprig of wild mint
> Picked from the verge of this pond
> A child gave me
> Yet she was not that
> But a woman, bosomed, mature...

And Adrian was indeed noticing the womanly shape of Sighile;
on one occasion he wondered, when she wore something new, if
she did so for his appreciation. His 'pal' as he called her, dominated
his thoughts. She was an integral part of the Green Bond he had
written about, he thought he saw the spirit of the wild wood

reflected in her green eyes. In his imagination, she was a magical, mystical embodiment of all the primal elements he worshipped.

There is no evidence that the friendship was anything but platonic, but Adrian's sister Stephanie came away from a visit to Barsham, telling her family that her brother was in love. And she was pleased. It was no secret among the Bell relatives that Stephanie thought Marjorie didn't look after him properly, saw her efforts to moderate his diet in the hope of staving off headaches as starvation.

In the village too, and in the Arts Trust, people were nudging each other and speculating. But Marjorie had seen it all before in her fanciful husband; these pensive silences, the humming of tunes and faraway smiles. She had no qualms about asking Sighile to take Adrian in while she was away helping Helene with her new baby daughter.

In his newspaper article of 11<sup>th</sup> January 1975, he wrote 'So now I dwell temporarily at the other end of our lane, I wake to the church tower seen from a different angle. To the postbox is a mere stroll...' He describes a walk he takes with Sighile, and as they stop to discuss which way to go, he remembers an American tourist he once saw in the churchyard. 'O my candy-coloured American, you should aim your camera at what makes English gardens grow, and English lawns look trim, and an English pond, unchoked by sedge, shine clear as a pane of sky - at an English countrywoman, member of the W.I., always "on the make" not of money but of things woven, things grown and cooked slowly with all their juices conserved. The title of this imagined study in brown - brown hair, brown jumper, brown skirt, before brown ploughland carpeting the view to the horizon - would be at this moment "Where is the Path?"'

If Adrian had summed up all that he liked about Sighile in that passage, he wrote a great deal more in his little red books that served as diaries, including a page of doodlings with ciphers of the initials A and S.

Even the editor of the *Eastern Daily Press* had noticed that this woman Sighile was cropping up in the *Countryman's Notebook* rather frequently. In October 1975 Adrian needed to take a break for a couple of weeks and he suggested that his pal could submit an article in his place. Sighile's piece, which was about Adrian, was introduced thus: 'With Adrian Bell taking a short holiday from *Countryman's Notebook* who better to fill this week's gap than Sighile, the figure who flits so tantalisingly through the notebook's pages? Sighile (pronounced "Siheelie" and derived from the old Irish) pens her own tribute to "a great talker, a dreamer, an enchanter."'

And Sighile went on to write more, putting the stories together in a booklet eventually, with a foreword by Adrian that suggests he hoped his calling her 'Sighile' rather than her real name had helped her find her true nature again, formerly submerged by her arduous life. Referring to a corn dolly she made called Earth Mother, he ended, 'When on my walk I see Sighile digging her garden and not pausing to take breath, I do not interrupt her with "Hallo", I murmur to myself "Earth Mother" and continue on my way.'

Perhaps Adrian's friendship was a liberating one. Certainly he had found a source of many stories in his talks with Sighile. But if he was merely projecting onto her all that he wished a woman to be, the mirage, as they do when one draws closer, would one day vanish.

In his book *The Green Bond* published in 1976 Adrian collected together a number of his recent articles, several of them featuring Sighile. It includes one that describes a day when he was not welcome to call, as she had a male visitor. The story is told in a way that suggests Sighile had no interest in this man and was glad when he was gone. Had they been for lunch together, Adrian had asked, or her favourite ginger wine at the Woolsack? (This a pseudonym for the Fleece in Bungay)

'No, sherry at some brash place opposite the service station. Do you suppose I'd take him to the chimney-corner of our conversations?'

Again, the exchange may have been fabrication and over-laden with intimacy. But Adrian was determined in his pursuit of friendship with this woman and even when he was told not to call, he would leave a note in her postbox or some firewood just inside her gate, so she would know he had passed by.

This was to be Adrian's last book, and it is described in the jacket as a celebration of the 'green bond' between people and the world around them. 'A rich world where present colours and past memories intermingle, seen through the eyes of a man who declares himself "a peasant at heart: I prefer mould under my feet, and to cross a watercourse in my own way, sniffing wild mint and bruised sheep's parsley, and meeting a beetle eye to eye in the process."'

The stories he chose and edited, and which his daughter Anthea typed out for him, had all appeared in the newspaper previously, but for no apparent reason he also made up a tale about a girl he had loved, Annabel, who had given herself to him as a twenty-first birthday present. They had made love in the long grass on his farm, and sworn their betrothal. But then she had died tragically in an accident, and he'd had to live on without her.

None of the family has heard of Annabel. The timing does not fit. There is no record in the local newspapers of such an accident. Sometimes Adrian's romantic old heart simply got carried away, and it seems he had latched onto 'Annabel's paddock' that was on Sighile's land, and made use of a story she had told him.

But eventually his fictional notions began to be tempered by reality. Sometimes Sighile would turn to him and her expression would not be all joy and welcome, but it would have a sterner 'cat-like' stare, he said. One day he was racked with concern because she had not waved to him. Would the 'loveliness of nothingness' they had admired become an epitaph to their friendship?

In the early days their mutual volubility was something they had in common, but now their need to chatter could cause conflict. That gabbling habit of his, at first so amusing, seemed to needle her. He felt he had embarrassed her in company, and apologised. But similarly her perfectionist eye, her fanatical extermination of every weed she found in her garden, did not really accord with his 'green bond' theory.

His balloon had deflated. The relationship settled into a down-to-earth, companionable one and Sighile continued to be a welcome guest of Adrian and Marjorie.

Adrian was ageing rapidly now and his wife worried about him wobbling round the lanes on his bike, a crossword grid propped in the front basket. She cared for his every need, tailoring their diet to his conservative palate, helping with his work, tucking a blanket round his legs as he lay on his couch dozing. Relatives on her side of the family had thought she did too much, felt that she waited on him too diligently. But the couple were happy: that was what counted.

By 1978 Adrian had started to feel his end might be within sight. If one of the cats suddenly startled and raised its hackles, he wondered if they had had a premonition, if perhaps they could see an apparition, come to call him home. A notice in the post office declaring 'Cold Kills the Old' did nothing to cheer him. Then he had fumbled about with his money, bought the wrong postage for a letter, and felt like a fool, an old fuddy-duddy.

He caught sight of himself in a shop window, and the decrepit old geezer who looked back at him sent a wave of alarm crashing over his morale. He had become one of those doddery old men who took forever in the public lavatory, while youngsters zoomed in, unzipped, performed, zipped and had gone before he'd finished unbuttoning his coat. His shuffling gait, his stiff, creaky bones, his uncertain digestion all signified a decline, the downhill road to the terminus, he might have said. The hand of Fate was reaching for the bell.

# 19.  Enduring Images

If Adrian's body was letting him down, his mind was standing steadfastly by him. Still alert, witty and perceptive, he would sit by his open window and occasionally creep around his garden, but otherwise he would lie on his couch or sit out in the summerhouse he'd made from the old stable, and there, in his big wicker basket chair, he would doze and dream.

His fans still loved his beautiful, evocative newspaper articles, his puzzle-fanatics still gnashed their teeth at his convoluted clues. He had compiled around 4,500 of them so far, and there was talk of a special celebration in 1980 for the golden anniversary of his first puzzle.

What a half-decade it would have been by then, spent picking his way through a minefield of morals and ethics, trying not to upset anyone, trying to get every spelling right, every fact. And then twisting and turning, punning and anagramming until he had his black and white grid complete. Each puzzle took him around twelve hours to compose, he once said, and he wore out a dictionary a year. He could never sit at a desk and grind out the clues, he had to be doing something rhythmic like walking, cycling, gardening, or, in the old days, harrowing on his farm.

For most of those years he had remained anonymous but now, the doyen of a team of ten as one report described him, his secret was well-known. In one article he revealed how his craft had brought him to the attention of M.I.5 when his answers and clues had seemed to contain a code that pointed to him knowing about the planned escape of the spy George Blake from Wormwood Scrubs prison in 1966. He had laughed at the suggestion that it was more than a coincidence clue 27 across 'What a row it makes in London and anywhere' gave the answer Artillery Row, the narrow lane that ran past the Scrubs. And yes, 4 down did lead to the answer 'Gaol' - what of it? He agreed that a compiler could be offered money to insert a code into his puzzle, but Adrian had met none, he said, in Never-Never Land.

Still on the fairytale theme he had commented to an interviewer that he reckoned one day he would disappear and all that would be left was the smile, like the Cheshire Cat.

But now he lived in fear, too. Fear that if anything happened to Marjorie, he would be lost, helpless. Fear that soon they would have to admit defeat and move out of their beloved farmhouse, which was becoming too much for Marjorie to cope with, and the stairs too difficult for him to climb. They had kind neighbours who helped with the garden, but the sight of it degenerating and Adrian too feeble to tackle it, distressed him. He had become a stranger in paradise, he thought; it was all beyond his control.

Martin was living in America now, as the B.B.C.'s Washington correspondent, although he came to see them when he could. Sylvia was in Saskatchewan but had visited in the summer of 1978. Anthea came down from Leicester whenever possible, but they certainly didn't want to become a burden to her. She was busy supporting herself, she had won awards for her translating work and was always in demand. Her boys, his grandsons, were deep-voiced young men now, and she might be termed 'middle aged'. It was frightening.

He didn't like to ring her too often, because his loquaciousness would override his thoughts of phone bills and before he knew it he'd been on there an hour. 'Telephones are not for the likes of me,' he'd concluded.

Adrian kept feeling headachey again. His legs gave him terrible pain. He could only walk by leaning heavily on his wife. In shops, he was the old boy sitting stiffly on the chair by the counter. But so few shops had chairs nowadays. 'I felt ashamed of myself' he wrote after one excursion. 'My - if not decrepitude - my less than crepitude.'

And when he had inadvertently asked a lady for some ten-shilling pieces, she had kindly explained to him in simple terms that they were called fifty p's now. As if he was a time traveller, just landed in Suffolk. To another assistant he had said that he only wanted a small tube of toothpaste because he might be dead before he'd used up the big one.

Marjorie herself had turned seventy now and could not be expected to keep up this pace of housekeeping, nursemaiding, caring for everyone and everything. He must try and think of her needs too, he realised. She gave meaning to his whole world, his life, his work. Every day now his thoughts ran back and forth over the years, over the events of his seventy-seven years on earth. He felt so old and yet, thanks to Marjorie, he still felt so beloved.

An article entitled *Ladybird, Ladybird*, contains some of Bell's most eloquent prose in his description of a ladybird making its way across grass and pebbles near to his sentry post in the old stable. 'The sun put a star on her polished wing-case, which led my eyes to follow her progress', he said. The next day he found the ladybird dead. Life could be so ephemeral, it seemed.

The previous week, on 8th April 1978, his regular article had again been a view from his seat, but this time he had lain back under the old walnut tree and mused on the saying 'Carpe Diem - Seize the Day'. He was enjoying gazing up through the canopy of leaves, he said 'Until someone who still loves you in spite of yourself and has paused on her way to the potato store to peer through the larch-lap to count if you blink, and if you don't seem to blink, comes toward you saying "Are you all right, dear?" in case you had simply passed away with so little fuss that people would be saying, "But what a lovely way to die - so quietly in the arms of nature"'. But he hoped that day was some way off yet.

They determined to go on a car journey around all the old haunts of their married life, but kept putting it off. Could they make it all the way to West Suffolk, to the Stour Valley where he had careered the lanes with Munnings, or paddled up river with Nash? Or perhaps tour Stradishall again, and see it in their mind's eye as it was when he had clumped out in his boots onto frozen furrows.

What would he find there? He had already written, 'I see combines like buses complete a harvest in hours, traversing prairie-like areas that once were many close-hedged fields'. He had mused then on the heaps of old farm tools he saw at auctions, usually described as *Lot 1 - All That You See Before You*, which was the title of an article on the subject. Some of them would be bought simply to adorn pub walls, he had realised, ignorant of the human hands that had brought them to life. *Lot 1 - All That You See Before You*. He concluded that he too could be labelled thus.

Once he had wished he could live again at the Old Vicarage at Redisham, now he simply wanted to see it one more time. A recent film he had seen about Lancaster bombers had reminded him of the night when the bombers had assembled as usual over his farm in preparation for a raid. The crew had switched on their lights too soon and were shot down by enemy fighters as Adrian and Marjorie stood on their front doorstep, seeing the fiery crosses in the night sky. The peace of the European Community was a miracle, he decided. At last he could feel that his children were safe now. Well, except when Martin rang to say he was off to Nicaragua, where a reporter had just been shot dead. He had survived Northern Ireland and Vietnam, so they must go on hoping his luck would last.

When Adrian had a note saying he needed a doctor's certificate to enable him to keep driving, his morale nose-dived. Well, he would just stay home and potter around the garden in his dressing gown, he decided with a defiant nod. 'Yet the heart is young' he consoled himself. And it was, in his case. The sight of a dew-glistening rose could still lift his spirit on high and give rise to a mental blessing that he had lived another day to see it. And every day he felt blessed for having Marjorie by his side.

Mostly they were happy to stay at home, in this house among the fields that they loved so much, wishing the days did not rush past so hastily. Neither of them slept very well these days, Adrian was restless and Marjorie, hearing him on another trip to the bathroom, would make him a cup of tea and lay a hand of love on him to soothe him back to sleep. Dressing in the morning and undressing at night could only be achieved by a series of contortions and gymnastics.

But this would not do. Winter was coming, and with it another enormous heating bill. They would have to go in search of the dreaded bungalow.

On the day that Margaret Thatcher moved into number 10 Downing Street (Adrian had voted for the Ecology Party), a buyer was found for Crakes Hall, High Common. Soon after, Adrian and Marjorie looked at a six year old bungalow in nearby Gillingham and decided that it was not so bad at all, even though its location on the north side of the River Waveney meant they would be moving out of Suffolk and into Norfolk.

Its garden was compact and surrounded by others, but he would be able to sit out on the little patio and doze in the sun, or even use the shed as a summerhouse. Its rooms were of a decent size, but they would have to clear out many of their accumulated possessions before they could fit in.

They gave away or sold much of their furniture, and even some trinkets that had held such meaning. The scent bottles Adrian had given Marjorie when they were engaged went to an antiques dealer, the family chose some pictures and books, and Sighile received a china basket that had been a present from Dolores. They gave Sylvia's old baby chair to her daughter, and she was pleased to accept it as an 'antique'.

Adrian began burning a heap of his old papers, his letters from friends long dead, his reviews, his scribblings for books and articles that had not borne fruit. It was a bonfire of future regret for his fans. He called it 'A great shedding of inessentials'. And Marjorie burned a portrait of herself she had never liked. The sight of her image collapsing and melting in a closing fist of flames was eerie, to say the least.

The day loomed when they must move to their new home, their antechamber to Kingdom Come, as Adrian viewed it. Martin and his family had come home for a while and helped to clear the house, Anthea was back and forth, helping Marjorie with the packing, and throughout it all Adrian could only sit or shuffle, creating an obstacle to the workforce. He felt desperately frustrated by his immobility and infirmity, noting in his diary, 'At times I feel I may be deposited at the "crem" on the way, on removal day.'

Instead he was to be billeted at Sighile's house and with his packed bag standing by his front door, he crept out the back to say goodbye to his garden. Goodbye to the pond, and its microcosm of life. Goodbye to the willow that drooped its tresses into the cool water. Goodbye and thanks to the vine-house where he had sat and dreamed so many dreams.

Never again would his morning ablutions be graced by that view of the great walnut tree. Their new bathroom window had frosted glass.

He climbed stiffly into the car and went up the lane he knew so well. He would rest peacefully in Sighile's big double bed with the frilled, rose patterned pillows. She would bring him breakfast there and open the curtains onto a day of glorious sunshine.

Anthea collected him at midday and drove him to the Quay at Beccles for a drink. They sat on the green by the water and remembered, until it was time to go.

Like a hamster in a new cage, Adrian was set free in his bungalow and left to make a nest for himself among his books and his belongings. He wondered what he might write about from now on, or would he indeed write at all?

As a gift from the children, Adrian and Marjorie took possession of their first colour television set, and it was a revelation to them. Adrian, who had for so long resisted any new-fangled thing, enjoyed seeing the spectacle of entertainment on the small screen, and yet still he could see the greatest show of all - the sunset - from his window.

Adrian continued writing his articles for the *Eastern Daily Press*, continued delighting readers with his thoughts and memories. Still he received letters from appreciative fans all over the country - devotees often passed on his articles to friends and relatives who admired his work but were out of the paper's area of circulation.

He didn't go far from home now, except the occasional trip to favourite spots, like Minsmere on the coast, and the commons around Barsham, the Country of the *Green Bond,* he recorded, adding 'What a foolish old heart mine is.' And yet he felt that the 'longing' of his youth was still imprisoned inside him, still searching for a means of expression.

'I've wanted everything' he told Sighile. 'You shall have everything,' she assured him. But he felt it was too late. This whole-sky view, the great stretched canvas of heaven and earth, was beyond his reach in Gillingham. He missed every inch of it, every tree, every leaf.

At first he was quite settled in this 'Toy Town' estate. He could creep along on two sticks as far as the post office, although trying it alone one day gave Marjorie a terrible fright when she found him gone. Darn it, he used to be so independent. Now all that stood between him and an old people's home was Marjorie's everlasting patience and love.

Was it a blessing or a cruel sentence that granted Adrian a clear, active brain until the final days of his life? Perhaps it was the mental agility required by all those crossword puzzles, perhaps it was genetic, or a wholesome diet, or just luck. Even as he sat in his garden, hoping for the inspiration to write something for his *Countryman's Notebook*, he saw the funny side of the carousels of washing that surrounded him in his neighbours' gardens. Baby clothes on one, bloomers on another, turning round and round in the breeze.

In his dreams he was fit again, virile even, with a spade in his hand and no arthritis to stop him using it. And he dreamed a lot now. In an article which appeared on 5th January 1980 he wrote,

'Since I have become rather lame, I find I dream all night of taking long country walks, striding o'er hill and dale. There are old packways along which I wander, and pass abbeys and convents enclosed in their own dream as I am in mine.'

He stood again by the dashing water of the Wye Valley, chatted with Aunt Ada in her hovel, smiled at her tame rabbits released in the jungle of her garden. He thought of his friends Henry Warren, Edmund Blunden, and Victor Savage, and of all those characters of his *Corduroy* days. When Rob Parfitt came to call, he had been dreaming he was in Paris, says Rob. 'Then we had this great conversation about Red Poll cattle', he adds.

But Adrian knew something was going seriously wrong with him. When he had begun his diary for the new year, 1980, he wondered if he would ever need another. He felt so ill, so sluggish, so trapped in this failing body. Car journeys were so painful now, and not to be undertaken lightly. The handfuls of pills he took did little to ease the agony in his legs and hips, and finally he was put on strychnine to give his system a jolt. 'If I had not stirred into life,' he wrote, recalling his tortuous birth, 'I should not at some later date be under the painful necessity of dying.'

He would not give up yet. He was having trees planted in his garden. He would learn to walk again, and then, if he could only manage to guide the little electric mower round their tiny patch of grass, he could consider himself a man once more. His embarrassment at having to be washed by nurses, or 'angels' as he looked upon them, had been acute and in his mind he envisaged telling them 'I can manage now, thank you.'

He was still writing articles, still composing crosswords, and on Saturday 26th July he noted in his diary that he had enjoyed a fine meal out with Martin and family.

There are no more entries after that.

In his last article, entitled *Portrait in a Mirror*, he said, 'In a diary there is no such thing as time past: it is all time present as you read'. That was published on 22nd August and the cutting is pasted into a scrapbook like all the hundreds of others, and dated in his own painfully-executed writing.

Illness took hold of Adrian again and this time no amount of drugs could help. By the end of August Marjorie was calling her daughters to their father's side. Sylvia came over from Canada; Anthea commuted between Suffolk and Leicester almost daily.

Adrian was almost completely paralysed, and becoming confused. Morphine helped him sleep, helped them all to rest, but when he was semi-awake he cried out for Marjorie. As long as she was there, he felt safe.

Adrian Bell took his last breath just after seven o'clock on the morning of Friday, the fifth day of September 1980. Marjorie was holding his hand.

Sonnet.

Mortality thy patient moment stands
Unshaken in the midst of silent fears.
I gather pearls where thou hast planted tears
I gather up delight with both my hands.

Strive on, ye streaming banners of the night
Sing forth, ye silver trumpets of the moon.
On the dim waters doth my soul go down
To meet my love upon the rivers of light.

What though the sunset folds her wings of fire
What though the curtain of the night is drawn
Fades not the loveliness of my desire,
The lips of darkness and the eyes of dawn.
And he shall follow Death and live who knows
What vision is remembered in the rose.

Adrian Bell.

# Books by Adrian Bell

| | | |
|---|---|---|
| Corduroy | Cobden-Sanderson | 1930 |
| Silver Ley | Cobden-Sanderson | 1931 |
| The Cherry Tree | Cobden-Sanderson | 1932 |
| Folly Field | Cobden-Sanderson | 1933 |
| The Balcony | Cobden-Sanderson | 1934 |
| Seasons (poems) | Centaur Press | 1934 |
| The Open Air: An Anthology of English Country Life (Editor) | Faber and Faber | 1936 |
| By-Road | Cobden-Sanderson | 1937 |
| Men and the Fields | B.T. Batsford Ltd | 1939 |
| The Shepherd's Farm | The Bodley Head | 1939 |
| Apple Acre | The Bodley Head | 1942 |
| Sunrise to Sunset | The Bodley Head | 1944 |
| The Budding Morrow | The Bodley Head | 1946 |
| The Black Donkey | Blandford Press | 1949 |
| The Flower and the Wheel | The Bodley Head | 1949 |
| The Path by the Window | The Bodley Head | 1952 |
| Music in the Morning | The Bodley Head | 1954 |
| A Young Man's Fancy | The Bodley Head | 1955 |
| A Suffolk Harvest | The Bodley Head | 1956 |
| The Mill House | The Bodley Head | 1958 |
| My Own Master | Faber and Faber | 1961 |
| A Street in Suffolk | Faber and Faber | 1964 |
| A Countryman's Notebook | Boydell Press Ltd | 1975 |
| The Green Bond | Boydell Press Ltd | 1976 |

# Bibliography

Carswell, John, *The Exile   A Life of Ivy Litvinov,*   Faber and Faber 1983

Gollin, A.M., *The Observer and J.L. Garvin 1908-1914  A Study in Great Editorship,*   Oxford University Press 1960

Griffiths, Dennis, *Plant Here the Standard,* Macmillan Press 1996

Lawn, G.R., *Music in State Clothing   The Story of the Kettledrummers, Trumpeters and Band of the Life Guards,* Pen and Sword Books 1995

Looker, Samuel J., *Richard Jefferies  Man of the Fields,* John Baker Publishers 1965

Matthews, Brian, *By God's Grace   A History of Uppingham School,* Whitehall Press 1984

Millington, Roger, *The Strange World of the Crossword* Book Club Associates 1975

Thompson, David, *Harry Becker (1865 - 1928),* Ipswich Borough Council 1993

(Various), *The Sun in the East  -  Norfolk and Suffolk Fairs,* R.B. Photographics  1983

Warren, Geoffrey, *The Contented Countryman  The Best of C.Henry Warren,* Alan Sutton 1991

Webb, Barry  *Edmund Blunden  A Biography,* Yale University Press 1990

Williamson, Anne  *Henry Williamson  Tarka and the Last Romantic,* Sutton Publishing 1995

# Index